A
HORACE
Workbook

Teacher's Manual

LLWS

Latin Literature Workbook Series

A Series Edited by LeaAnn A. Osburn

A HORACE Workbook

Teacher's Manual

David J. Murphy
& Ronnie Ancona

Bolchazy-Carducci Publishers, Inc.
Mundelein, Illinois USA

Series Editor: LeaAnn A. Osburn
Volume General Editor: Donald E. Sprague
Volume Contributing Editor: LeaAnn A. Osburn
Design & Typography: Adam Phillip Velez

A Horace Workbook
Teacher's Manual

David J. Murphy & Ronnie Ancona

Bolchazy-Carducci Publishers, Inc.
1570 Baskin Road
Mundelein, Illinois 60060
www.bolchazy.com

Printed in the United States of America
2010
by CreateSpace

ISBN 978-0-86516-649-3

CONTENTS

FOREWORD

All Latin teachers want their students to read ancient authors in the original. Yet to study the authentic Latin of an ancient Roman author is a complex task. It requires comprehension of the text and its grammatical underpinnings; an understanding of the world events and the culture in which the work of literature was produced; an ability to recognize the figures of speech the author uses and to grasp the impact they have on the text; sensitivity to the way sound effects, including meter if a passage is poetry, interact with the meaning of the text; and the ability to probe whatever thoughts and ideas the author may be expressing. To be successful in this multifaceted task, students need not only a comprehensive textbook but also exercises of different kinds in which to practice their newly developing literary and critical skills.

Students often need extensive drill and practice material—something not available in the traditional Latin author textbook—to help them master the grammar and syntax of the Latin text as well as the literary skills that the text demands of its readers. Teachers, too, no matter how many questions they ask in class to help their students analyze the syntax and the literary qualities of the text, often need and want more questions to be available. Realizing this need on the part of both students and teachers, Bolchazy-Carducci Publishers developed a series of workbooks to accompany Latin author textbooks. There will be six workbooks in the series: Caesar, Catullus, Cicero, Horace, Ovid, and Vergil. A team of authors—one, a university scholar with special expertise in the Latin literary text and the other, a high school Advanced Placement* Latin teacher—will write each workbook.

Workbooks in this series contain the Latin text for the material on the former Advanced Placement* Syllabus (Catullus, Cicero, Horace, Ovid, Vergil) and the 2013 syllabus (Caesar, revised Vergil) and exercises that drill grammar, syntax, and figures of speech. In addition, multiple-choice questions will be included and will focus on the student's comprehension of the passage and on items of literary analysis. The workbooks will also feature scansion practice, essays to write, and other questions that are appropriate to the author being studied. By reading and answering these types of questions, students will gain experience with the types of questions that are found on the Advanced Placement* Examinations. Students at the college level will also benefit from the additional practice offered in the workbooks.

These workbooks contain neither textual notes nor vocabulary on the page with the text nor on the facing page. The absence of these traditional features of textbooks will allow students, after reading the Latin passage in the textbook, to practice in the workbook what they have learned and to assess how much they have mastered already and what needs more study. The workbooks will, however, contain a Latin to English Vocabulary at the back of the book.

We are confident that this series of workbooks has a unique role to play in fostering students' understanding of authentic Latin text and will be a significant addition to the Advanced Placement* and college materials that already exist.

LeaAnn A. Osburn
Series Editor

---

* AP is a registered trademark of the College Entrance Examination Board, which was not involved in the production of, and does not endorse, this product.

PREFACE TO THE STUDENT WORKBOOK

We are grateful to Bolchazy-Carducci Publishers for giving us the opportunity to collaborate on *A Horace Workbook*, one in the series of workbooks originally planned for Advanced Placement* Latin authors. The challenge of devising exercises to help students understand and write about Horace has been a most enjoyable one. We had already worked together on Horace in the past when Ronnie Ancona visited David Murphy's Latin Literature AP* class to discuss her work on Horace *Ode* 1.23 (the "Chloe Ode") and when Murphy was a peer reviewer of the Teacher's Guide to Ancona's *Horace: Selected Odes and Satire 1.9* for Bolchazy-Carducci Publishers. This project has allowed us to extend that earlier common engagement with Horace. With one of us teaching high school and the other college, we have shared differing perspectives to our benefit. Of course, one always profits by testing one's ideas against another, informed mind. That endeavor was all the more rewarding in this case, for it was accompanied by shared sensibilities, goals, and respect. We hope we have produced a workbook that will enhance students' reading of Horace. Its writing was a pleasure for the authors.

This workbook is designed to provide high school and college students with exercises to accompany their reading in Latin of selected poems of Horace. It provides extensive practice with the Latin, which will develop and reinforce the students' skills in a variety of ways. The audience for which the book is intended is the advanced high school Horace student or the college level student of Horace. The workbook can be used in conjunction with any textbook or edition of Horace. The text printed and the complete Latin Vocabulary included are those of Ronnie Ancona, *Horace: Selected Odes and Satire 1.9* (Wauconda, Il.: Bolchazy-Carducci Publishers, 1999, second edition, 2005).

For each poem we provide the following types of exercises:

I.   Short Answer Questions
II.   Multiple Choice Questions
III.   Translation
IV.   Short Analysis Questions
V.   Essay
VI.   Scansion

II–V are similar to questions found on the Latin Advanced Placement* Examinations. For these, we suggest time limits in line with those suggested for similar questions on the AP* Exam. We do not suggest time limits for I and VI, since they provide needed practice but are not patterned after types of questions used on the AP* Exam. These questions assist upper level Latin students build thier skills.

---

* AP is a registered trademark of the College Entrance Examination Board, which was not involved in the production of, and does not endorse, this product.

I. Short Answer Questions

These questions ask, in line-by-line order, for analysis of grammatical or syntactical points (e.g. case and use of nouns), identification of figures of speech, and translation of words or phrases. They can be completed by students working alone, in pairs or groups, or together as a class "advancing the text at sight." This exercise is particularly useful for the student who is translating the poem for the first time.

A note on terminology—when we ask for the "function" of a word, the student's task is to explain the word's grammatical or syntactical use in its context. For example, on *Ode 1.24.9*, we ask "what is the case and use of *bonis*, and what is its function?" The answer would be, "dative of reference with *flebilis*; adjective used as a substantive."

II. Multiple Choice Questions

These questions ask about the same features as the multiple-choice questions on the former Advanced Placement* Examination: translation or interpretation, grammar, lexical details, allusions or references, metrics, and figures of speech. Each exercise concerns a passage of up to sixteen lines.

The multiple-choice section of the former Latin Literature Advanced Placement* Exam consisted of four passages: three "unseen" passages (usually one prose and two poetry) and one "seen" passage from the Catullus syllabus. On the Advanced Placement* Exam, students did not encounter multiple-choice questions on poems from the Horace syllabus. Nevertheless, we have included a multiple-choice exercise for each poem because students generally find multiple-choice AP* questions difficult, and they profit from extensive practice.

We intend the multiple-choice questions for students who have already translated the poem. Their degree of difficulty resembles that of Advanced Placement* multiple-choice questions on passages of Catullus that students have read. For that reason, our suggested time is shorter than what is allowed on the Advanced Placement* Exam for the same number of questions on an "unseen" passage. Teachers who want to give our multiple-choice exercises to students who have not yet read the passage should supply unfamiliar vocabulary and allow at least 1.2 minutes per question.

Finally, in the Appendix we provide students with four practice multiple-choice exercises, with answers, on "unseen" passages to add to their experience with this type of exercise.

III. Translation

These exercises test translation skills of students who have already translated the poem. Passages are of approximately the same length as translation passages on the Advanced Placement* Exams. The directions call for a translation that is as literal as possible. For that reason, one should not switch active voice verbs to passive voice or vice versa, or alter verb tenses. In rendering the historical present, one should either use the English present tense for Latin present or convert to past tense in English consistently. Students should stay within the range of accepted definitions of words and not impose from context a sense that the word does not have.

IV. Short Analysis Questions

These questions, similar to what have informally been called "spot" questions on the Advanced Placement* Exams, ask the student to address several detailed issues in a passage: translation, interpretation, scansion, analysis of figurative language, identification of historical or literary allusions. They are designed for students who have already read/translated the poem. Having discussed it already in class is helpful as well.

---

* AP is a registered trademark of the College Entrance Examination Board, which was not involved in the production of, and does not endorse, this product.

V. Essay

Aimed at students who have already read/translated and discussed the poem in class, the essay questions call for in-depth analysis of a feature of a passage or entire poem. The grading scheme suggested in the Teacher's Guide evaluates responses on a scale of 0–6.

The essay should:

- address the question exactly as it is asked, especially if it entails more than one task
- analyze, not merely describe, the passage so as to answer the question
- address the passage as a whole
- support assertions with evidence from the Latin. This means copy the Latin or cite the line numbers AND translate or paraphrase closely enough that it is clear the Latin is understood.

VI. Scansion

Once they have learned its meter, students can practice scansion from a poem whether or not they have translated it. Following the format of the Advanced Placement˙ Exams, we do not provide macrons/long marks in the lines to be scanned.

A Word on Figures of speech

In this workbook, we use the term "figure of speech" to refer to figurative uses of language in general, whether they involve non-standard senses of words (tropes or figures of thought) or arrangements of words (rhetorical figures or figures of speech). We use the term in this broad sense to encompass not only all the literary devices that are designated "figures of speech" to be learned for the former Advanced Placement˙ Examination, but also some devices which do not appear on the current Advanced Placement˙ list of figures of speech. Because we aim this workbook beyond an audience of AP˙ students, and because lovers of Latin literature always want to dig more deeply when they can, we call attention to some of these devices with the designation "figure of speech (non-AP)." These include juxtaposition, repetition for pathos or pathetic effect, meiosis, and rhetorical question. When students are asked to identify a figure of speech on the Advanced Placement˙ Examination, though, as opposed to discussing Horace's technique in an essay, we believe they are best advised to select only those on the Advanced Placement˙ list.

It is our hope that this workbook will facilitate and strengthen the reading of Horace in Latin for both high school and college students. Horace's Latin can be difficult at times, but with work and with practice we trust that reading it will be a rewarding experience as it has been for both of us.

In conclusion, we would like to acknowledge several individuals for their direct and indirect help with this project. LeaAnn Osburn, our editor, gave us the opportunity to write this workbook and offered help, advice, and encouragement at various stages of the writing process. The manuscript benefited from her careful reading and commenting as well as that of Donald Sprague, who joined the editorial

˙ AP is a registered trademark of the College Entrance Examination Board, which was not involved in the production of, and does not endorse, this product.

effort towards the end, and that of the two anonymous peer reviewers for Bolchazy-Carducci Publishers. To Panayotes Dakouras, David Murphy's colleague at The Nightingale-Bamford School, we owe thanks for his willingness to test in the classroom some of our workbook materials-in-progress, and to his Advanced Placement Latin Literature students and David Murphy's Advanced Placement Vergil students of 2004–05 we say thank you for providing us with feedback on various exercises. Without our Horace teachers we would probably not have written this book. Finally, our own students, past and present, by serving as an ideal audience as we wrote, helped to ground our work in the pedagogical framework for which it was meant.

David J. Murphy, Ph.D.,
The Nightingale-Bamford School

Ronnie Ancona, Ph.D.,
Hunter College and The Graduate Center (CUNY)

PREFACE TO THE TEACHER'S MANUAL

The purpose of *A Horace Workbook Teacher's Manual* is to provide the instructor with material that will help evaluate students' performance on the workbook exercises and to suggest ways of adapting those exercises to meet various teaching and assessment objectives. Sections I and VI provide exercise in the important skills of reading and scanning Horace's poetry. While originally written with the AP* Latin Literature Exam in mind, the selected passages and the workbook exercises provide all upper level Latin students an opportunity to enhance their Latin skills.

Section I. Answers to the Short Answer Questions

The authors have exercised their best, considered judgment in deciding between plausible alternatives, as, for example, between dative and ablative, or among uses of the ablative or genitive. Occasionally we have proposed more than one correct answer when we believe that a strong case can be made for it (cf., e.g., on 1.1.8). In some questions, when we require a student to provide a certain number of features as a minimum, more choices may be possible. The fact that we may suggest alternative choices does not exclude even further possibilities. Teachers must always use their discretion in applying the guidelines of this manual to their classroom needs.

Section VI. Scansion of the Passage Presented and Meter Identification

The following meters were not required for the former Advanced Placement* Examination, but we include exercises on them: first or lesser Asclepiadean (1.1, 3.30), fourth Asclepiadean (1.5, 1.23, 3.13), fifth or greater Asclepiadean (1.11), second Asclepiadean (1.13, 3.9), third Asclepiadean (1.24), and first Archilochian (4.7).

Scoring Guidelines for Sections II–V

These exercises are similar to questions written for the Advanced Placement* Examinations, and therefore the scoring guidelines are similar to those used for the Advanced Placement* exams. By following them, instructors can inform themselves and their students about the expectations that usually shape the scoring of the Advanced Placement* exams. Alternatively, instructors are free to devise their own grading schemes for these exercises. Information on the scoring of the Advanced Placement* Latin Exams can be found in the College Board's publications, *Released Exams 1999, 2005 AP® Latin Literature and Latin: Vergil Released Exams*, on The College Board website, AP Central, http://apcentral.collegeboard.com/, and in the reports on the grading of the Exams in *Classical Outlook.*

The following grading scheme yields a grade expressed as a fraction. Some Advanced Placement* teachers find it helpful to establish a fractional grade for all the questions on a test taken together (e.g., 30 out of 45 possible points) and then use this scheme to assign rough equivalents to the Advanced Placement* grading scale of 1–5:

    *   AP is a registered trademark of the College Entrance Examination Board, which was not involved in the production of, and does not endorse, this product.

0 to 1/3 (33%) correct: 1
1/3 to 1/2 (33% to 50%) correct: 2
1/2 to 2/3 (50% to 67%) correct: 3
2/3 to 4/5 (67% to 80%) correct: 4
4/5 and above correct: 5

Multiple Choice

Award one point for each right answer. Do not subtract points for either a blank or a wrong answer, simply total the number correct. (AP* policy beginning with May 2011 exams.)

Translation

Each passage is broken into sixteen or eighteen segments or chunks. Award one point for each segment that is completely correct. Any error within the segment makes the *whole* segment wrong. For example, if the segment were *"si me satis"*, omission of *"me"* would make the *whole* segment wrong and the student would not get credit for that segment. There is no partial credit awarded within a segment. Require active voice verbs to be active, passive to be passive, objective case substantives to be governed by the correct word, and definitions to fall within the range offered by the textbook's vocabulary or by a dictionary.

Total the correct segments and divide by sixteen or eighteen. Reduce the result by dividing dividend and divisor by two, after rounding up the dividend to an even number if it is an odd number. For example, if a student translates fifteen of eighteen segments correctly, round to 16 and divide by 18, i.e., 8/9, or 88%. By the rough scale set forth under Multiple Choice, this student's translation would rate 5 on a scale of 1–5.

To consult a translation, see Ronnie Ancona, *Horace: Selected Odes and Satire 1.9, Teacher's Guide* (Wauconda, IL: Bolchazy-Carducci Publishers, 1999, 2nd edition, 2005).

Short Analysis Questions

These are collections of four or five items that feature short-answer translation, identification, or brief analysis. Where asked, students must offer Latin support from the text for their assertions. Scoring guidelines are set forth in detail within the body of this Teacher's Guide.

Essay

Detailed guidelines accompany each essay question. The twenty-minute essay should be graded holistically on a scale of 0 to 6, with a dash (—) reserved for off-task answers or blank papers.

Major features of an essay to consider in grading:

1. Does the student answer the question as the directions frame it?
2. Does the student discuss all features of a question adequately, or are some features given short shrift or even neglected? For example, in *Ode 1.5*, the question breaks into two elements: how weather and seafaring imagery represents Pyrrha's treatment of men AND how it represents the men's reaction to that treatment.

---

3. Does the student treat all the parts of the poem that are relevant to the question? Many students, for example, skip over parts of the text that are hard to translate.

4. Does the essay develop and conclude an argument?

5. Does the student correctly cite and translate or paraphrase Latin words or phrases that support his or her argument? Are Latin citations liberal or scanty? How well do they reflect mastery of the language? Assertions that lack correct Latin support cannot contribute to the student's grade.

6. Discussion of major features of a poem, like propositional content, structure, and imagery, usually contribute more to an essay's argument than discussion of details like sound effects or isolated figures of speech.

In general, do not "take off" for errors. Award credit for what is correct. You need not agree with the student's interpretation, but that interpretation should be plausible, well argued, and well supported.

In two Appendices we offer examples of how to apply the essay grading scale described in this Teacher's Guide. Appendix A presents six increasingly faulty versions of a sample answer to the essay question on *Ode 1.5*. The six versions of the sample essay serve as models for the kind of responses that may earn a 6, a 5, and so on when graded according to the standards outlined in this Teacher's Guide. After each essay we explain briefly why we believe it merits the assigned grade. In Appendix B we print five actual student responses to the essay question on *Ode 2.3*. High school Advanced Placement* students wrote them in about 20 minutes. We and the Advanced Placement* teacher agreed on the grades awarded to each paper. After each essay we explain briefly why we assigned its grade.

Suggestions for Using the Workbook

Although the poems are printed by their order in the Horatian corpus, the instructor may teach them in any order. In all likelihood, our workbook will provide more exercises than the available time in a term allows. They can be used as homework assignments, in-class assignments, instruments for oral drill, or test questions.

Part I, Short Answer Questions, is good as an alternative to a straight translation assignment when students first read a poem. This section (or parts of it) can also make for good in-class drill.

Part II, Multiple Choice Exercises, is good for in-class use. For students who have already read the poem and learned the vocabulary, the degree of difficulty resembles that of Advanced Placement* Latin Literature multiple choice questions on passages from the Catullus syllabus, which students are to have read. Our suggested times therefore are briefer than what is allowed on the Advanced Placement* Exam for the same number of questions on an "unseen" passage. Teachers who want to give our multiple choice exercises to students who have not yet read the passage should supply unfamiliar vocabulary and allow at least 1.2 minutes per question.

An Appendix in the back of the (Student) Workbook provides four multiple choice exercises, with a key, based on "unseen" passages. Students can practice and check their own answers.

Part III, Translation, is designed to assess the accuracy of student translation. It is best not to allow students access to vocabulary lists for this exercise in order to best imitate the actual Advanced Placement* testing situation.

Part IV, Short Answer Analysis, is designed to assess students' mastery of translation, comprehension, and scansion, as well as their familiarity with references and allusions. It is best assigned as an in-class exercise or as part of a test.

---

* AP is a registered trademark of the College Entrance Examination Board, which was not involved in the production of, and does not endorse, this product.

Part V, Essay, may be assigned as a take-home assignment or as an in-class exercise or test question. If students preparing for the Advanced Placement* Exam write the essay unproctored, it is in their interest to time themselves, so that they practice finishing within the time limit suggested on the Exam's Horace essay. This limit at present is 20 minutes.

Part VI, Scansion, is good for homework or as in-class drill to be done singly, in pairs or small groups, or by the whole class.

Instructors who want to set review tests for their students may use the three review tests in Appendix C in their entirety or may select questions from them in any order. The free-response portion of each review test is designed for administration within 40 minutes, including a five-minute reading period. Further instructions and suggestions are found at the beginning of Appendix C. Note: the multiple choice questions added to the beginning of each review test are based on an "unseen" passage. This is to give students practice for the bulk of the multiple-choice section of the Advanced Placement* Exam.

As we state in the Preface to the Workbook, our exercises lay heavy emphasis on literary devices, broadly called by us "figures of speech," that appeared on the syllabus for the Advanced Placement* Exam in Latin Literature. Nevertheless, on occasion in the Short Answer Questions, Part I, we ask for "figure of speech (non-AP)": viz. juxtaposition, repetition for pathos or pathetic effect, meiosis, and rhetorical question. Teachers may wish to expose their students to even more devices, such as priamel, which we do not mention (e.g., in *Ode 1.1*), or pathetic fallacy (e.g., in *Ode 2.3*), or *schema Horatianum*, which several of the actual student essays of Appendix B discuss (i.e., *pinus ingens albaque populus* implies also "dark pine" and "short poplar"). When students are asked to *identify* a figure of speech on the Advanced Placement* Examination, as opposed to discuss Horace's technique in an essay, we believe they are best advised to select only those on the Advanced Placement* list of figures. For that reason, we rarely ask students to identify "figures of speech" that do not appear on the list.

We would like to make some additions to the acknowledgments we have already made in the Preface to the Workbook itself.

Donald Sprague, editor for the Teacher's Manual, provided us with excellent help and advice throughout the editing process. His good humor and prompt responses via e-mail made our job that much easier and more pleasant. LeaAnn Osburn, coeditor with Donald Sprague for the Workbook, continued to help us, when needed, on the Teacher's Manual. We thank Dr. Panayotes Dakouras, David Murphy's colleague at The Nightingale-Bamford School, for supplying us with "real" student essays and for sharing with us his grading of them. We are grateful to the following Advanced Placement* Latin students who gave us permission to use their essays: Adwoa Serwaa-Adusei, Jenna Bass, Jing Jin, Emma Lipari, and Jessica Taylor. In addition, we would like to thank former staff member at Bolchazy-Carducci, Michelle Wu, for writing the sample essay for *Ode 1.5*. Finally, a great debt is owed to the peer reviewers for Bolchazy-Carducci, Karen Lee Singh, Florida State University School, and Elizabeth Sutherland, University of Tennessee, whose knowledge and helpful feedback improved both the Workbook and this Teacher's Manual.

D.J.M. and R.A.

TEXT OF
SATIRE 1.9
WITH EXERCISES
AND ANSWERS

SATIRE 1.9.1–37

Ibam forte via sacra, sicut meus est mos,
nescio quid meditans nugarum, totus in illis.
accurrit quidam notus mihi nomine tantum,
arreptaque manu: 'quid agis, dulcissime rerum?'
5   'suaviter, ut nunc est' inquam, 'et cupio omnia, quae vis.'
cum adsectaretur: 'numquid vis?' occupo, at ille
'noris nos' inquit, 'docti sumus.' hic ego: 'pluris
hoc' inquam 'mihi eris.' misere discedere quaerens
ire modo ocius, interdum consistere, in aurem
10   dicere nescio quid puero, cum sudor ad imos
manaret talos. 'o te, Bolane, cerebri
felicem' aiebam tacitus, cum quidlibet ille
garriret, vicos, urbem laudaret. ut illi
nil respondebam: 'misere cupis' inquit 'abire;
15   iam dudum video. sed nil agis; usque tenebo.
persequar hinc, quo nunc iter est tibi.' 'nil opus est te
circumagi: quendam volo visere non tibi notum;
trans Tiberim longe cubat is prope Caesaris hortos.'
'nil habeo, quod agam, et non sum piger: usque sequar te.'
20   demitto auriculas, ut iniquae mentis asellus,
cum gravius dorso subiit onus. incipit ille:
'si bene me novi, non Viscum pluris amicum,
non Varium facies: nam quis me scribere pluris
aut citius possit versus? quis membra movere
25   mollius? invideat quod et Hermogenes ego canto.'
interpellandi locus hic erat: 'est tibi mater,
cognati, quis te salvo est opus?' 'haud mihi quisquam;
omnis composui.' 'felices! nunc ego resto.
confice! namque instat fatum mihi triste, Sabella
30   quod puero cecinit divina mota anus urna:
hunc neque dira venena, nec hosticus auferet ensis,
nec laterum dolor aut tussis, nec tarda podagra:
garrulus hunc quando consumet cumque. loquaces,
si sapiat, vitet, simul atque adoleverit aetas.'
35   ventum erat ad Vestae, quarta iam parte diei
praeterita, et casu tum respondere vadato
debebat, quod ni fecisset, perdere litem.

Short Answer Questions

Line 1   What is the case and use of *via sacra*? **ablative of place where**

Line 2   What is the case and use of *nugarum*? **partitive genitive with *nescio quid***

Line 3   What is the case and use of *nomine*? **ablative of means with *notus***

Line 4   What is the case and use of *manu*? **ablative absolute with *arrepta***

Line 5   What is the form of *vis*? **second person singular present active indicative of *velle***

Line 7   What is the translation of *hic*? **"here, at this point"**

Line 10   What is the case and use of *puero*? **dative, indirect object of *dicere***

Line 12   What is the case and use of *quidlibet*? **cognate accusative with *garriret***

Line 14   What does *misere* modify? ***cupis***

Line 16   What is the translation of *quo*? **"to where, where, whither"**

            What is the case and use of *tibi*? **dative of possession with *est***

Line 17   What form is *circumagi*? **present passive infinitive of *circumagere***

            What is the case and use of *quendam*? **accusative adjective acting as substantive, direct object of *visere***

Line 18   What is the case and use of *is*? **nominative, subject of *cubat***

            What is the case and use of *hortos*? **accusative, object of *prope***

Line 19   What is a good, idiomatic translation of *nil habeo, quod agam*? **"I have nothing to do," "I've got nothing to do."**

Line 20   What figure of speech is in this line? ***ut* etc., simile**

            What is the case and use of *mentis*? **genitive of quality**

Line 21   What is a good, idiomatic translation of *gravius*? **"rather heavy, too heavy"**

            What is the case and use of *dorso*? **ablative of means**

Lines 23–24 What figure of speech (non-AP) is in these lines? **rhetorical question**

Line 26   What part of speech is *interpellandi,* and what other word in the sentence provides the cause for its grammatical case? **gerund, genitive depending on *locus***

            What is the case and use of *tibi*? **dative of possession with *est***

Line 29   What is the case and use of *fatum*? **nominative, subject of *instat***

            What is the case and use of *Sabella*? **nominative adjective modifying the subject, *anus***

Line 31	To what does *hunc* refer? **the speaker, who represents himself as the subject of prophecy**
	What is the case and use of *venena?* **nominative, subject of implied *auferet***
	What two figures of speech are in this line? *neque ... nec ...* **etc.: anaphora; *ensis auferet:* personification or metaphor**
Line 32	What is the case and use of *laterum?* **subjective genitive with *dolor aut tussis***
	What figure of speech is in this line? *tarda podagra:* **transferred epithet**
Line 33	What is the case and use of *loquaces?* **adjective acting as substantive, accusative, direct object of *vitet***
Line 34	What is the translation of *si sapiat, vitet,* and by what name do we classify this kind of conditional sentence? **"if he should/were to have sense, he would avoid," future less vivid condition**
	What is the tense of *adoleverit?* **future perfect**
Line 35	What is the case and use of *diei?* **partitive genitive with *parte***
Line 36	What is the case and use of *casu?* **ablative of means**
Line 37	What is the case and use of *quod?* **accusative, direct object of *fecisset***
	What is the best translation in its context of *ni fecisset?* **"if he did not do/unless he did" or "if he had not done/unless he had done."**

Multiple Choice Questions *Suggested time: 15 minutes*

  Ibam forte via sacra, sicut meus est mos,
  nescio quid meditans nugarum, totus in illis.
  accurrit quidam notus mihi nomine tantum,
  arreptaque manu: 'quid agis, dulcissime rerum?'
5 'suaviter, ut nunc est' inquam, 'et cupio omnia, quae vis.'
  cum adsectaretur: 'numquid vis?' occupo, at ille
  'noris nos' inquit, 'docti sumus.' hic ego: 'pluris
  hoc' inquam 'mihi eris.' misere discedere quaerens
  ire modo ocius, interdum consistere, in aurem
10 dicere nescio quid puero, cum sudor ad imos
  manaret talos. 'o te, Bolane, cerebri
  felicem' aiebam tacitus, cum quidlibet ille
  garriret, vicos, urbem laudaret. ut illi
  nil respondebam: 'misere cupis' inquit 'abire;

             Satire 1.9.1–14

1. From lines 1–2, we learn that Horace was
    a. going to make sacrifices
    b. taking an unaccustomed route
    c. lost in thought
    d. setting out bravely

2. The character mentioned in line 3 was
    a. a friend of Horace
    b. a recent acquaintance of Horace
    c. a professional associate of Horace
    d. a man Horace knew only by name

3. The behavior of the character described in lines 3–4 is best described as
    a. considerate
    b. hostile
    c. presumptuous
    d. tentative

4. From lines 5–6, we may infer that Horace hopes that the man will
    a. go away
    b. want all the same things he wants
    c. follow him
    d. speak pleasantly

5. In line 4, the best translation of *quid agis* is
    a. how are you doing
    b. which are you doing
    c. what are you driving
    d. why are you doing

6. The words *hic ego: 'pluris hoc . . . mihi eris'* (lines 7–8) are translated
    a. I say this: you will be more to me than this
    b. I am this one: you will be full with this for me
    c. here I say: you will be worth more to me because of this
    d. I say at this point: you will be more valuable to me than to him

7. Horace's mood in lines 8–11 is best described as
    a. desperate
    b. frightened
    c. sad
    d. angry

8. In line 8, *misere* modifies
    a. *discedere* (line 8)
    b. *quaerens* (line 8)
    c. *ire* (line 9)
    d. *consistere* (line 9)

9. The case of *puero* (line 10) is determined by
    a. *quid* (line 10)
    b. *nescio* (line 10)
    c. *dicere* (line 10)
    d. *aurem* (line 9)

10. The person described as *puero* (line 10) is Horace's
    a. slave
    b. son
    c. young friend
    d. student

11. The metrical pattern of the first four feet of line 12 is

    a. dactyl-dactyl-dactyl-spondee
    b. spondee-spondee-dactyl-spondee
    c. dactyl-spondee-dactyl-spondee
    d. spondee-spondee-spondee-dactyl

12. A figure of speech found in line 13 is

    a. syncope
    b. hyperbole
    c. hysteron proteron
    d. asyndeton

13. The case and number of *illi* (line 13) are

    a. genitive singular
    b. dative singular
    c. nominative plural
    d. ablative singular

Translation *Suggested time: 10 minutes*

Translate the passage below as literally as possible.

> 'si bene me novi, non Viscum pluris amicum,
> non Varium facies: nam quis me scribere pluris
> aut citius possit versus? quis membra movere
> mollius? invideat quod et Hermogenes ego canto.'
> 5   interpellandi locus hic erat: 'est tibi mater, . . . ?'

Satire 1.9.22–26

18 chunks. 9 points, 1/2 point each. Round up to nearest whole point.

si bene	if well/or: as certainly as
me novi	I know myself
non Viscum . . . amicum	not Viscus (as a) friend (*amicum* may be in apposition to Viscum or may be predicate accusative)
pluris . . . facies	you will regard/consider (not "make") (as) worth more
non Varium	not Varius
nam quis	for who
me	than I (must be ablative of comparison)
scribere . . . possit	could/would be able to write
pluris . . . versus	more verses (*pluris* must be accusative)
aut citius	or more quickly/faster
quis membra	who (his) limbs
movere mollius	(could) move more softly/gently/flexibly
invideat . . . et Hermogenes	let/may/would even (not "and") Hermogenes envy
quod	that which/what
ego canto	I sing/recite/sing about
interpellandi locus	a place/opportunity of/for interrupting/breaking in
hic erat	here/at this point (not "this") was
est tibi mater	do you have a mother/is there a mother to/for you

Short Analysis Questions *Suggested time: 10 minutes*

interpellandi locus hic erat: 'est tibi mater,
cognati, quis te salvo est opus?' 'haud mihi quisquam;
omnis composui.' 'felices! nunc ego resto.
confice! namque instat fatum mihi triste, Sabella
5   quod puero cecinit divina mota anus urna:
hunc neque dira venena, nec hosticus auferet ensis,
nec laterum dolor aut tussis, nec tarda podagra:
garrulus hunc quando consumet cumque. loquaces,
si sapiat, vitet, simul atque adoleverit aetas.'

Satire 1.9.26–34

Eight points total.

1. a. Where are the family members of the person talking to the speaker?

    One point for saying the family members of the poet's interlocutor are dead or buried or in the grave.

  b. What does the speaker hope to accomplish by bringing up this person's family?

    One point for saying that the speaker hopes to spur his interlocutor to go away to conduct some family business.

2. What does the speaker reveal about his feelings when he says *"felices! nunc ego resto"* (line 3)? Write out and translate a Latin word or phrase and explain how it supports your answer.

    One point for identifying the speaker's tone as sarcastic or ironical or sardonic.

    One point for supporting Latin, such as *felices*, "happy/lucky": the interlocutor's family members are lucky to be dead, because they don't have to listen to him anymore. Students may add that the explanation on the surface is a wish for the happy repose of the dead.

    OR

    ***nunc ego resto*, "now I remain/am left": the speaker is stuck having to listen with no one else to distract the interlocutor. Students may add that the polite construal is that the speaker remains at the interlocutor's service in default of family members.**

3. According to lines 4–9, a prophecy was made about the speaker.

  a. Who made this prophecy?

    One point for identifying the prophet as the Sabine old woman.

  b. When was this prophecy made?

    One point for fixing the time of the prophecy as the speaker's boyhood.

  c. What does the prophecy foretell will be the cause of the speaker's death?

    One point for identifying foretold cause of death as a talkative/garrulous person or as listening to such a person.

4. Copy and scan line 5 (*quod . . . urna*).

One point for copying out and correctly scanning the line:

_ ∪∪ |_ ∪∪| _ _| _ _| _ ∪∪ |_ ×
quod puero cecinit divina mot(a) anus urna

(dactyl-dactyl-spondee-spondee-dactyl-spondee, elision of *a* in *mota*)

Essay *Suggested time: 20 minutes*

```
          accurrit quidam notus mihi nomine tantum,
          arreptaque manu: 'quid agis, dulcissime rerum?'
  5       'suaviter, ut nunc est' inquam, 'et cupio omnia, quae vis.'
          cum adsectaretur: 'numquid vis?' occupo, at ille
          'noris nos' inquit, 'docti sumus.' hic ego: 'pluris
          hoc' inquam 'mihi eris.' misere discedere quaerens
          ire modo ocius, interdum consistere, in aurem
 10       dicere nescio quid puero, cum sudor ad imos
          manaret talos. 'o te, Bolane, cerebri
          felicem' aiebam tacitus, cum quidlibet ille
          garriret, vicos, urbem laudaret. ut illi
          nil respondebam: 'misere cupis' inquit 'abire;
 15       iam dudum video. sed nil agis; usque tenebo.
          persequar hinc, quo nunc iter est tibi.' 'nil opus est te
          circumagi: quendam volo visere non tibi notum;
          trans Tiberim longe cubat is prope Caesaris hortos.'
          'nil habeo, quod agam, et non sum piger: usque sequar te.'
 20       demitto auriculas, ut iniquae mentis asellus,
          cum gravius dorso subiit onus. . . .
```

Satire 1.9.3–21

One of the elements that contributes to the humor of this satire is the conflict within the speaker between the desire to be polite to the person who addresses him and the desire to get rid of him. In a **brief,** well-organized essay, show how Horace represents this conflict.

Support your assertions with references drawn from **throughout** the passage. All Latin words must be copied or their line numbers provided, AND they must be translated or paraphrased closely enough so that it is clear you understand the Latin. It is your responsibility to convince your reader that you are basing your conclusions on the Latin text and not merely on a general recollection of the passage. Direct your answer to the question; do not merely summarize the passage. Please write your essay on a separate piece of paper.

The question asks the student to show how Horace represents the speaker's conflict between the desire to be polite and the desire to get rid of his unnamed interlocutor. Students can draw inferences from what the poet says about himself as speaker and from the words he puts in the speaker's mouth. They may point out, for example, that the speaker's sweating (10–11) is a sign of his stress, or that his

silence (12–14) aims to discourage further conversation without his saying so. Rather than look to see whether an essay enumerates all the speaker's character qualities, the grader should consider whether it presents analysis or merely description, shows insight, reveals mastery of the Latin evidence, and in broad outline, does justice to the whole passage.

6 – A fully-developed essay, which analyzes how Horace represents the speaker's conflict between the urge to politeness and the urge to escape conversation. The analysis ranges over the whole passage. The student makes ample reference to specific aspects of the Latin text to support his analysis and his position. Latin references are properly cited. Even though there may be occasional mistakes, the discussion is coherent and of high quality.

5 – A strong essay. Although the piece has good analysis, it is not as fully developed nor as supported with references to the text as a 6 paper. Latin references are properly cited. The essay reflects familiarity with the poem. A few parts of the passage may receive thin treatment.

4 – A competent response. There may be uneven development of the two opposing desires. Although they are limited in quantity, the essay includes accurate and relevant references in responding to the topic. The discussion may rely more on identifying and describing Horace's opposing desires than on showing how the poet depicts them. Some parts of the passage may be glossed over or omitted. Latin support is accurate but not extensive.

3 – A limited response. The Latin support is weak and/or inappropriate. Latin references are not properly cited. The answer is descriptive and does not reach the level of analysis. In some 3 papers, the student demonstrates an understanding of the passage but cites no Latin to support his answer.

2 – Some understanding of the passage, but the essay is general and/or vague. The discussion is flawed. The Latin cited demonstrates very limited comprehension.

1 – An incoherent response. While it does contain some relevant information, no substantive argument is presented. The student demonstrates no understanding of the poem.

0 – A response that is off-topic, completely incorrect, or irrelevant. Responses that merely restate the question are also a 0.

Scansion

Scan the following lines and name the meter. **The meter is dactylic hexameter.**

_ _ | _ ᴗ ᴗ|_ _ | _ _|_ ᴗᴗ|_ ×
Ibam forte via sacra, sicut meus est mos,

_ ᴗᴗ| _ ᴗᴗ|_ _|_ _ | _ᴗ ᴗ|_×
nescio quid meditans nugarum, totus in illis.

_ _ |_ _|_ _| _ ᴗᴗ| _ ᴗᴗ|_ ×
accurrit quidam notus mihi nomine tantum,

_ _ | _ ᴗ ᴗ|_ ᴗ ᴗ|_ _ |_ ᴗ ᴗ|_ ×
arreptaque manu: 'quid agis, dulcissime rerum?'

5   _ ᴗᴗ| _ _ |_ _| _ ᴗ ᴗ | _ ᴗᴗ| _ ×
'suaviter , ut nunc est' inqu(am), 'et cupi(o) omnia, quae vis.'

_ _ |_ _|_ _ | _ _ | _ ᴗ _ ᴗ|_ ×
c(um) adsectaretur: 'numquid vis?' occup(o), at ille

Satire 1.9.1–6

SATIRE 1.9.38–78

'si me amas' inquit, 'paulum hic ades.' 'inteream, si
aut valeo stare aut novi civilia iura,
40 et propero, quo scis.' 'dubius sum, quid faciam' inquit,
'tene relinquam, an rem.' 'me, sodes.' 'non faciam' ille,
et praecedere coepit. ego, ut contendere durum
cum victore, sequor. 'Maecenas quomodo tecum?'
hinc repetit, 'paucorum hominum et mentis bene sanae;
45 nemo dexterius fortuna est usus. haberes
magnum adiutorem, posset qui ferre secundas,
hunc hominem velles si tradere. dispeream, ni
summosses omnis.' 'non isto vivimus illic,
quo tu rere, modo. domus hac nec purior ulla est,
50 nec magis his aliena malis. nil mi officit, inquam,
ditior hic aut est quia doctior: est locus uni
cuique suus.' 'magnum narras, vix credibile.' 'atqui
sic habet.' 'accendis, quare cupiam magis illi
proxumus esse.' 'velis tantummodo: quae tua virtus,
55 expugnabis, et est, qui vinci possit, eoque
difficilis aditus primos habet.' 'haud mihi dero:
muneribus servos corrumpam; non, hodie si
exclusus fuero, desistam; tempora quaeram,
occurram in triviis, deducam. nil sine magno
60 vita labore dedit mortalibus.' haec dum agit, ecce
Fuscus Aristius occurrit, mihi carus et illum
qui pulchre nosset. consistimus. 'unde venis?' et
'quo tendis?' rogat et respondet. vellere coepi
et pressare manu lentissima brachia, nutans,
65 distorquens oculos, ut me eriperet. male salsus
ridens dissimulare, meum iecur urere bilis:
'certe nescio quid secreto velle loqui te
aiebas mecum.' 'memini bene, sed meliore
tempore dicam: hodie tricesima sabbata. vin tu
70 curtis Iudaeis oppedere?' 'nulla mihi' inquam
'religio est.' 'at mi! sum paulo infirmior, unus
multorum. ignosces; alias loquar.' huncine solem
tam nigrum surrexe mihi! fugit inprobus ac me
sub cultro linquit. casu venit obvius illi
75 adversarius et 'quo tu, turpissime?' magna
inclamat voce, et 'licet antestari?' ego vero
oppono auriculam. rapit in ius: clamor utrimque,
undique concursus. sic me servavit Apollo.

Short Answer Questions

Line 39   What is the case and use of *civilia iura*?   **accusative, direct object of *novi***

Line 40   What part of speech is *quo*?   **adverb: "whither, to what place"**

Line 41   What is the tense and mood of *faciam*?   **future indicative**

          What figure of speech is in this line?   **ellipsis of *inquit***

Line 42   What figure of speech is in this line?   **ellipsis of *est***

          Translate *ut*.   **"as"**

Line 45   Translate *dexterius*.   **"more skillfully, more dexterously"**

Line 46   What two figures of speech (one non-AP) are in this line?   ***posset qui:* postposition/ anastrophe; *ferre secundas:* metaphor**

Line 48   What word does *isto* modify?   ***modo* (line 49)**

          To what does *illic* refer?   **the house or circle of Maecenas**

Line 49   What is the case and use of *hac*?   **ablative of comparison with *purior***

Line 50   What does *magis* modify?   ***aliena***

Line 51   To what does *hic* refer?   **any randomly chosen member of Maecenas' circle**

          What is the case and use of *uni*?   **dative of possession with *est locus***

Line 52   What is the case and use of *magnum*?   **accusative substantival adjective, direct object of *narras***

Line 53   What is the tense and mood of *cupiam*?   **present subjunctive**

          What is the case and use of *illi*?   **dative with adjective *proxumus***

Line 54   What is the tense and mood of *velis*?   **present subjunctive**

Line 55   What is the object of *expugnabis*?   **an understood *eum*, i.e., *Maecenatem***

          What figure of speech is in this line?   ***expugnabis:* metaphor**

Line 56   What is the case and use of *aditus*?   **accusative, direct object of *habet***

Line 57   What is the case and use of *muneribus*?   **ablative of means with *corrumpam***

Line 58   To what does *tempora* refer?   **times in which the speaker may meet Maecenas**

Line 59   What is the case and use of *nil*?   **accusative, direct object of *dedit* (line 60)**

Line 60   What is the case and use of *mortalibus*?   **dative, indirect object of *dedit***

Line 61   To what does *illum* refer?   **Horace's unnamed interlocutor**

Line 64   What is the case and use of *manu*? **ablative of means with *pressare***

            What does *lentissima* modify? ***brachia***

Line 65   What type of clause does *ut* introduce? **a purpose clause**

            What does *salsus* modify? **the subject of *dissimulare*, who is Aristius Fuscus**

Line 66   What two figures of speech are in this line? ***dissimulare, meum:* asyndeton; *iecur urere bilis:* metaphor**

Line 67   What is the case and use of *te*? **accusative subject of *velle* in indirect statement depending on *aiebas* (line 68)**

Line 69   What is the case and use of *tempore*? **ablative of time when**

Line 70   What is the case and use of *mihi*? **dative of possession with *religio est* (line 71)**

Line 71   What is the case and use of *paulo*? **ablative of degree of difference with *infirmior***

Line 73   What is the case and use of *mihi*? **dative of reference or disadvantage with *solem surrexe***

            What does *inprobus* modify? **the subject of *fugit*, who is Aristius Fuscus**

Line 74   What figure of speech is in this line? ***sub cultro linquit:* metaphor**

            To what does *illi* refer? **Horace's unnamed interlocutor**

Line 77   What is the direct object of *rapit*? **an understood *illum* or *eum*, i.e., the interlocutor**

Multiple Choice Questions *Suggested time: 15 minutes*

'si me amas' inquit, 'paulum hic ades.' 'inteream, si
aut valeo stare aut novi civilia iura,
et propero, quo scis.' 'dubius sum, quid faciam' inquit,
'tene relinquam, an rem.' 'me, sodes.' 'non faciam' ille,
5 et praecedere coepit. ego, ut contendere durum
cum victore, sequor. 'Maecenas quomodo tecum?'
hinc repetit, 'paucorum hominum et mentis bene sanae;
nemo dexterius fortuna est usus. haberes
magnum adiutorem, posset qui ferre secundas,
10 hunc hominem velles si tradere. dispeream, ni
summosses omnis.'

Satire 1.9.38–48

1. In line 1, *inteream* appears in a clause that expresses
    a. purpose   b. condition
    c. deliberation   **d. wish**

2. In line 2, *novi* is translated
   - a. of the new
   - **b. I know**
   - c. I knew
   - d. the new ones

3. The case and number of *civilia* (line 2) are
   - **a. accusative plural**
   - b. nominative plural
   - c. nominative singular
   - d. ablative singular

4. In line 3, *quo* is translated
   - a. by which
   - b. for whom
   - **c. to what place**
   - d. as

5. In lines 1–3, Horace does NOT say that he
   - a. is in a hurry
   - **b. is bored with the conversation**
   - c. is not able to appear as an advocate
   - d. has no legal knowledge

6. From lines 3–5, we learn that Horace's interlocutor is willing to
   - a. abandon the conversation
   - b. hold Horace to his word
   - c. stop and consider what to do
   - **d. lose his case in court**

7. The expression closest in meaning to *sodes* (line 4) is
   - a. *comes*
   - **b. *si vis***
   - c. *amice*
   - d. *se audis*

8. A figure of speech that occurs in line 6 is
   - **a. ellipsis**
   - b. chiasmus
   - c. hyperbole
   - d. apostrophe

9. The case of *mentis* (line 7) is determined by
   - a. *paucorum* (line 7)
   - b. *bene* (line 7)
   - **c. an understood *homo***
   - d. *hominum* (line 7)

10. The metrical pattern of the first four feet of line 7 is
    - **a. dactyl-spondee-dactyl-spondee**
    - b. dactyl-dactyl-dactyl-spondee
    - c. spondee-spondee-dactyl-spondee
    - d. dactyl-spondee-spondee-dactyl

11. In lines 8–10, Horace's interlocutor promises to
    - a. listen enthusiastically
    - **b. be a help**
    - c. bring second-best things
    - d. receive a mutual friend

12. In line 10, *hominem* refers to
    a. the poet
    b. Maecenas
    c. the slave
    d. the person speaking to Horace

13. In line 11, the case of *omnis* is
    a. nominative
    b. accusative
    c. genitive
    d. ablative

14. The tense and mood of *summosses* (line 11) are
    a. pluperfect subjunctive
    b. future indicative
    c. imperfect subjunctive
    d. present indicative

Translation *Suggested time: 10 minutes*

Translate the passage below as literally as possible.

> '. . . nil mi officit, inquam,
> ditior hic aut est quia doctior: est locus uni
> cuique suus.' 'magnum narras, vix credibile.' 'atqui
> sic habet.' 'accendis, quare cupiam magis illi
> 5   proxumus esse.' 'velis tantummodo: quae tua virtus,
> expugnabis, et est, qui vinci possit, . . . '

Satire 1.9.50–56

18 chunks. 9 points, 1/2 point each. Round up to nearest whole point.

nil mi	**nothing to me/me (must be governed by *officit*)**
officit, inquam	**is an interference/impedes/interferes with I say/said**
hic . . . est quia	**because this one is**
ditior . . . aut . . . doctior	**richer/wealthier or more learned/educated**
est locus . . . suus	**there is his own place**
uni . . . cuique	**to/for each one OR *est . . . suus* may be translated "each one has his own place"**
magnum narras	**you relate/tell/narrate a big thing/something big**
vix credibile	**scarcely/hardly/with difficulty believable/credible**
atqui	**but/nevertheless/and yet**
sic habet	**thus/so it holds itself/it is OR that's how/the way it is**
accendis . . . quare	**you kindle/set on fire (an object like "reasons" or "me" may be supplied) why/wherefore/for which reason**
cupiam magis	**I desire/want more**
illi proxumus esse	**to be nearest/next to him/that one**
velis tantummodo	**you would only wish it/you only need wish it**
quae tua virtus	**virtue/valor which is your(s) OR such is your valor**
expugnabis	**you will take (him) by assault/storm, you will conquer/overcome (him)**
et est	**and he is**
qui vinci possit	**(a person) who could/would be able to/can be overcome/won (over)/defeated**

Short Analysis Questions *Suggested time: 10 minutes*

> . . . casu venit obvius illi
> adversarius et 'quo tu, turpissime?' magna
> inclamat voce, et 'licet antestari?' ego vero
> oppono auriculam. rapit in ius: clamor utrimque,
> 5   undique concursus. sic me servavit Apollo.

Satire 1.9.74–78

Eight points total.

1. In lines 1–2,

   a. who is the *adversarius?*

      One point for identifying the *adversarius* as the opponent in court of Horace's interlocutor.

   b. to whom is he speaking?

      One point for identifying Horace's interlocutor as the person to whom the *adversarius* is speaking.

   c. why does he address this person as *turpissime?*

      One point for explaining *turpissime* as motivated by Horace's interlocutor's intention to continue following Horace rather than appearing in court as required.

2. In line 3, what does the *adversarius* want to happen?

   One point for saying that the *adversarius* wants to call Horace as a witness to his dragging the interlocutor.

3. Copy and scan line 4 (*oppono . . . utrimque*) and name the meter.

   One point for copying out and correctly scanning the line:

   $$\_ \ \_ \ | \ \_\cup\cup| \_ \ \ \cup\cup|\_ \ \_ \ | \ \_ \ \cup \ \cup|\_ \ \ \times$$
   oppon(o) auriculam. rapit in ius: clamor utrimque

   One point for identifying the meter as dactylic hexameter.

4. In line 4,

   a. what action is meant by *oppono auriculam?*

      One point for explaining *oppono auriculam*: Horace offers his ear so that the *adversarius* may touch it.

   b. what is the legal significance of this action?

      One point for explaining legal significance as an indication of Horace's willingness to stand as a witness (on behalf of the *adversarius*).

Essay *Suggested time: 20 minutes*

```
        . . . haec dum agit, ecce
        Fuscus Aristius occurrit, mihi carus et illum
        qui pulchre nosset. consistimus. 'unde venis?' et
        'quo tendis?' rogat et respondet. vellere coepi
   5    et pressare manu lentissima brachia, nutans,
        distorquens oculos, ut me eriperet. male salsus
        ridens dissimulare, meum iecur urere bilis:
        'certe nescio quid secreto velle loqui te
        aiebas mecum.' 'memini bene, sed meliore
  10    tempore dicam: hodie tricesima sabbata. vin tu
        curtis Iudaeis oppedere?' 'nulla mihi' inquam
        'religio est.' 'at mi! sum paulo infirmior, unus
        multorum. ignosces; alias loquar.' huncine solem
        tam nigrum surrexe mihi! fugit inprobus ac me
  15    sub cultro linquit. . . .
```

Satire 1.9.60–74

One of the elements that contribute to the humor of *Satire* 1.9 is Horace's representation of character. In a **brief,** well-organized essay, discuss the ways in which Horace creates an impression of the character of Aristius Fuscus, and show how this depiction of Fuscus' character contributes to the satire's humor.

Support your assertions with references drawn from **throughout** the passage. All Latin words must be copied or their line numbers provided, AND they must be translated or paraphrased closely enough so that it is clear you understand the Latin. It is your responsibility to convince your reader that you are basing your conclusions on the Latin text and not merely on a general recollection of the passage. Direct your answer to the question; do not merely summarize the passage. Please write your essay on a separate piece of paper.

The essay asks the student to do two things: show how Horace develops the character of Aristius Fuscus; show how that development aims to contribute to the humor of the satire. The need for a student to analyze rather than merely describe is acute, for simply recounting what happens in the passage is not enough to answer either element of the two-part question. Perhaps the easiest evidence for students to pick out are the three adjectives that describe Fuscus (*mihi carus,* 2; *male salsus,* 6; *inprobus,* 14); sensitivity to Horace's tone will mark a sophisticated analysis of Horace's use of these adjectives. Much of the student's material for an analysis of Fuscus' character must come by infer-ence. Conclusions about Fuscus' character can be drawn from what he says (9–11 and 12–13), what he does (3–7 passim, 14–15), and the fact that he knows the unnamed interlocutor well (3). There is no single answer to the question, how this depiction of Fuscus' character contributes to the satire's humor. The student can pick out comic elements in the material cited above and in the predicament in which Fuscus leaves Horace by line 15.

Some analysis for each "element" of the two-part question, supported with accurate Latin, is neces-sary for a 4. A 6 reveals itself by the success with which it analyzes the whole passage to answer both parts of the question and by the mastery it betrays of the Latin support.

6 – A fully-developed essay, which analyzes how Horace represents Fuscus' character AND how that representation contributes to the humor of the poem. The analysis ranges over the whole passage. The student makes ample reference to specific aspects of the Latin text to support his analysis and his position. Latin references are properly cited. Even though there may be occasional mistakes, the discussion is coherent and of high quality.

5 – A strong essay. Although the piece has good analysis, it is not as fully developed nor as supported with references to the text as a 6 paper. Latin references are properly cited. The essay reflects familiarity with the poem. A few parts of the passage may receive thin treatment.

4 – A competent response. There may be uneven development of the two parts of the question. Although limited in quantity, the essay includes accurate and relevant references in responding to the topic. The discussion may rely more on describing Fuscus' character than on showing how its representation contributes to the humor, but some attempt at analysis of this second point must be made and supported from the Latin. Some parts of the passage may be glossed over or omitted. Latin support is accurate but not extensive.

3 – A limited response. The Latin support is weak and/or inappropriate. Latin references are not properly cited. The answer is descriptive and does not reach the level of analysis. In some 3 papers, the student demonstrates an understanding of the passage but cites no Latin to support his answer.

2 – Some understanding of the passage, but the essay is general and/or vague. The discussion is flawed. The Latin cited demonstrates very limited comprehension.

1 – An incoherent response. While it does contain some relevant information, no substantive argument is presented. The student demonstrates no understanding of the poem.

0 – A response that is off-topic, completely incorrect, or irrelevant. Responses that merely restate the question are also a 0.

Scansion

Scan the following lines and name the meter. **The meter is dactylic hexameter.**

$$\_\ \_\ |\ \_\ \cup\cup|\_\ \ \_\ |\ \_\ \ \_\ \ \ \ \_\ \ \cup\ \ \cup|\ \_\ \times$$
nemo dexterius fortuna (e)st usus. haberes

$$\_\ \ \ \ \ \ \_\ |\ \_\ \_|\ \_\ \ \ \ \_\ |\ \_\ \ \ \ \_\ |\ \_\ \cup\ \cup|\ \ \times$$
magn(um) adiutorem, posset qui ferre secundas,

$$\_\ \ \ \ \cup\ \cup|\ \_\ \ \ \_\ |\ \_\ \ \ \_\ |\ \_\ \cup\cup|\ \_\ \cup\cup|\ \ \times$$
hunc hominem velles si tradere. dispeream, ni

$$\_\ \ \ \_\ |\ \_\ \ \_\ \ |\ \_\ \ \ \ \_\ |\_\ \ \_\ |\ \_\ \cup\ \cup|\ \_\ \times$$
summosses omnis.' 'non isto vivimus illic,

5   $$\_\ \ \_\ |\ \_\ \cup\ \ \cup|\ \_\ \ \ \cup\ \cup|\ \_\ \ \ \_\ |\ \_\cup\cup|\ \_\ \times$$
quo tu rere, modo. domus hac nec purior ulla (e)st,

$$\_\ \ \ \cup\ \cup|\ \_\ \cup\cup|\_\cup\ \ \cup|\_\ \ \ \ \_\ |\ \ \ \ \_\ \cup\cup|\ \_\ \ \times$$
nec magis his aliena malis. nil m(i) officit, inquam,

Satire 1.9.45–50

TEXT OF
ODES
WITH EXERCISES
AND ANSWERS

ODE 1.1

Maecenas atavis edite regibus,
o et praesidium et dulce decus meum:

sunt, quos curriculo pulverem Olympicum
collegisse iuvat metaque fervidis

5   evitata rotis palmaque nobilis
terrarum dominos evehit ad deos;

hunc, si mobilium turba Quiritium
certat tergeminis tollere honoribus,

illum, si proprio condidit horreo,
10   quicquid de Libycis verritur areis.

gaudentem patrios findere sarculo
agros Attalicis condicionibus

numquam demoveas, ut trabe Cypria
Myrtoum pavidus nauta secet mare;

15   luctantem Icariis fluctibus Africum
mercator metuens otium et oppidi

laudat rura sui, mox reficit rates
quassas indocilis pauperiem pati.

est, qui nec veteris pocula Massici
20   nec partem solido demere de die

spernit, nunc viridi membra sub arbuto
stratus, nunc ad aquae lene caput sacrae;

multos castra iuvant et lituo tubae
permixtus sonitus bellaque matribus

25   detestata; manet sub Iove frigido
venator tenerae coniugis inmemor,

seu visa est catulis cerva fidelibus,
seu rupit teretes Marsus aper plagas.

          me doctarum hederae praemia frontium
30   dis miscent superis, me gelidum nemus

          Nympharumque leves cum Satyris chori
          secernunt populo, si neque tibias

          Euterpe cohibet, nec Polyhymnia
          Lesboum refugit tendere barbiton.

35   quodsi me lyricis vatibus inseres,
          sublimi feriam sidera vertice.

Short Answer Questions

Line 1   What figure of speech is in this line? **interlocked word order/synchysis**

                What is the case and use of *atavis?* **ablative of source or origin with *edite***

                What is the case and use of *edite?* **vocative, modifying *Maecenas***

                What is the case and use of *regibus?* **ablative, used adjectivally to modify *atavis***

Line 2   What is the case and use of *praesidium?* **vocative in apposition to *Maecenas***

                What figure of speech is in this line? ***praesidium et dulce decus:* alliteration;
                praesidium: metaphor is also acceptable**

Line 3   What is the case and use of *curriculo?* **ablative of means with *collegisse***

Line 4   What is the form of *collegisse?* **perfect active infinitive**

          · What is the case and use of *meta?* **nominative, a second subject of *iuvat* (line 4), or
                a subject of *evehit,* line 6, along with *palma* (cf. Ronnie Ancona, *Horace. Selected
                Odes and Satire 1.9* [Wauconda, IL: Bolchazy-Carducci, 1999, 2nd edition, 2005]
                ad loc.)**

Lines 4–5 What figure of speech is present in these lines? ***meta fervidis evitata rotis:*
                interlocked word order/synchysis/synchesis**

Lines 5–6 What three figures of speech are in these lines? ***metaque … palmaque … evehit ad
                deos:* metaphor; *palma nobilis:* metonymy for victory; *nobilis:* transferred epithet
                (cf. Ancona, *Horace,* 1999, 2nd edition, 2005 *ad loc.*)**

Line 6   What is the case and use of *terrarum?* **objective genitive or genitive of possession
                with *dominos***

Line 8   What figure of speech is in this line? **use of t's: alliteration**

                What is the case and use of *honoribus?* **ablative of means or ablative of manner with
                *tollere***

Lines 9–10   What is the direct object of *condidit*? **the noun clause** *quicquid de Libycis verritur areis*

Line 11   What is the function of *gaudentem*? ***gaudentem* is a present participle acting as a substantive, the direct object of *demoveas***

On what other word in the sentence does *findere* depend? ***gaudentem* (*findere* is a complementary infinitive, denoting an action performed by the person represented as *gaudentem*)**

What is the case and use of *sarculo*? **ablative of means with *findere***

Line 12   What two figures of speech are in this line? ***Attalicis condicionibus*: hyperbole, metonymy (for the wealth that the conditions would secure)**

What is the case and use of *condicionibus*? **ablative of means with *demoveas***

Line 13   What is the case and use of *trabe*? **ablative of means with *secet***

Line 14   What figure of speech is in this line? ***Myrtoum pavidus nauta . . . mare*: chiasmus**

Line 15   What two figures of speech are in this line? **chiasmus; *luctantem*: personification**

Line 16   What is the direct object of *metuens*? ***Africum***

What is the case and use of *oppidi*? **genitive of possession with *rura***

Line 17   What are the direct objects of *laudat*? ***otium* and *rura***

Line 18   What is the case and use of *indocilis*? **nominative modifying *mercator* (line 16)**

What is the case and use of *pauperiem*? **accusative, direct object of *pati***

Lines 20–21   What figure of speech is in these lines? ***spernit*: enjambment**

On what other word in the sentence does *demere* depend? ***demere* is a complementary infinitive with *spernit***

Lines 21–22   What two figures of speech are in these lines? ***nunc . . . nunc*: anaphora; *stratus*: enjambment**

What is the case and use of *membra*? **Greek medial accusative with *stratus*, a passive form used reflexively, or accusative of respect with *stratus***

Line 22   What does *stratus* modify? **the person who may be understood as subject of *est* and *spernit***

What figure of speech is in this line? ***aquae lene caput sacrae*: chiasmus**

Line 23   What is the case and use of *multos*? **accusative, adjective used as substantive, direct object of *iuvant***

What are the subjects of *iuvant*? ***castra, sonitus,* and *bella***

What is the case and use of *tubae*? **subjective genitive with *sonitus***

Lines 24–25   What figure of speech is in these lines? ***detestata*: enjambment**

Line 26	What figure of speech is present in this line? *venator tenerae coniugis inmemor:* **chiasmus**
	What is the case and use of *coniugis?* **genitive with *inmemor*, which governs that case**
Line 27	What is the case and use of *catulis?* **with *visa est*, dative of agent or ablative of agent without preposition, or dative of reference**
Line 28	What figure of speech is in this line? *teretes Marsus aper plagas:* **chiasmus**
Line 29	What is the case and use of *me?* **accusative, direct object of *miscent***
	What is the case and use of *hederae?* **nominative, subject of *miscent***
	What is the case and use of *praemia?* **nominative in apposition to *hederae***
	What is the case and use of *frontium?* **genitive of possession with *praemia***
	What two figures of speech are in this line? *doctarum:* **transferred epithet;** *frontium:* **synecdoche for the poet**
Lines 29–30	What two figures of speech are in these lines? *me . . . me:* **anaphora;** *(hederae) miscent:* **metaphor**
Line 32	What are the subjects of *secernunt?* **nemus and chori**
	What is the case and use of *populo?* **ablative of separation with *secernunt***
Line 35	What is the case and use of *vatibus?* **dative with *inseres***
Lines 35–36	What tense are *inseres* and *feriam?* Name the type of conditional sentence that is in these lines. **inseres and feriam are future indicative in a future more vivid conditional sentence**
Line 36	What does *sublimi* modify? **vertice**
	What two figures of speech are in this line? *feriam sidera vertice:* **hyperbole; metaphor for gaining eternal fame or immortality or divine status**
	What is the case and use of *vertice?* **ablative of means with *feriam***

Multiple Choice Questions *Suggested time: 15 minutes*

gaudentem patrios findere sarculo
agros Attalicis condicionibus
numquam demoveas, ut trabe Cypria
Myrtoum pavidus nauta secet mare;
5 luctantem Icariis fluctibus Africum
mercator metuens otium et oppidi
laudat rura sui, mox reficit rates
quassas indocilis pauperiem pati.
est, qui nec veteris pocula Massici

10   nec partem solido demere de die
        spernit, nunc viridi membra sub arbuto
        stratus, nunc ad aquae lene caput sacrae;

Ode 1.1.11–22

1. In line 1, *gaudentem* describes a person who rejoices because he
    a. found his father's fields
    c. becomes a sailor
    b. was paid a fortune
    d. **farms his native soil**

2. The case of *condicionibus* (line 2) is determined by
    a. *numquam* (line 3)
    c. *findere* (line 1)
    b. *Attalicis* (line 2)
    d. *demoveas* **(line 3)**

3. In line 3, *demoveas* is translated
    a. you move away
    c. in order that you move away
    b. **you would move away**
    d. so that you may move away

4. A figure of speech contained in line 3 is
    a. **synecdoche**
    c. personification
    b. hyperbole
    d. transferred epithet

5. The words *luctantem . . . metuens* (lines 5–6) are translated
    a. **the merchant, fearing the African wind wrestling with the Icarian waves**
    c. amidst the Icarian waves, the merchant fearing the African wind wrestling
    b. with the Icarian winds flowing, the merchant fearing the struggling African wind
    d. the African wind contends with the Icarian waves as the merchant fears

6. From lines 7–8, we learn that the merchant
    a. praises commerce
    c. **rebuilds ships**
    b. is poor
    d. prefers the countryside to the sea

7. The case and number of *indocilis* (line 8) are
    a. ablative plural
    c. genitive singular
    b. **nominative singular**
    d. accusative plural

8. The form *pati* (line 8) is
    a. perfect participle
    c. **present infinitive**
    b. perfect indicative
    d. present imperative

9. In line 9, *veteris* modifies
    a. *qui* (line 9)
    c. the subject of *spernit* (line 11)
    b. the subject of *est* (line 9)
    d. *Massici* **(line 9)**

10. The person described in lines 9–12 (*est . . . sacrae*)

   a. **takes time out from business**
   b. despises drinking
   c. steals metal
   d. works in his garden

11. The case of *membra* (line 11) is determined by

   a. *arbuto* (line 11)
   b. *viridi* (line 11)
   c. **stratus (line 12)**
   d. *sub* (line 11)

12. In line 12, *caput* refers to a

   a. person's life
   b. **source**
   c. body part
   d. chief

13. A description of a person who devotes time to relaxation is

   a. *luctantem Icariis fluctibus Africum mercator metuens* (lines 5–6)
   b. **nec partem solido demere de die spernit (lines 10–11)**
   c. *pavidus nauta secet mare* (line 4)
   d. *mox reficit rates quassas* (lines 7–8)

Translation *Suggested time: 15 minutes*

Translate the passage below as literally as possible.

> multos castra iuvant et lituo tubae
> permixtus sonitus bellaque matribus
> detestata; manet sub Iove frigido
> venator tenerae coniugis inmemor,
> 5   seu visa est catulis cerva fidelibus,
> seu rupit teretes Marsus aper plagas.
> me doctarum hederae praemia frontium
> dis miscent superis, . . .

Ode 1.1.23–30

18 chunks. 9 points total, 1/2 point each. Round up to nearest whole point.

multos castra iuvant	**the (military) camp pleases many**
et . . . tubae . . . sonitus	**and the sound of the (straight) trumpet**
lituo . . . permixtus	**mixed (together) with the (curved cavalry) trumpet**
bellaque . . . detestata	**and wars prayed against/cursed/detested/abhorred**
matribus	**by mothers**
manet . . . venator	**the hunter remains/stays**
sub Iove frigido	**beneath/under frigid/cold Jupiter/Jove/sky/(open) air**
inmemor	**unmindful/forgetful**
tenerae coniugis	**of (his) tender/delicate/soft/young wife/spouse**
seu . . . seu	**whether . . . or**
visa est . . . cerva	**a deer/doe was seen/(has) appeared**
catulis . . . fidelibus	**by/to faithful (young) dogs**

rupit . . . Marsus aper	**a Marsian boar (has) broken/shattered/destroyed (perfect tense of verb must be rendered)**
teretes . . . plagas	**rounded/smooth/polished nets (must be object of *rupit*)**
me . . . miscent	**mix/mingle me**
hederae praemia	**ivy/ivies, (the) reward/s. *Hederae* and the words coordinate to it may be translated as singular.**
doctarum . . . frontium	**of learned foreheads**
dis . . . superis	**with/among the gods above/on high/the higher ones**

Short Analysis Questions *Suggested time: 10 minutes*

> sunt, quos curriculo pulverem Olympicum
> collegisse iuvat metaque fervidis
> evitata rotis palmaque nobilis
> terrarum dominos evehit ad deos;
> 5   hunc, si mobilium turba Quiritium
> certat tergeminis tollere honoribus,
> illum, si proprio condidit horreo,
> quicquid de Libycis verritur areis.

Ode 1.1.3–10

Eight points total.

1.   What is the achievement of the people who are described in lines 1–4? Cite and translate or paraphrase closely two Latin words or phrases that support your answer.

Three points total.

One point for identifying the accomplishment as winning a chariot race. Students may add that the victory is in the Olympic games.

One point for each of two items of Latin support correctly cited and translated or closely paraphrased: *curriculo pulverem (Olympicum) collegisse* (to have collected [Olympic] dust with/on a chariot), *metaque (fervidis) evitata rotis* (and the turning post avoided by burning-hot wheels), *palmaque nobilis evehit ad deos* (and the noble palm carries out/raises to the gods), etc.

2.   Identify a figure of speech contained in lines 2–3 and write out the Latin words that illustrate it.

One point for identifying a figure of speech and citing the accompanying Latin: interlocked word order/synchysis/synchesis (*metaque fervidis evitata rotis*); metonymy (*palma* stands for victory).

3.   In lines 5–6,

a.   what is the *turba Quiritium*?

One point for identifying the *turba Quiritium* as (a crowd of Roman) citizens.

b. what does it do that pleases the person referred to by the word *hunc* (line 5)?

One point for stating that the crowd confers political honors, which the student may further characterize as "triple" or as election as aedile, praetor, and consul, or as triple or reiterated applause.

4. To what does *quicquid* in line 8 refer? Cite and translate or paraphrase closely the Latin words that support your answer.

One point for identifying what is described in line 8 as grain. The student may add that it is from Libya.

One point for Latin support, which must include *verritur areis*.

Essay *Suggested time: 20 minutes*

> me doctarum hederae praemia frontium
> dis miscent superis, me gelidum nemus
> Nympharumque leves cum Satyris chori
> secernunt populo, si neque tibias
> 5   Euterpe cohibet, nec Polyhymnia
> Lesboum refugit tendere barbiton.
> quodsi me lyricis vatibus inseres,
> sublimi feriam sidera vertice.

Ode 1.1.29–36

In the passage above, Horace suggests that his poetic gifts win him special status. In a short, well-organized essay, explain what this status is and show how the poet expresses his claims to deserve it.

Support your assertions with references to the Latin text **throughout** the passage above. All Latin words must be copied or their line numbers provided, AND they must be translated or paraphrased closely enough so that it is clear you understand the Latin. It is your responsibility to convince the reader that you are basing your conclusions on the Latin text and not merely on a general recollection of the passage. Direct your answer to the question; do not merely summarize the passage. Please write your essay on a separate piece of paper.

The student is asked to do two things: explain the special status for which Horace claims his poetic gifts qualify him; show how he expresses his claims that his poetry qualifies him to deserve that status. An excellent paper will analyze the rich imagery of these lines to show their significance for Horace's representation of his status and role as a poet, and it will support its arguments with a generous amount of Latin evidence, accurately translated or paraphrased. A student may draw inferences like these: poetic gifts confer on Horace a privileged position (*secernunt populo*); references to myth and literary history put Horace on a level with great poets of Greece (*Nympharum . . . cum Satyris chori*), including Sappho and/or Alcaeus (*Lesboum . . . barbiton*); he benefits from inspiration (*si neque . . . Euterpe cohibet . . . nec Polyhymnia . . . refugit*); approbation or collaboration of his patron/reader helps him achieve poetic immortality (*quodsi . . . feriam sidera vertice*). If students make value judgements about the way Horace represents his poetic vocation, they should offer argument and support for

them. For example, someone may point to the way a playful tone lessens the boastful quality: e.g., the humor in the picture of Horace's head bumping the stars. Some students may point to instances of good writing in the poem as support for Horace's assertion of his own talent: e.g., Horace's word choice, word position, or use of figures of speech (superior papers will explain their effect and not merely note their presence).

6 – Excellent, perceptive, analytical account of the nature of Horace's special status and of how he expresses his claims that his poetry qualifies him to deserve it. The whole passage is discussed. Liberal, appropriate and accurate use of Latin support, correctly cited.

5 – Good, not as analytical or as organized a discussion of Horace's status and of how he expresses his claims that his poetry entitles him to deserve it. May offer less full Latin support, but what appears is accurate and appropriate.

4 – Satisfactory, adequate analysis of Horace's claims to special status and of how his poetic gifts justify them. The essay may be thinner and tend more toward description than analysis, although some analysis is present. For example, even if it may include statements that go no further than to assert something like "Horace says that nymphs and satyrs will separate him from the people," with supporting Latin adduced, the essay must make some attempt to show how such statements bear on the question. Alternatively, a satisfactory essay may present a convincing analysis, with strong Latin support, but omit discussion of major parts of the passage.

3 – Superficial, may be rambling, too general, or uneven. Unlike a satisfactory essay, a superficial one will have inadequate analysis; the paper may amount to a restatement of the Latin. If attempted, analysis engages only one part of the question. Alternatively, the essay may offer good analysis but lack correctly cited and translated/paraphrased Latin support.

2 – Scanty, vague, faulty discussion of the question. The student provides some correct information but may betray a major misconception about the poem. Very scanty Latin support or even no Latin correctly cited.

1 – Only one or two correct things in response to the question and based on the passage.

0 – The student says nothing correct or meaningful derived from the passage, although something may be guessed at from the wording of the question itself.

Scansion

Scan the following lines and name the meter. **The meter is first or lesser Asclepiadean.**

gaudentem patrios findere sarculo

agros Attalicis condicionibus

numquam demoveas, ut trabe Cypria

Myrtoum pavidus nauta secet mare;

15 luctant(em) Icariis fluctibus Africum

mercator metuens oti(um) et oppidi

laudat rura sui, mox reficit rates

quassas indocilis pauperiem pati.

Ode 1.1.11–18

ODE 1.5

Quis multa gracilis te puer in rosa
perfusus liquidis urget odoribus
   grato, Pyrrha, sub antro?
      cui flavam religas comam

5   simplex munditiis? heu quotiens fidem
mutatosque deos flebit et aspera
   nigris aequora ventis
      emirabitur insolens,

qui nunc te fruitur credulus aurea,
10   qui semper vacuam, semper amabilem
   sperat, nescius aurae
      fallacis. miseri, quibus

intemptata nites. me tabula sacer
votiva paries indicat uvida
15   suspendisse potenti
      vestimenta maris deo.

Short Answer Questions

Line 1   What figure of speech is in this line? **extended chiasmus (ABCBA)**

What is the case and use of *te*? **accusative, direct object of *urget***

Line 4   What is the case and use of *cui*? **dative of reference with *religas***

What is the subject and translation of *religas*? **Pyrrha understood "you (s.) tie back, bind back, untie"**

Line 5   What is the case and use of *munditiis*? **ablative of specification**

Line 7   What is the case and use of *ventis*? **ablative of cause with *aspera***

Line 8   What is the subject and translation of *emirabitur*? **the *puer,* translation: he will be amazed at, marvel at**

Line 9   What is the case and use of *te*? **ablative (of means) with *fruitur,* which governs the ablative**

Line 10   What two figures of speech are in this line? *semper . . . semper:* **anaphora; asyndeton**

What is the translation of *vacuam* and what does it modify? **translation: available; modifies an understood accusative *te* (Pyrrha)**

Line 11   What is the case and use of *aurae*? **genitive with adjective of knowledge** *(nescius)*

Line 12   What is the antecedent, case, and use of *quibus*? **antecedent:** *miseri;* **dative of reference with** *nites*

Line 13   What is the translation of *intemptata*? What does it modify? **translation: untried, unassailed; modifies Pyrrha**

             What figure of speech (non-AP) is in this line? **assonance**

             What is the case and use of *me*? **accusative subject of** *suspendisse* **in indirect statement**

             What is the case and use of *tabula*? **ablative of means with** *indicat*

             What is the case and use of *sacer*? **nominative adjective modifying** *paries*

Line 14   What is the subject of *indicat*? ***paries;*** **("the wall declares that I have hung up")**

Lines 13–14   What figure of speech is in these lines? *tabula sacer votiva paries:* **interlocked word order/synchysis/synchesis**

Line 15   Why must *suspendisse* appear in the infinitive form? **because it appears in an indirect statement**

Line 16   What is the case and use of *deo*? **dative, indirect object or dative of reference with** *suspendisse*

Multiple Choice Questions *Suggested time: 12 minutes*

> Quis multa gracilis te puer in rosa
> perfusus liquidis urget odoribus
>   grato, Pyrrha, sub antro?
>   cui flavam religas comam
>
> 5   simplex munditiis? heu quotiens fidem
> mutatosque deos flebit et aspera
>   nigris aequora ventis
>   emirabitur insolens,
>
> qui nunc te fruitur credulus aurea,
> 10 qui semper vacuam, semper amabilem
>   sperat, nescius aurae
>   fallacis. miseri, quibus
>
> intemptata nites. me tabula sacer
> votiva paries indicat uvida
> 15   suspendisse potenti
>   vestimenta maris deo.

Ode 1.5

1. In line 1, *multa gracilis . . . puer in rosa* is translated
   a. many slender boys in the roses
   b. boy among many graceful roses
   c. slender boy in a large rose
   d. slender boy among many a rose

2. From lines 1–3, we learn that the boy
   a. is urging Pyrrha to accept perfume
   b. is mixing scents with liquids
   c. has put much perfume on himself
   d. is pouring perfume on Pyrrha

3. The subject of *emirabitur* (line 8) is
   a. the boy
   b. Pyrrha
   c. the sea
   d. the god

4. The case of *te* (line 9) is determined by
   a. *fruitur* (line 9)
   b. *aurea* (line 9)
   c. *credulus* (line 9)
   d. *sperat* (line 11)

5. In its context, *vacuam* (line 10) implies
   a. empty-headed
   b. not stylish
   c. with few possessions
   d. available

6. A figure of speech that appears in line 12 is
   a. poetic plural
   b. ellipsis
   c. transferred epithet
   d. simile

7. In line 12, *miseri* refers to
   a. Pyrrha's past lovers
   b. those who have yielded to temptation
   c. men whose advances fail to tempt Pyrrha
   d. those who are attracted to Pyrrha without experience of her

8. In line 14, *uvida* modifies
   a. *tabula* (line 13)
   b. *votiva* (line 14)
   c. *paries* (line 14)
   d. *vestimenta* (line 16)

9. The subject of *suspendisse* (line 15) is
   a. *me* (line 13)
   b. *paries* (line 13)
   c. *vestimenta* (line 16)
   d. *deo* (line 16)

10. What is **not** implied in lines 13–16?
    a. the speaker had an inscription put up
    b. the speaker dedicated his clothes in a temple
    c. the speaker's clothes are dripping
    d. Neptune saved the speaker

Translation *Suggested time: 10 minutes*

Translate the passage below as literally as possible.

> qui nunc te fruitur credulus aurea,
> qui semper vacuam, semper amabilem
> sperat, nescius aurae
> fallacis. miseri, quibus
>
> 5   intemptata nites. me tabula sacer
> votiva paries indicat uvida
> suspendisse potenti
> vestimenta maris deo.

Ode 1.5.9–16

16 chunks. 8 points, 1/2 point each. Round up to nearest whole point.

qui nunc . . . fruitur	**who now enjoys/delights in**
te aurea	**you (as) golden**
credulus	**(can modify *qui* or can be rendered adverbially with *fruitur*)**
	too easily believing/too trusting/credulous (not "believing")
qui . . . sperat	**who hopes/ expects**
semper vacuam	**(*vacuam* must understand *te esse* or *te futuram esse*) that you**
	are/will be always available/at leisure/free
semper amabilem	**always lovely/pleasant/attractive**
nescius aurae fallacis	**ignorant/without knowledge (must modify *qui* or *puer*) of the**
	deceiving/deceptive/deceitful breeze/breath of air (not simply "air")
miseri, quibus	**unfortunate/wretched/unhappy/miserable to/for whom**
intemptata nites	**you gleam/shine untested/untried/untouched/unattempted**
	(not "untempted")
sacer . . . paries	**(the) sacred wall**
tabula votiva	**with (its) votive tablet (must be construed as ablative)**
indicat	**(subject must be *paries*) announces/proclaims (give credit for**
	"indicates" but point out why it is a weak rendering)
me . . . suspendisse	**that I have hung up (must be rendered as indirect statement)**
uvida . . . vestimenta	**(my) wet/moist/damp clothes**
potenti	**powerful (must modify the dative "god")**
maris deo	**to/for the god of the sea**

Short Analysis Questions *Suggested time: 10 minutes*

> simplex munditiis? heu quotiens fidem
> mutatosque deos flebit et aspera
>   nigris aequora ventis
>   emirabitur insolens,
>
> 5 qui nunc te fruitur credulus aurea,
>   qui semper vacuam, semper amabilem
>   sperat, nescius aurae
>   fallacis. miseri, quibus

Ode 1.5–12

Ten points total.

1. To whom does *simplex munditiis* refer in line 1? Translate the phrase and show how it contributes to the poet's characterization of this person.

    Three points.

    One point for identifying the reference to Pyrrha; one point for translation ("simple in your elegance" or, rendering as transferred epithet, "with elegant simplicity"); one point for explaining how the phrase serves as praise. Different approaches to this last point are possible, but the student must be convincing. E.g., "These words praise Pyrrha by showing that she is so classy that she does not need ostentatious attire or hair-styling; understatement shows off the elegance of her person."

2. What is the effect of the contrast between future and present time in lines 1–7? To support your answer, write out and translate two Latin words or phrases, one to show future and one to show present.

    Six points.

    One point for a Latin word or phrase identified as referring to the future and one point for a Latin word or phrase identified as referring to the present. One point for correct translation of each of these Latin words or phrases. Two points for explaining the effect of the contrast between future and present time. Lines 1–7 do not draw a contrast that involves past time.

    As markers of future time, the most obvious words are *flebit* and *emirabitur*. Another possibility is the future time implied in the indirect statement in lines 6–7, for which the student must cite and translate some combination of *sperat ... te semper vacuam/ amabilem (futuram esse)*. As markers of present time, the best words are *nunc* and *fruitur*. *Credulus* and *nescius* by themselves do not establish a reference to present time.

    The student may claim that the effect of the shift in tense is to contrast the boy's present happiness with Pyrrha with his future misery when she "turns on" him. Alternatively, the student may contrast the boy's false belief now that Pyrrha loves him with his future realization that she does not. Other analyses of the effect of the juxtaposition should be accepted if they are convincing and supported by the text.

3. Name a figure of speech that appears in lines 2–3 and write out the Latin that illustrates it.

One point for writing *aspera nigris aequora ventis* and identifying as interlocked word order/synchysis/synchesis.

Essay *Suggested time: 20 minutes*

> Quis multa gracilis te puer in rosa
> perfusus liquidis urget odoribus
> grato, Pyrrha, sub antro?
> cui flavam religas comam
>
> 5 simplex munditiis? heu quotiens fidem
> mutatosque deos flebit et aspera
> nigris aequora ventis
> emirabitur insolens,
>
> qui nunc te fruitur credulus aurea,
> 10 qui semper vacuam, semper amabilem
> sperat, nescius aurae
> fallacis. miseri, quibus
>
> intemptata nites. me tabula sacer
> votiva paries indicat uvida
> 15 suspendisse potenti
> vestimenta maris deo.

Ode 1.5

Imagery of weather and seafaring are major elements of *Ode* 1.5. In a **short** essay, discuss how the speaker uses this imagery to talk about Pyrrha's treatment of men and about the men's reactions to her treatment of them.

Support your assertions with references to the Latin text. All Latin words must be copied or their line numbers provided, AND they must be translated or paraphrased closely enough so that it is clear you understand the Latin. It is your responsibility to convince your reader that you are basing your conclusions on the Latin text and not merely on your recollection of the passage. Direct your answer to the question; do not merely summarize the passage. Please write your essay on a separate piece of paper.

It is not necessary that a student distinguish weather and seafaring imagery in this poem, since the weather imagery refers to weather at sea, and the seafaring imagery presupposes the effects of weather. To receive passing credit (4 on a scale of 6), however, students must discuss both elements of the question: the way this imagery represents Pyrrha's treatment of men and the way it represents their reactions to her treatment of them. Superior papers will discuss how the weather and seafaring imagery works in these two ways throughout lines 5–16. Answers that receive full credit will discuss how the imagery of clear, sunny weather at sea depicts Pyrrha as treating men favorably at first (cf. lines 9–10 and *nites*, line 13), how the "deceitful breeze" (11–12) shows her favor's fickleness, and how the

images of a storm (cf. lines 6–7) and shipwreck (*uvida vestimenta*, 14–16) show how she turns against the men. At the same time, full credit answers will show how the men who are hurt by Pyrrha trust her at first (9–11, 13) because they lack experience (8, 11–13) and cannot believe it when she withdraws her favor (7–8). On the other hand, the speaker's survival of shipwreck represents his recovery from rejection by Pyrrha; unlike her inexperienced lovers, he has knowledge of Pyrrha's true character, so that as a result he can escape being made wretched by her again (12–16).

6 – Perceptive discussion of sea/weather imagery's depiction both of Pyrrha's behavior toward lovers and of their reaction to it; liberal, appropriate and accurate use of Latin support, correctly cited; discussion of the imagery throughout lines 5–16.

5 – Solid discussion, not as full Latin support, and/or not as much depth of analysis of how the text creates its effect. One or two significant elements of the imagery may go unnoticed. One element of the question may receive somewhat fuller treatment.

4 – Adequate, "bare bones" treatment of both elements of the question. Latin support is apt and accurate but minimal. Although it may be heavy on description, the essay undertakes some analysis. Several parts of the passage may go without comment.

3 – Superficial, weak discussion of both elements of the imagery or adequate discussion of only one. Unlike a 4, a 3 will not convince you that the student has adequately undertaken any analysis. Latin citations may support only one element of the discussion or may be inadequate for both. Alternatively, a student may receive a 3 for writing a good essay but failing to provide correctly cited and translated/paraphrased Latin support.

2 – Inadequate, vague, faulty discussion of both elements of the question, or superficial discussion of one element and almost nothing or nothing on the second. Very scanty Latin or even no Latin correctly cited.

1 – The student says only one meaningful thing in response to the question and based on the passage.

0 – The student says nothing correct or meaningful derived from the passage, although something may be guessed at from the wording of the question itself.

Scansion

Scan the following lines and name the meter. **The meter is fourth Asclepiadean.**

‾ ‾ ‾ ∪∪‾ ‾ ∪∪ ‾ ∪ ×
Quis multa gracilis te puer in rosa

‾ ‾ ‾ ∪ ∪ ‾ ‾ ∪ ∪ ‾ ∪ ×
perfusus liquidis urget odoribus

‾ ‾ ‾ ∪ ∪ ‾ ×
grato, Pyrrha, sub antro?

‾ ‾ ‾ ∪∪ ‾ ∪ ×
cui flavam religas comam

5

‾ ‾ ‾ ∪∪‾ ‾ ∪∪‾ ∪ ×
simplex munditiis? heu quotiens fidem

‾ ‾ ‾ ∪ ∪‾ ‾∪∪ ‾ ∪ ×
mutatosque deos flebit et aspera

‾ ‾ ‾ ∪ ∪ ‾ ×
nigris aequora ventis

‾ ‾ ‾ ∪∪ ‾ ∪ ×
emirabitur insolens,

Ode 1.5.1–8

ODE 1.9

Vides, ut alta stet nive candidum
Soracte, nec iam sustineant onus
  silvae laborantes, geluque
    flumina constiterint acuto?

5 dissolve frigus ligna super foco
large reponens atque benignius
  deprome quadrimum Sabina,
    o Thaliarche, merum diota.

permitte divis cetera, qui simul
10 stravere ventos aequore fervido
  deproeliantis, nec cupressi
    nec veteres agitantur orni.

quid sit futurum cras, fuge quaerere, et
quem Fors dierum cumque dabit, lucro
15 adpone, nec dulcis amores
    sperne puer neque tu choreas,

donec virenti canities abest
morosa. nunc et campus et areae
  lenesque sub noctem susurri
20   composita repetantur hora,

nunc et latentis proditor intumo
gratus puellae risus ab angulo
  pignusque dereptum lacertis
    aut digito male pertinaci.

Short Answer Questions

Line 1   What is the translation of *ut*? **"how"**

          Why is *stet* subjunctive? ***stet* is subjunctive in an indirect question depending on *ut***

Line 3   What is the case and use of *gelu*? **ablative of means**

Line 4   What is the tense and mood of *constiterint*? **perfect subjunctive in indirect question**

Line 5   What is the case and use of *ligna*? **accusative, direct object of *reponens* (line 6)**

Line 6	What is the part of speech and translation of *benignius*? **comparative adverb, "more generously," i.e., a more generous supply of wine, modifying** *deprome* **("draw off, decant," taking** *diota* **in line 8 as ablative of separation)**
Line 9	What is the case and use of *divis*? **dative, indirect object of** *permitte*
	What is the translation of *simul*? *simul* = *simul atque*, **"as soon as"**
Line 10	What form is *stravere*? **an alternative ending of third person plural, perfect tense indicative (apocopated ending)**
Lines 10–11	What two figures of speech are in these lines? *ventos . . . deproeliantes:* **chiasmus; personification**
Line 13	For what reason is *sit* subjunctive? **subjunctive in indirect question**
Line 14	What is the case and use of *lucro*? **dative, indirect object after** *adpone*
Lines 17–18	What two figures of speech are in these lines? *canities . . . morosa:* **transferred epithet or personification, enjambment**
Line 20	Why is *repetantur* subjunctive? **jussive subjunctive**
	What is the case and use of *hora*? **ablative of time when**
Line 21	What is the case and use of *proditor*? **nominative, in apposition to the subject,** *risus*
Line 22	What is the case and use of *puellae*? **objective genitive with** *proditor*
	What is the case and use of *risus*? **nominative, one of the subjects of** *repetantur*
Line 23	What is the case and use of *pignus*? **nominative, one of the subjects of** *repetantur*
	What is the case and use of *lacertis*? **dative of separation with** *dereptum*

Multiple Choice Questions *Suggested time: 15 minutes*

permitte divis cetera, qui simul
stravere ventos aequore fervido
   deproeliantis, nec cupressi
     nec veteres agitantur orni.

5   quid sit futurum cras, fuge quaerere, et
quem Fors dierum cumque dabit, lucro
   adpone, nec dulcis amores
     sperne puer neque tu choreas,

donec virenti canities abest
10   morosa. nunc et campus et areae
   lenesque sub noctem susurri
     composita repetantur hora,

> nunc et latentis proditor intumo
> gratus puellae risus ab angulo
> 15   pignusque dereptum lacertis
>   aut digito male pertinaci.

Ode 1.9.9–24

1. The case and number of *cetera* (line 1) are
   a. accusative plural   b. ablative singular
   c. nominative singular   d. nominative plural

2. The winds in lines 2–3 are described as
   a. seething   b. spreading
   c. sailing   **d. fighting**

3. The events that happen to the trees in lines 3–4 are cited as an example of how the gods
   a. destroy the proud   **b. grant tranquillity**
   c. create new life   d. contend in rivalry

4. One piece of advice found in lines 5–7 is to
   a. flee from tomorrow's dangers   b. seek knowledge of the future
   c. imitate the lucky   **d. consider each day a gain**

5. The case and number of *dulcis* (line 7) are
   a. accusative plural   b. ablative plural
   c. nominative singular   d. vocative singular

6. The case of *virenti* (line 9) is determined by
   a. *canities* (line 9)   b. *morosa* (line 10)
   c. *donec* (line 9)   **d. *abest* (line 9)**

7. The activity that the speaker has in mind in lines 10–12 is
   a. study   **b. love affairs**
   c. attending the theatre   d. voting

8. In line 12, *composita hora* is an ablative of
   a. cause   b. manner
   c. specification   **d. time**

9. A figure of speech found in lines 13–14 is
   a. hyperbaton   b. zeugma
   c. asyndeton   d. hendiadys

10. Context makes clear that the *pignus* in line 15 is

    a. a sum of money

    b. a piece of jewelry

    c. a document

    d. a tree

11. The case of *digito* (line 16) is determined by

    a. *pignus* (line 15)

    b. *male* (line 16)

    c. *dereptum* (line 15)

    d. *lacertis* (line 15)

Translation *Suggested time: 10 minutes*

Translate the passage below as literally as possible.

> Vides, ut alta stet nive candidum
> Soracte, nec iam sustineant onus
>   silvae laborantes, geluque
>   flumina constiterint acuto?
>
> 5   dissolve frigus ligna super foco
> large reponens atque benignius
>   deprome quadrimum Sabina,
>   o Thaliarche, merum diota.

Ode 1.9.1–8

16 chunks. 8 points, 1/2 point each. Round up to nearest whole point.

vides, ut	**do you see how**
alta . . . nive	**with deep/high snow (*alta* must modify *nive*)**
stet candidum Soracte	**Soracte stands white/bright/radiant**
nec iam	**and no longer/and not now**
silvae laborantes	**the laboring/suffering woods/forests**
sustineant onus	**sustain/withstand/hold up the burden/load**
-que flumina constiterint	**and the rivers have stood still (-*que* can be placed with *gelu acuto* but must be translated for either chunk to receive credit)**
gelu . . . acuto	**with severe/sharp chill/ice/cold/frost**
dissolve frigus	**dissolve/undo the chill/cold**
super foco	**on/over the hearth/fireplace (not "fire")**
ligna . . . large	**wood/pieces of wood generously/lavishly**
reponens atque	**restoring/putting anew (not "putting back") and/and also**
benignius deprome	**more generously/quite liberally bring forth/take down**
quadrimum merum	**four-year-old wine/pure wine**
Sabina diota	**in OR from its/a Sabine (two-handled) jar/jug**
o Thaliarche	**oh Thaliarchus (must be vocative)**

Short Analysis Questions *Suggested time: 10 minutes*

> quid sit futurum cras, fuge quaerere, et
> quem Fors dierum cumque dabit, lucro
> adpone, nec dulcis amores
> sperne puer neque tu choreas,
>
> 5   donec virenti canities abest
> morosa. nunc et campus et areae
> lenesque sub noctem susurri
> composita repetantur hora,

Ode 1.9.13–20

Twelve points total.

1. In line 2,

   a. translate *Fors*.

      One point for identifying Fors as chance or fortune.

   b identify the gift given by *Fors*.

      One point for identifying the gift as a day or days.

2. To what does *canities* (line 5) refer literally and metaphorically?

   One point for *canities* as literal reference to grey or white hair, greyness or whiteness.

   One point for metaphorical reference to old age.

3. What are two actions that the speaker proposes in lines 3–4? Write out and translate the Latin that refers to each action.

   One point for each of two actions if the Latin word that supports it is also given (e.g., *amores* for love affairs, *choreas* for dancing).

4. Name a figure of speech in line 2 and write out the Latin that illustrates it.

   One point for tmesis.

   One point for the Latin that illustrates that figure: *quem . . . cumque*.

5. In what situation does the speaker envision the boy in lines 7–8? Cite two Latin words or phrases that support your answer.

   Four points.

   One point for stating that the boy is envisioned as meeting a lover/girl.

   One point for stating another feature: at evening, or by arrangement, or whispering, or at close distance.

   One point for each of two Latin citations.

Essay Question *Suggested time: 20 minutes*

Vides, ut alta stet nive candidum
Soracte, nec iam sustineant onus
   silvae laborantes, geluque
      flumina constiterint acuto?

5   dissolve frigus ligna super foco
    large reponens atque benignius
      deprome quadrimum Sabina,
        o Thaliarche, merum diota.

    permitte divis cetera, qui simul
10   stravere ventos aequore fervido
      deproeliantis, nec cupressi
        nec veteres agitantur orni.

    quid sit futurum cras, fuge quaerere, et
    quem Fors dierum cumque dabit, lucro
15   adpone, nec dulcis amores
        sperne puer neque tu choreas,

    donec virenti canities abest
    morosa. nunc et campus et areae
      lenesque sub noctem susurri
20   composita repetantur hora,

    nunc et latentis proditor intumo
    gratus puellae risus ab angulo
      pignusque dereptum lacertis
        aut digito male pertinaci.

Ode 1.9

In a **short** essay, discuss how the imagery of the poem contributes to the advice about time and love given in the third and fourth stanzas.

Support your assertions with references to the Latin text. All Latin words must be copied or their line numbers provided, AND they must be translated or paraphrased closely enough so that it is clear you understand the Latin. It is your responsibility to convince your reader that you are basing your conclusions on the Latin text and not merely on your recollection of the passage. Direct your answer to the question; do not merely summarize the passage. Please write your essay on a separate piece of paper.

This question about the effect of Horace's imagery is very open-ended. Students can develop varied and original interpretations of such a rich poem. To receive at least 4 points on a scale of 6, students must produce an adequate discussion of how the imagery illustrates both parts of the question: advice about time and love. They must support their points about each part with several appropriate

references to the Latin, which they cite and translate accurately. Superior papers will discuss how the imagery throughout the poem represents the workings or effects of time and love, and they will show how it expands on the advice about time and love given in stanzas three and four.

6 – Perceptive discussion of how the imagery illustrates the speaker's advice in stanzas three and four about both time and love; liberal, appropriate and accurate use of Latin support, correctly cited; discussion of the imagery throughout the poem.

5 – Solid discussion, not as full Latin support, and/or not as much depth of analysis of how the imagery illustrates the advice about time and love given in stanzas three and four. One or two significant images may go unnoticed; for example, students may connect imagery of stanzas five and six more successfully to the poem's advice than they do the imagery of stanzas one and two. One focus of the imagery (time or love) may receive somewhat fuller treatment.

4 – Adequate, "bare bones" treatment of both foci of the imagery. Latin support is apt and accurate but minimal. Although it may be heavy on description, the essay undertakes some analysis. Several parts of the passage may go without comment.

3 – Superficial, weak discussion of both foci of the imagery or adequate discussion of only one. Unlike a 4, a 3 will not convince you that the student has adequately undertaken analysis. Latin citations may support only one element of the discussion or may be inadequate for both. Alternatively, a student may receive a 3 for writing a good essay but failing to provide correctly cited and translated/paraphrased Latin support.

2 – Inadequate, vague, faulty discussion of both elements of the question, or superficial discussion of one element and almost nothing or nothing on the second. Very scanty Latin or even no Latin correctly cited.

1 – The student says only one meaningful thing in response to the question and based on the passage.

0 – The student says nothing correct or meaningful derived from the passage, although something may be guessed at from the wording of the question itself.

Scansion

Scan the following lines and name the meter. **The meter is Alcaic.**

‾ ‾ ◡ ‾ ‾ ‾ ◡◡ ‾ ◡ ×
permitte divis cetera, qui simul

      ‾ ‾◡ ‾ ‾ ‾ ◡◡ ‾ ◡ ×
10   **stravere ventos aequore fervido**

‾ ‾◡ ‾ ‾ ‾ ◡ ‾ ×
deproeliantis, nec cupressi

‾ ◡◡ ‾ ◡ ◡ ‾ ◡ ‾ ×
nec veteres agitantur orni.

      ‾ ‾ ◡ ‾ ‾ ‾ ◡ ◡ ‾ ◡ ×
quid sit futurum cras, fuge quaerer(e), et

      ‾ ‾ ‾ ◡ ‾ ‾ ◡ ◡ ‾ ◡ ×
quem Fors dierum cumque dabit, lucro

      ‾ ‾ ‾ ◡ ‾ ‾ ‾ ◡ ‾ ×
15   **adpone, nec dulcis amores**

      ‾ ◡ ◡ ‾ ◡ ◡ ‾ ◡ ‾×
sperne puer neque tu choreas,

Ode 1.9.9–16

ODE 1.11

Tu ne quaesieris (scire nefas), quem mihi, quem tibi
finem di dederint, Leuconoe, nec Babylonios

temptaris numeros. ut melius, quidquid erit, pati!
seu pluris hiemes, seu tribuit Iuppiter ultimam,

5   quae nunc oppositis debilitat pumicibus mare
Tyrrhenum: sapias, vina liques et spatio brevi

spem longam reseces. dum loquimur, fugerit invida
aetas: carpe diem, quam minimum credula postero.

Short Answer Questions

Line 1	The verb *quaesieris* is an alternative of what verb form? ***quaesiveris***
	What figure of speech is in this line? ***quem mihi, quem tibi:* asyndeton or *quem . . . quem:* anaphora or ellipsis of *est***
	What part of speech is *quem*? **(interrogative) adjective**
	What is the case and use of *mihi* and *tibi*? **dative, indirect object (alternatively, dative of reference) of *dederint* (line 2)**
Line 3	What is the case and use of *quidquid*? **nominative, subject of *erit***
	What form is *pati*? **present infinitive of deponent verb *patior***
Line 4	What is the case and use of *hiemes*? **accusative, direct object of *tribuit***
Line 5	What are the antecedent, case, and use of *quae*? ***hiems/hiemem* understood from *ultimam,* line 4; nominative, subject of *debilitat***
	What is the case and use of *oppositis . . . pumicibus*? **ablative of means**
Lines 5–6	What figure of speech is in these lines? ***Tyrrhenum:* enjambment**
Line 6	What figure of speech is in this line? ***sapias, vina liques:* asyndeton**
Line 7	What two figures of speech are in this line? ***spem longam reseces:* metaphor; *invida (aetas):* personification**
Lines 7–8	What figure of speech is in these lines? ***aetas:* enjambment**
Line 8	What is the case and use of *postero*? **dative with adjective that governs dative (*credula*)**

Multiple Choice Questions *Suggested time: 11 minutes*

Tu ne quaesieris (scire nefas), quem mihi, quem tibi
finem di dederint, Leuconoe, nec Babylonios

temptaris numeros. ut melius, quidquid erit, pati!
seu pluris hiemes, seu tribuit Iuppiter ultimam,

5   quae nunc oppositis debilitat pumicibus mare
Tyrrhenum: sapias, vina liques et spatio brevi

spem longam reseces. dum loquimur, fugerit invida
aetas: carpe diem, quam minimum credula postero.

Ode 1.11

1. Lines 1–2 state that it is a crime to
   a. ignore the future
   c. tempt Babylonian numbers
   b. question the gods' will
   d. know what end the gods have given

2. The case of *mihi* (line 1) is determined by
   a. *quem* (line 1)
   c. *finem* (line 2)
   b. *di* (line 2)
   d. *dederint* (line 2)

3. *Pati* (line 3) is a form of
   a. pateo
   c. patior
   b. parco
   d. pasco

4. The case and number of *pluris* (line 4) are
   a. accusative plural
   c. nominative singular
   b. genitive singular
   d. dative plural

5. From lines 4–5, we learn that
   a. the sea weakens the pumice stones
   c. the rocks break the force of the sea
   b. Jupiter is worn out by the winter storm
   d. the sea opposes the god

6. In line 7, *fugerit* is literally translated as
   a. has fled
   c. flees
   b. will have fled
   d. will flee

7. In line 8, *quam minimum* is translated as
   a. which the smallest
   c. which least
   b. than the least
   d. as little as possible

8. In line 8, *credula* modifies
   a. the understood subject of *carpe* (line 8)   b. *diem* (line 8)
   c. *aetas* (line 8)   d. *quam* (line 8)

9. A figure of speech that appears in line 8 is
   a. hyperbole   **b. metaphor**
   c. transferred epithet   d. metonymy

Translation *Suggested time: 10 minutes*

Translate the passage below as literally as possible.

> Tu ne quaesieris (scire nefas), quem mihi, quem tibi
> finem di dederint, Leuconoe, nec Babylonios
>
> temptaris numeros. ut melius, quidquid erit, pati!
> seu pluris hiemes, seu tribuit Iuppiter ultimam,
>
> 5   quae nunc oppositis debilitat pumicibus mare
> Tyrrhenum: sapias, vina liques et spatio brevi

Ode 1.11.1–6

18 chunks. 9 points, 1/2 point each. Round up to nearest whole point.

Tu ne quaesieris	**(You) do not seek/ask/inquire**
scire nefas	**(it is) a sin/sacrilege/crime to know**
quem ... quem ... finem	**what (end) ... what end (must be accusative)**
mihi ... tibi ... Leuconoe	**to/for me ... to/for you ... Leuconoe**
di dederint	**the gods have given/gave ("will have given" is not acceptable)**
nec ... temptaris	**and do not/nor make trial of/try/attempt**
Babylonios ... numeros	**Babylonian numbers (must be direct object of *temptaris*)**
ut melius ... pati	**how (much) better (it is) to endure/suffer/undergo/experience**
quidquid erit	**whatever will be (clause must be object of *pati*)**
seu ... seu	**whether ... or**
pluris hiemes	**more winters/storms/winter storms (must be object of *tribuit*)**
tribuit Iuppiter	**Jupiter allots/assigns (tense may be rendered as perfect; *tribuit* must govern both *pluris hiemes* and *ultimam*)**
ultimam	**the last/final (one)**
quae nunc ... debilitat	**which now weakens/breaks the force of**
mare Tyrrhenum	**the Tyrrhenian/Etruscan sea (must be object of *debilitat*)**
oppositis ... pumicibus	**with/by means of (placed) opposite/hostile/facing pumice stones/rocks**
sapias, vina liques	**(you should) be wise/have taste, (you should) strain the wine/s**
ex spatio brevi	**and in/because of a short/brief space/period of time**

Short Analysis Questions *Suggested time: 10 minutes*

Tu ne quaesieris (scire nefas), quem mihi, quem tibi
finem di dederint, Leuconoe, nec Babylonios

temptaris numeros. ut melius, quidquid erit, pati!
seu pluris hiemes, seu tribuit Iuppiter ultimam,

5   quae nunc oppositis debilitat pumicibus mare
Tyrrhenum: sapias, vina liques et spatio brevi

spem longam reseces. dum loquimur, fugerit invida
aetas: carpe diem, quam minimum credula postero.

Ode 1.11

Nine points total.

1. State two things Leuconoe is told not to do in lines 1–3. Cite and translate or accurately paraphrase the Latin that describes each action.

   Two points. Latin and translation/accurate paraphrase of each phrase required. Minimal Latin underlined.

   One point: *Tu ne quaesieris ... quem mihi, quem tibi finem di dederint* "You, do not seek/ask ... what end the gods have given to me, what end to you" "Knowing" is not an acceptable substitute for "seeking/asking."

   One point: *nec Babylonios temptaris numeros.* "and do not try/attempt Babylonian numbers/astrology." "Trying numbers" is an insufficient answer.

2. In line 4 the speaker contrasts two outcomes that Jupiter may assign.

   a. Name these outcomes. Cite and translate or accurately paraphrase the Latin that describes each outcome.

   Two points. Latin and translation or accurate paraphrase of each phrase required.

   One point: *seu pluris hiemes (Iuppiter tribuit)* "or whether Jupiter assigns/has assigned more winters/storms"

   One point: *seu Iuppiter tribuit ultimam* "or whether Jupiter/he assigns/has assigned the last (one)"

   b. What outcomes for the lives of Leuconoe and the speaker are represented by these alternatives?

   One point for explaining that the alternatives represent whether the speaker and Leuconoe have more time or just the present.

3. Describe three things that the speaker tells Leuconoe to do in lines 6–7. Name the figure of speech in these lines.

   Three points.

   One point: be wise, strain the wine(s)

   One point: cut back long hope in/because of (our) short time

   One point: identifying tricolon crescens/crescendo

4. What does the speaker say will happen while they speak (line 7)?

   One point for saying that life or the time of one's life will depart/flee/will have fled.

Essay *Suggested time: 20 minutes*

Tu ne quaesieris (scire nefas), quem mihi, quem tibi
finem di dederint, Leuconoe, nec Babylonios

temptaris numeros. ut melius, quidquid erit, pati!
seu pluris hiemes, seu tribuit Iuppiter ultimam,

5   quae nunc oppositis debilitat pumicibus mare
Tyrrhenum: sapias, vina liques et spatio brevi

spem longam reseces. dum loquimur, fugerit invida
aetas: carpe diem, quam minimum credula postero.

Ode 1.11

This ode makes a contrast between things in life that the individual cannot control and things that the individual **can** control. In a **short** essay, discuss how the speaker develops this contrast to help him set forth advice about how to live. The quality of your essay will depend on the coherence of your interpretation, your ability to account for the poem as a whole, and your use of the Latin to support your interpretation.

Support your assertions with references to the Latin text **throughout** the poem. All Latin words must be copied or their line numbers provided, AND they must be translated or paraphrased closely enough so that it is clear you understand the Latin. It is your responsibility to convince your reader that you are basing your conclusions on the Latin text and not merely on a general recollection of the passage. Direct your answer to the question; do not merely summarize the passage. Please write your essay on a separate piece of paper.

The question first asks students to explain how the poem makes a contrast between aspects of life over which the individual has no control and other aspects over which he or she does exert control. Students may enumerate these uncontrollable and controllable things in an initial paragraph or two, or incorporate identification within line-by-line analysis, or choose other essay designs. Uncontrollable things include the end of our life (line 2), the number of years or winters we will see (line 4), time (*aetas*, line 8), and the future (*postero*, line 8). Things over which we have some control include

the actions of the subjunctive verbs in lines 6–7 (be wise, strain the wine, cut back long hope) and of the imperative *carpe diem*, line 8. Some students may also say that the decisions not to demand knowledge of our future (lines 1–2), to endure whatever will be (line 3), and to cease idle chat and act (line 7) also lie within our control.

The second task is to show how the speaker makes use of this contrast as he advises Leuconoe how to live. Essays that range between the superficial and the satisfactory may do little beyond repeat the wording of the poem, e.g., "he tells her to seize the day." Good to excellent essays will attempt richer analysis of the import of Horace's advice, perhaps by giving more content to that maxim: e.g., she should seek to be happy by refusing to worry over the future ("better to endure whatever will be" than to worry!) and by finding pleasure in what the present moment provides. Perceptive students may analyze the imagery to clarify what it implies about life choices. For example, the grim storms (lines 4–6) convey the mood of dread which worry over the future produces, and the image of plucking the day (line 8) evokes the rapidity with which unused resources of the present can fade like blossoms. Students who think that the poem is a disguised piece of seduction rhetoric may argue that the speaker tries to convince Leuconoe that she can be happy by exerting her will in a decision to take up with him rather than wait for a future lover, who may never come, or they may see lines 1–3 as the speaker's way of saying, "Don't seek a future for our 'relationship.' All we've got is right now." The quality of a paper will reveal itself in the coherence and perception of its argument, its discussion of the whole poem, its mastery of Latin, and its use of the Latin text to support points.

6 – Perceptive account both of what the speaker wants Leuconoe to do and of what his aims appear to be in trying to persuade her. Liberal, appropriate and accurate use of Latin support, correctly cited; discussion of the entire speech. An excellent essay may be apparent by virtue of the student's ability to support probable inferences about the speaker's interests from the surface meaning of his words.

5 – Solid discussion, not as full Latin support, and/or not as much insight into how the speaker's words reveal his personal interest. One or two significant elements of the speaker's argument may go unnoticed. One element of the question may receive somewhat fuller treatment.

4 – Adequate, "bare bones" treatment of both elements of the question. Latin support is apt and accurate but minimal. Although it may rely largely on restating the speaker's words, the essay undertakes some analysis of them. Several parts of the passage may go without comment.

3 – Superficial, weak discussion of both elements of the question or adequate discussion of only one. Unlike a satisfactory paper, a superficial one will not convince you that the student has adequately undertaken analysis; the paper may amount to a restatement of the Latin. Latin citations may support only one element of the discussion or may be inadequate for both. Alternatively, an essay may be judged "superficial" because it lacks correctly cited and translated/paraphrased Latin support.

2 – Scanty, vague, faulty discussion of both elements of the question, or superficial discussion of one element and almost nothing or nothing on the second. Very scanty Latin or even no Latin correctly cited.

1 – The student says only one meaningful thing in response to the question and based on the passage. It is highly likely that this one thing will be the observation that Leuconoe is advised to "seize the day."

0 – The student says nothing correct or meaningful derived from the passage, although something may be guessed at from the wording of the question itself.

Scansion

Scan the following lines and name the meter. **The meter is fifth or greater Asclepiadean.**

5   ‒ ‒ ‒ ᴗ ᴗ ‒ ‒ ᴗᴗ ‒ ‒ ᴗᴗ ‒ ᴗ ×
     quae nunc oppositis debilitat pumicibus mare

     ‒ ‒ ‒ ᴗ ᴗ ‒ ‒ ᴗ ᴗ ‒ ‒ ᴗᴗ ‒ ᴗ ×
     Tyrrhenum: sapias, vina liques et spatio brevi

     ‒ ‒ ‒ ᴗ ᴗ ‒ ‒ ᴗ ᴗ ‒ ‒ ᴗᴗ ‒ ᴗ ×
     spem longam reseces. dum loquimur, fugerit invida

     ‒ ‒ ‒ ᴗ ᴗ ‒ ‒ ᴗᴗ ‒ ‒ ᴗᴗ ‒ ᴗ ×
     aetas: carpe diem, quam minimum credula postero.

Ode 1.11.5–8

ODE 1.13

Cum tu, Lydia, Telephi
    cervicem roseam, cerea Telephi
laudas brachia, vae meum
    fervens difficili bile tumet iecur.

5   tunc nec mens mihi, nec color
    certa sede manet, umor et in genas
furtim labitur arguens,
    quam lentis penitus macerer ignibus.

uror, seu tibi candidos
10   turparunt umeros inmodicae mero
rixae, sive puer furens
    inpressit memorem dente labris notam.

non, si me satis audias,
    speres perpetuum dulcia barbare
15   laedentem oscula, quae Venus
    quinta parte sui nectaris imbuit.

felices ter et amplius,
    quos inrupta tenet copula, nec malis
divolsus querimoniis
20   suprema citius solvet amor die.

Short Answer Questions

Line 2	What is the case and use of *cervicem?* **accusative, direct object of *laudas* (line 3)**
Line 4	What is the case and use of *bile?* **ablative of means with *tumet***
Line 5	What is the case and use of *mihi?* **dative of reference or dative of possession**
Line 6	What is the case and use of *sede?* **ablative of place where**
	What two figures of speech (one non-AP) are in these lines? **umor et: anastrophe/ postposition; umor: metonymy for tears**
Line 7	What is the translation of *labitur?* **"glides/slips/passes"**
Line 8	What is the part of speech and translation of *quam?* **adverb modifying *penitus,* "how"**
	For what reason is *macerer* subjunctive? **subjunctive in indirect question**
	What is the case and use of *ignibus?* **ablative of means**

Line 9   What figure of speech is in this line? **uror: metaphor**

What is the case and use of *tibi*? **dative of reference or disadvantage with *turparunt* or dative of possession**

Line 10   What is the case and use of *mero*? **ablative of cause with *inmodicae***

Line 12   What is the case and use of *dente*? **ablative of means with *inpressit***

What is the case and use of *labris*? **dative with *inpressit* (verb taking dative after direct object)**

Line 14   What is the tense and mood of *speres*? **present subjunctive**

What is the translation of *perpetuum*, and what does it modify? **"permanent, long-lasting," modifying understood *eum*, i.e., the boy**

What is the part of speech and use of *barbare*? **adverb modifying *laedentem***

Line 15   What are the translation, case, and use of *laedentem*? **"harming, bruising, injuring"; accusative in apposition to *eum* understood (cf. on line 14 above)**

What is the case and use of *oscula*? **accusative, direct object of *laedentem***

What is the antecedent of *quae*? **oscula**

Line 16   What is the case and use of *parte*? **ablative of means with *imbuit***

What is the case and use of *nectaris*? **partitive genitive with *parte***

Line 17   What figure of speech is in this line? **ellipsis of *sunt ei***

What is the part of speech of *ter* and *amplius*? What do they modify? **adverbs; *ter* modifies *felices*, *amplius* modifies *ter***

Line 18   What are the antecedent, case, and use of *quos*? **understood *ei*; accusative direct object of *tenet***

Line 19   What is the translation of *divolsus*, and what does it modify? **"(having been) torn apart," modifies *amor***

What is the case and use of *querimoniis*? **ablative of cause or means with *divolsus***

Line 20   What is the translation and part of speech of *citius*? **"more quickly"; adverb in comparative degree**

What is the tense of *solvet*? What is its direct object? **future indicative; its direct object is *quos* (line 18)**

What is the case and use of *die*? **ablative of comparison (i.e., love will not untie the lovers more quickly than the last day of their lives will untie them) or ablative of time when (i.e., sooner than on the last day)**

Multiple Choice Questions *Suggested time: 15 minutes*

Cum tu, Lydia, Telephi
    cervicem roseam, cerea Telephi
laudas brachia, vae meum
    fervens difficili bile tumet iecur.

5   tunc nec mens mihi, nec color
    certa sede manet, umor et in genas
furtim labitur arguens,
    quam lentis penitus macerer ignibus.

uror, seu tibi candidos
10   turparunt umeros inmodicae mero
rixae, sive puer furens
    inpressit memorem dente labris notam.

non, si me satis audias,
    speres perpetuum dulcia barbare
15   laedentem oscula, quae Venus
    quinta parte sui nectaris imbuit.

felices ter et amplius,
    quos inrupta tenet copula, nec malis
divolsus querimoniis
20   suprema citius solvet amor die.

Ode 1.13

1. In line 1, *cum* is translated

    a. when

    c. since

    b. with

    d. although

2. In line 3, *meum* modifies

    a. *fervens*

    c. *bile*

    b. *vae*

    d. *iecur*

3. The case and number of *difficili* (line 4) are

    a. nominative plural

    c. ablative singular

    b. genitive singular

    d. dative singular

4. In lines 6–8, the speaker says that Lydia's praise of Telephus makes him

    a. stumble

    c. argue

    b. speechless

    d. weep

5. The case of *ignibus* (line 8) is determined by
   a. *penitus* (line 8)
   b. ***macerer* (line 8)**
   c. *lentis* (line 8)
   d. *quam* (line 8)

6. The best translation of *tibi . . . turparunt umeros . . . rixae* (lines 10–11) is
   a. for you they broke the back of the quarrel
   b. **quarrels disfigured your shoulders**
   c. having quarreled, they bared their shoulders to you
   d. your shoulders grew ugly in the quarrel

7. In lines 13–14, *non . . . speres* is translated
   a. you may not hope
   b. you do not hope
   c. you should not hope
   d. **you would not hope**

8. In line 15, *laedentem* modifies
   a. *me* (line 13)
   b. **the boy understood from line 11**
   c. *barbare* (line 14)
   d. an understood *te*

9. Lines 15–16 tell us that Venus
   a. **sweetens Lydia's lips**
   b. bestows kisses
   c. flavors her own nectar
   d. strikes Lydia's mouth

10. The antecedent of *quos* (line 18) is
    a. the speaker and the *puer*
    b. the *puer* and Lydia
    c. **an understood *ei***
    d. *malis*

11. The case of *querimoniis* (line 19) is determined by
    a. *malis* (line 18)
    b. *citius* (line 20)
    c. *solvet* (line 20)
    d. ***divolsus* (line 19)**

12. The tense and mood of *solvet* (line 20) are
    a. present subjunctive
    b. present indicative
    c. **future indicative**
    d. imperfect subjunctive

13. In line 20, *suprema die* is the day of
    a. **death**
    b. a religious festival
    c. the wedding
    d. love's declaration

Translation *Suggested time: 15 minutes*

Translate the passage below as literally as possible.

> uror, seu tibi candidos
>   turparunt umeros inmodicae mero
> rixae, sive puer furens
>   inpressit memorem dente labris notam.
>
> 5   non, si me satis audias,
>   speres perpetuum dulcia barbare
> laedentem oscula, quae Venus
>   quinta parte sui nectaris imbuit.

Ode 1.13.9–16

18 chunks. 9 points, 1/2 point each. Round up to nearest whole point.

uror	**I burn/I am burned/I am on fire**
seu tibi	**whether your/for you**
turparunt . . . rixae	**quarrels/brawls (have) disfigured/made ugly**
candidos . . . umeros	**(shining) white shoulders (must be object of *turparunt*)**
inmodicae mero	**immoderate/uncontrolled because of/with wine**
sive . . . furens	**or whether the raging/mad/wild**
puer . . . inpressit	**boy (has) pressed/impressed**
memorem . . . notam	**a remembering/mindful mark (must be object of *inpressit*)**
dente	**with (his) tooth/teeth**
labris	**on/upon (your) lips**
non . . . speres	**you would not hope/expect**
si me satis audias	**if you should hear/listen to me enough/sufficiently**
perpetuum	**continuing/permanent/long lasting/forever yours The translation must make clear that this adjective is predicate in indirect statement with some substantive and copula like *eum fore* (e.g., "that he would be continuing") or with *laedentem* as the substantive (i.e., "that the one injuring your lips . . . would be continuing").**
dulcia . . . oscula	**sweet mouth/lips/kisses**
barbare laedentem	**barbarously/like a barbarian injuring/striking/harming**
quae Venus . . . imbuit	**which Venus wet/filled/imbued or wets/fills/imbues (*quae* must be accusative and refer to *oscula*)**
quinta parte	**with the fifth part/one fifth**
sui nectaris	**of her (own) nectar**

Short Analysis Questions *Suggested time: 10 minutes*

> tunc nec mens mihi, nec color
> > certa sede manet, umor et in genas
> furtim labitur arguens,
> > quam lentis penitus macerer ignibus.

> 5 uror, seu tibi candidos
> > turparunt umeros inmodicae mero
> rixae, sive puer furens
> > inpressit memorem dente labris notam.

> non, si me satis audias,
> 10 speres perpetuum dulcia barbare
> laedentem oscula, quae Venus
> > quinta parte sui nectaris imbuit.

> felices ter et amplius,
> > quos inrupta tenet copula, nec malis
> 15 divolsus querimoniis
> > suprema citius solvet amor die.

Ode 1.13.5–20

Nine points total.

1. a. State **one** fact about **each** of these relationships: Lydia and Telephus; the speaker and Lydia.

   Two points. One point for one fact about each relationship.

   Examples: Telephus gets into drunken quarrels with Lydia; the speaker weeps because Lydia ignores him for Telephus.

   b. As support for what you say, cite and translate or accurately paraphrase **one** Latin phrase for **each** fact (two Latin phrases in all).

   Two points. One point for each Latin phrase correctly cited and translated or paraphrased.

   Examples: "quarrels immoderate because of pure wine have disfigured your white shoulders," lines 5–7; "and moisture glides stealthily onto my cheeks, proving how deeply I am weakened by slow fires," lines 2–4.

2. Identify a figure of speech found in lines 7–8 and write out the Latin words that illustrate it.

   Two points. One point for identifying the figure of speech; one for citing the Latin.

   transferred epithet or personification: *memorem . . . notam*

3. In lines 9–11, what does the speaker advise Lydia not to do? Cite the Latin words that contain this advice.

One point for stating that the speaker advises Lydia not to hope that the boy will be long-lasting, or a long-lasting lover.

One point for citing *non speres* (sc. *eum*) *perpetuum* (*fore*).

4. In the last stanza, how does the speaker describe those lovers who do not break up?

One point for saying that lovers who do not break up are "three times happy and more."

Essay *Suggested time: 20 minutes*

> Cum tu, Lydia, Telephi
>   cervicem roseam, cerea Telephi
> laudas brachia, vae meum
>   fervens difficili bile tumet iecur.
>
> 5   tunc nec mens mihi, nec color
>   certa sede manet, umor et in genas
> furtim labitur arguens,
>   quam lentis penitus macerer ignibus.
>
> uror, seu tibi candidos
> 10   turparunt umeros inmodicae mero
> rixae, sive puer furens
>   inpressit memorem dente labris notam.
>
> non, si me satis audias,
>   speres perpetuum dulcia barbare
> 15   laedentem oscula, quae Venus
>   quinta parte sui nectaris imbuit.

Ode 1.13.1–16

In these stanzas, the speaker makes frequent reference to physical appearance or physical suffering as he tries to dissuade Lydia from her relationship with Telephus. In a **short** essay, discuss how the speaker uses references to physical appearance **and** to physical suffering to try to enhance the persuasive force of his speech.

Support your assertions with references to the Latin text **throughout** the passage. All Latin words must be copied or their line numbers provided, AND they must be translated or paraphrased closely enough so that it is clear you understand the Latin. It is your responsibility to convince your reader that you are basing your conclusions on the Latin text and not merely on a general recollection of the passage. Direct your answer to the question; do not merely summarize the passage. Please write your essay on a separate piece of paper.

The student is asked to analyze references to the body as elements of Horace's representation of a lover's rhetoric in stanzas one through four. The best papers will confront how Lydia is supposed to react as the speaker refers to Telephus' appearance, Lydia's appearance before and after quarrels and hard kisses, and his own symptoms of emotion. Excellent responses will discuss examples in more than one of these spheres, thereby accounting for a good deal of the poem. Skillful interpretations will go beyond the prompt in the question to point out that the speaker clearly wants Lydia to be in love with him. They may make points like these: description of the speaker's anger and grief at Lydia's praise of Telephus bespeaks his own passion for Lydia, to which she should respond; description of Telephus' rough treatment of Lydia proves he is an unworthy lover; the speaker's admiration of Lydia's beauty (cf. *candidos ... umeros*, lines 9–10) aims to advance his purpose. Although the question does not ask the student to evaluate the effectiveness of the speaker's rhetoric, many better papers will do this. Acceptable but less sophisticated papers may focus more on recounting what the speaker says about bodily states than on analyzing how he refers to them as a tactic to persuade Lydia. Such papers also will offer less Latin support and discuss fewer examples. Papers that fall below the acceptable standard will offer no analysis and/or no Latin support.

6 – Excellent, perceptive account of how the speaker tries to dissuade Lydia from being in love with Telephus. Discussion of some rhetorical use of each of the three spheres of talk about the body: Telephus' appearance, the speaker's passions, and the abuse Lydia suffers from Telephus. Liberal, appropriate and accurate use of Latin support, correctly cited, from throughout the passage. An excellent paper may "leap out at you" by virtue of the student's ability to support probable inferences about the speaker's interests from the speaker's choice of examples and imagery.

5 – Good, solid discussion of the speaker's talk about physical appearance and physical suffering. One sphere of the speaker's talk about suffering (i.e., his own or Lydia's) may receive thin treatment. Perhaps not as full Latin support, and/or not as much insight into how the speaker's words are designed to persuade Lydia.

4 – Satisfactory, adequate, "bare bones" treatment of both physical appearance and physical suffering. Latin support is apt and accurate but minimal. Although it may rely largely on restating the speaker's words, the essay undertakes some analysis of them. One sphere of the speaker's talk about physical suffering may go without comment.

3 – Superficial, limited response that deals superficially with the speaker's talk about physical appearance and physical suffering, or adequate discussion of only one. Unlike a satisfactory essay, a superficial one will not convince you that the student has adequately undertaken analysis; the paper may amount to a restatement of the Latin. Latin citations may support only one element of the discussion or may be inadequate for both. Alternatively, an essay may be judged superficial because it lacks correctly cited and translated/paraphrased Latin support.

2 – Vague, weak, faulty discussion of both elements of the question, or superficial discussion of one element and almost nothing or nothing on the second. Very scanty Latin or even no Latin correctly cited.

1 – The student tries to direct an answer to the question but says only one meaningful thing in response to it and based on the passage. It is highly likely that this one thing will be description of a bodily state derived from a single word, such as "I am on fire."

0 – The student says nothing correct or meaningful derived from the passage, although something may be guessed at from the wording of the question itself.

Scansion

Scan the following lines and name the meter. **The meter is second Asclepiadean.**

$$\text{—} \quad \text{—} \quad \text{—} \overset{\smile\smile}{} \text{—} \overset{\smile}{} \times$$
Cum tu, Lydia, Telephi

$$\text{—} \quad \text{—} \text{—} \quad \overset{\smile}{} \overset{\smile}{} \text{—} \quad \text{—} \overset{\smile\smile}{} \text{—} \overset{\smile}{} \times$$
cervicem roseam, cerea Telephi

$$\text{—} \text{—} \quad \text{—} \overset{\smile\smile}{} \text{—} \overset{\smile}{} \times$$
laudas brachia, vae meum

$$\text{—} \quad \text{—} \quad \text{—} \overset{\smile\smile}{} \text{—} \overset{\smile}{} \overset{\smile}{} \text{—} \overset{\smile}{} \times$$
fervens difficili bile tumet iecur.

$$\text{—} \quad \text{—} \quad \text{—} \overset{\smile\smile}{} \text{—} \overset{\smile}{} \times$$
5   **tunc nec mens mihi, nec color**

$$\text{—} \quad \text{—} \quad \text{—} \overset{\smile}{} \overset{\smile}{} \text{—} \quad \text{—} \overset{\smile}{} \overset{\smile}{} \text{—} \overset{\smile}{} \times$$
certa sede manet, umor et in genas

$$\text{—} \quad \text{—} \quad \text{—} \overset{\smile\smile}{} \text{—} \overset{\smile}{} \times$$
furtim labitur arguens,

$$\text{—} \quad \text{—} \quad \text{—} \overset{\smile}{} \overset{\smile}{} \text{—} \quad \text{—} \overset{\smile\smile}{} \text{—} \overset{\smile}{} \times$$
quam lentis penitus macerer ignibus.

Ode 1.13.1–8

ODE 1.22

Integer vitae scelerisque purus
non eget Mauris iaculis neque arcu,
nec venenatis gravida sagittis,
    Fusce, pharetra,

5   sive per Syrtis iter aestuosas
sive facturus per inhospitalem
Caucasum, vel quae loca fabulosus
    lambit Hydaspes.

namque me silva lupus in Sabina,
10   dum meam canto Lalagen et ultra
terminum curis vagor expeditis,
    fugit inermem,

quale portentum neque militaris
Daunias latis alit aesculetis,
15   nec Iubae tellus generat, leonum
    arida nutrix.

pone me, pigris ubi nulla campis
arbor aestiva recreatur aura,
quod latus mundi nebulae malusque
20   Iuppiter urget,

pone sub curru nimium propinqui
solis in terra domibus negata:
dulce ridentem Lalagen amabo,
    dulce loquentem.

Short Answer Questions

Line 1   What figure of speech is in this line? *Integer vitae scelerisque purus:* **chiasmus**

What is the case and use of *vitae?* **genitive of reference**

Line 2   What is the case and use of *iaculis* and *arcu?* **ablative with *eget,* which governs ablative**

Line 4   What is the case and use of *Fusce?* **vocative, direct address**

What is the case and use of *pharetra?* **ablative with *eget* (line 2)**

Line 5   What is the translation of *aestuosas,* and what does it modify? **"hot/sweltering; agitated"; modifies *Syrtis***

Line 6	What does *facturus* modify? **the understood subject of *eget*, i.e., the person described in the stanza**
Line 7	What is the translation of *fabulosus,* and what does it modify? **"storied/fabled"; modifies *Hydaspes***
Lines 5–8	What figure of speech is in these lines? **tricolon crescens/crescendo**
Line 9	What did the wolf do in this stanza? **The wolf fled from the unarmed poet. Students may add: as the poet was roaming in the Sabine woods beyond the boundary of his land, singing of his beloved Lalage.**
	What is the case and use of *me*? **accusative, direct object of *fugit* (line 12)**
Line 10	What is the case and use of *Lalagen*? **Greek accusative, direct object of *canto***
Line 11	Of what preposition is *terminum* the object? **object of preposition *ultra***
	What is the case and use of *curis . . . expeditis*? **ablative absolute**
Line 12	What is the translation of *inermem* and what does it modify? **"unarmed"; modifies *me* (line 9)**
Line 13	To what in the preceding lines does the phrase *quale portentum* refer? ***lupus* or the fleeing of the wolf**
Line 14	What is the case and use of *Daunias*? **nominative, subject of *alit***
	What is the translation of *latis aesculetis*? **"in broad/wide oak forests/groves"**
Line 15	What is the object of *generat*? ***portentum* (line 13)**
	What is the case and use of *leonum*? **objective genitive with *nutrix***
Line 16	What three figures of speech are in this line? ***arida nutrix*: oxymoron; *nutrix*: metaphor, personification**
Line 17	What is the form of *pone*? **present active imperative singular of *ponere***
	What does *nulla* modify? ***arbor* (line 18)**
	What is the case and use of *campis*? **ablative of place where**
Line 18	What is the translation of *aestiva,* and what does it modify? **"summer (adj.), summertime's, summer's"; modifies *aura***
	What is the case and use of *aura*? **ablative of means**
Line 19	Of what verb is *nebulae* the subject? **the subject of *urget* (line 20), which is attracted to singular by *Iuppiter***
Line 20	What figure of speech is in this line? ***Iuppiter*: metonymy**
	What is the translation of *urget,* and what is its object? **"pressure(s), press(es) upon"; its object is *(quod) latus***

Line 21   What part of speech is *nimium,* and what does it modify? **adverb, "excessively/too much/too/very," modifies *propinqui***

Line 22   What is the case and use of *solis?* **genitive of possession with *curru***

What is the case and use of *domibus?* **dative with *negata***

Lines 23–24 What part of speech is *dulce* and what does it modify in each instance? **adverb modifying *ridentem* and *loquentem***

Lines 23–24 What figure of speech is in these lines? ***dulce ... dulce:* anaphora**

Multiple Choice Questions *Suggested time: 15 minutes*

Integer vitae scelerisque purus
non eget Mauris iaculis neque arcu,
nec venenatis gravida sagittis,
        Fusce, pharetra,

5   sive per Syrtis iter aestuosas
sive facturus per inhospitalem
Caucasum, vel quae loca fabulosus
        lambit Hydaspes.

namque me silva lupus in Sabina,
10   dum meam canto Lalagen et ultra
terminum curis vagor expeditis,
        fugit inermem,

quale portentum neque militaris
Daunias latis alit aesculetis,
15   nec Iubae tellus generat, leonum
        arida nutrix.

Ode 1.22.1–16

1. The case of *sceleris* (line 1) is determined by
    a. *eget* (line 2)   b. *vitae* (line 1)
    c. *integer* (line 1)   **d. *purus* (line 1)**

2. A figure of speech contained in lines 2–4 is
    a. metaphor   **b. tricolon crescens/crescendo**
    c. hendiadys   d. chiasmus

3. The case of *sagittis* (line 3) is determined by
    a. *venenatis* (line 3)   b. *eget* (line 2)
    c. *gravida* (line 3)   d. *pharetra* (line 4)

4. The imagery of lines 1–4 evokes
   a. the Caucasus
   c. Africa
   b. India
   d. Italy

5. In line 5, *iter* is the object of
   a. *facturus* (line 6)
   c. *lambit* (line 8)
   b. *per* (line 5)
   d. *aestuosas* (line 5)

6. The case and number of *Syrtis* (line 5) are
   a. nominative singular
   c. ablative plural
   b. genitive singular
   d. accusative plural

7. The word *quae* (line 7) refers to
   a. *Hydaspes* (line 8)
   c. *Syrtis* (line 5)
   b. *loca* (line 7)
   d. *Caucasum* (line 7)

8. In lines 1–8, the poet claims that
   a. he will journey to foreign lands
   c. virtue is better protection than weapons
   b. Fuscus does not need weapons
   d. god safeguards the lover

9. The best translation of the words *dum . . . ultra terminum curis vagor expeditis* (lines 10–11) is
   a. while I wander beyond the boundary line and lay aside my cares
   c. granted only that I lay aside my cares as I wander beyond the boundary line
   b. until I may wander beyond the boundary line, having laid aside my cares
   d. while I was wandering beyond the boundary line, with cares laid aside

10. From lines 9–12, we learn that the poet was
    a. near his home
    c. fleeing from a wolf
    b. in southern Italy
    d. singing with his beloved

11. The translation of *fugit* (line 12) is
    a. flees
    c. fled
    b. will flee
    d. may flee

12. In line 13, *militaris* modifies
    a. *Daunias* (line 14)
    c. *latis* (line 14)
    b. *aesculetis* (line 14)
    d. *portentum* (line 13)

13. The best translation of *alit* (line 14) is
    a. salts
    c. flies
    b. nourishes
    d. gets down

14. In line 16, *nutrix* refers to

    a. *arida* (line 16)
        b. *tellus* (line 15)
    c. *leonum* (line 15)
        d. *Iubae* (line 15)

15. From lines 13–16, we can infer that the poet thinks that

    a. omens are to be despised
        b. oak forests have been brought to southern Italy
    c. lions are not found in the land of Iuba
        d. he saw an abnormal phenomenon

Translation *Suggested time: 15 minutes*

Translate the passage below as literally as possible.

> Integer vitae scelerisque purus
> non eget Mauris iaculis neque arcu,
> nec venenatis gravida sagittis,
>   Fusce, pharetra,
>
> 5   sive per Syrtis iter aestuosas
> sive facturus per inhospitalem
> Caucasum, vel quae loca fabulosus
>   lambit Hydaspes.

Ode 1.22.1–8

16 chunks. 8 points, 1/2 point each. Round up to nearest whole point.

Integer vitae	he/the one/the man) wholesome/upright of/in life. Some substantive must be supplied, either here or below in line 2, to serve as the subject of *eget*.
scelerisque purus	and pure/free of sin/crime
non eget	does not need/have need of/want
Mauris iaculis	Moorish/African javelins (must be governed by *eget*)
neque arcu	nor a bow
nec . . . Fusce, pharetra	nor, Fuscus, a quiver
gravida	laden/weighed down/heavy. "Pregnant" should also be accepted. Must modify *pharetra*.
venenatis . . . sagittis	with poisoned arrows (must be ablative)
sive . . . sive	whether . . . or (if)
per Syrtis . . . aestuosas	through the sweltering/hot/agitated Syrtes (must be object of *per*)
iter . . . facturus	(he is) about to make a journey. Must govern *iter*, must modify subject of *non eget*.
per inhospitalem Caucasum	through the inhospitable Caucasus (range/mountains)
vel . . . loca	or (the) places. Must be understandable as object of *per*.
quae	which. May be rendered as relative pronoun following "places" or adjectivally, i.e., "or (through) what places the Hydaspes licks/washes."

fabulosus	**storied/fabled/legendary (not "fabulous"). Must modify Hydaspes.**
lambit Hydaspes	**the Hydaspes licks/washes. Hydaspes must be subject; must be clear that *loca* is object of *lambit*.**

Short Analysis Questions *Suggested time: 10 minutes*

> quale portentum neque militaris
> Daunias latis alit aesculetis,
> nec Iubae tellus generat, leonum
>   arida nutrix.
>
> 5   pone me, pigris ubi nulla campis
> arbor aestiva recreatur aura,
> quod latus mundi nebulae malusque
>   Iuppiter urget,
>
> pone sub curru nimium propinqui
> 10 solis in terra domibus negata:
> dulce ridentem Lalagen amabo,
>   dulce loquentem.

Ode 1.22.13–24

Eight points total.

1.   Write out and scan lines 3–4 (*nec Iubae . . . nutrix*).

    One point for writing out and correctly scanning lines 3–4 (Sapphic meter):

    ‾ ◡ ‾ ‾ ‾ ◡ ◡ ‾ ◡‾ ×
    nec Iubae tellus generat, leonum

    ‾ ◡◡ ‾ ×
    arida nutrix.

2.   In lines 5–10, the poet imagines himself in two different landscapes.

    a.   Describe **one** feature of **each** landscape.

    One point for each of two descriptions. The two landscapes are

    a) a cold or bleak landscape (lines 5–8)

    b) a torrid wasteland (lines 9–10).

b. Cite and either translate or accurately paraphrase the Latin that supports your description of each feature.

One point for each of two Latin phrases correctly cited and translated or paraphrased.

Examples of descriptions:

a) frozen plains (*pigris . . . campis*), no trees (*nulla . . . arbor*), cold (*nulla arbor aestiva recreatur aura*), misty/cloudy (*nebulae*), bad weather (*malus Iuppiter urget*)

b) hot/close to the sun/near the equator (*sub curru nimium propinqui solis*), uninhabited/no houses (*terra domibus negata*)

3. In lines 11–12, the poet declares his feelings about Lalage.

a. What are the poet's feelings about Lalage, and why does he feel this way?

One point for stating that the poet loves/will love Lalage.

One point for explaining the love as a response to Lalage's charming personality: her laughter and/or speech and/or charm/sweetness.

b. Refer specifically to the Latin that supports your answer.

One point for Latin support: (*Lalagen*) *amabo, ridentem, loquentem, dulce*

Essay *Suggested time: 20 minutes*

Integer vitae scelerisque purus
non eget Mauris iaculis neque arcu,
nec venenatis gravida sagittis,
    Fusce, pharetra,

5   sive per Syrtis iter aestuosas
sive facturus per inhospitalem
Caucasum, vel quae loca fabulosus
    lambit Hydaspes.

namque me silva lupus in Sabina,
10   dum meam canto Lalagen et ultra
terminum curis vagor expeditis,
    fugit inermem,

quale portentum neque militaris
Daunias latis alit aesculetis,
15   nec Iubae tellus generat, leonum
    arida nutrix.

> pone me, pigris ubi nulla campis
> arbor aestiva recreatur aura,
> quod latus mundi nebulae malusque
> 20   Iuppiter urget,
>
> pone sub curru nimium propinqui
> solis in terra domibus negata:
> dulce ridentem Lalagen amabo,
>   dulce loquentem.

Ode 1.22

This ode contains many references to and descriptions of places. In a **short** essay, discuss how the poet uses place references to enhance his representation of himself in the role of lover.

Support your assertions with references to the Latin text **throughout** the poem. All Latin words must be copied or their line numbers provided, AND they must be translated or paraphrased closely enough so that it is clear you understand the Latin. It is your responsibility to convince your reader that you are basing your conclusions on the Latin text and not merely on a general recollection of the passage. Direct your answer to the question; do not merely summarize the passage. Please write your essay on a separate piece of paper.

The question asks the student to analyze how Horace uses place references to help represent himself in the role of lover. The requirement that the student draw Latin support from "throughout the poem" requires that good essays offer some analysis of each of the three local realms of the poem: exotic, foreign places where, first, the pure man, and finally, the poet/lover travel unharmed; the Sabine forest near Horace's property, where a wolf fled from him; the violent places (southern Italy, the Mauretanian desert) that produce no portent to rival the wolf. Although they need not connect every place reference to the poet's talk about himself as a lover, papers that say nothing about how the place references help the poet talk about himself as a lover cannot earn a passing score. Some students may argue that the place references show how the lover or poet enjoys the special protection that he claims for the virtuous man, taking Horace's story of his escape from the wolf at face value as an example of divine protection of lovers. Others may highlight elements of bombast in the descriptions (pile-up of learned references, hyperbolic and high-flown language, exaggerated description of the wolf) to argue that Horace adopts a tongue-in-cheek tone toward the privileged status of poet/lover. Following the cue in the introduction in Ancona, *Horace*, 1999, 2nd edition, 2005, p. 47, some students may notice that the poem does not say what would happen to the poet's invulnerability if he were no longer involved with Lalage.

6 – Excellent, perceptive account of how the speaker uses geographical references to represent himself in the role of lover. Strong analysis of all three realms: bleak foreign destinations, Horace's Sabine neighborhood, and places of portents. Sophistication in handling tone (the implied attitude of the speaker toward his subject matter). Liberal, appropriate and accurate use of Latin support, correctly cited. An excellent essay may be apparent by virtue of the student's ability to support probable inferences about the speaker's interests from the speaker's examples and imagery.

5 – Good, solid discussion of how place references contribute to the speaker's talk about himself as a lover. One of the local realms may receive thinner treatment than the other two. Perhaps not as full Latin support, and/or not as much insight into how the geographical references form part of the speaker's claims about his status as a lover.

4 – Satisfactory, adequate, "bare bones" treatment of the way that place references contribute to the poet's representation of himself as a lover. The discussion may be more descriptive than analytical, although there must be some analysis in answer to the question. Latin support is apt and accurate but minimal. Two of the local realms may receive thin comment.

3 – Superficial, limited discussion that deals superficially with Horace's use of place references as he represents himself as a lover. There may be no attempt to tie discussion of place references to the topic of the question, or this may be done for only one of the three realms. Unlike a satisfactory essay, a superficial one will not convince you that the student has adequately undertaken analysis of the poem; the paper may amount to a restatement of the Latin. Latin citations may support only one element of the discussion or may be inadequate for all three.

2 – Vague, weak, faulty discussion of all three local realms or superficial discussion of one realm and almost nothing or nothing on the other two. Very scanty Latin or even no Latin correctly cited.

1 – The student tries to direct an answer to the question but says only one meaningful thing in response to it and based on the passage.

0 – The student says nothing correct or meaningful derived from the passage, although something may be guessed at from the wording of the question itself.

Scansion

Scan the following lines and name the meter.   **The meter is Sapphic.**

‾ ⏑ ‾ ‾ ‾ ⏑⏑ ‾ ⏑ ‾ ×
Integer vitae scelerisque purus

‾ ⏑ ‾ ‾ ‾ ⏑ ⏑ ‾ ⏑ ‾ ×
non eget Mauris iaculis nequ(e) arcu

‾ ⏑ ‾ ‾ ‾ ⏑⏑ ‾ ⏑ ‾ ×
nec venenatis gravida sagittis,

‾ ⏑ ⏑ ‾ ×
Fusce, pharetra,

‾ ⏑ ‾ ‾ ‾ ⏑⏑ ‾ ⏑ ‾ ×
5   **sive per Syrtis iter aestuosas**

‾ ⏑ ‾ ‾ ‾ ⏑ ⏑ ‾ ⏑ ‾ ×
sive facturus per inhospitalem

‾ ⏑ ‾ ‾ ‾ ⏑ ⏑ ‾ ⏑ ‾ ×
Caucasum, vel quae loca fabulosus

‾ ⏑ ⏑ ‾ ×
lambit Hydaspes.

Ode 1.22.1–8

ODE 1.23

Vitas inuleo me similis, Chloe,
quaerenti pavidam montibus aviis
matrem non sine vano
aurarum et siluae metu.

5   nam seu mobilibus veris inhorruit
adventus foliis, seu virides rubum
dimovere lacertae,
et corde et genibus tremit.

atqui non ego te tigris ut aspera
10   Gaetulusve leo frangere persequor:
tandem desine matrem
tempestiva sequi viro.

Short Answer Questions

Line 1   What is the case and use of *me?* **accusative, direct object of *vitas***

What figure of speech is in this line? *inuleo similis:* simile

Line 2   What word does *quaerenti* modify? *inuleo* (line 1)

Translate *pavidam.* **"panicky, trembling with fear, startled"**

What word does *pavidam* modify? **matrem**

What is the case and use of *montibus aviis?* **ablative of place where**

Line 3   For what word does *matrem* serve as object? **direct object of *quaerenti* (line 2)**

What word does *vano* modify? **metu (line 4)**

Lines 2–3   What figure of speech is in these lines? *pavidam montibus aviis matrem:* chiasmus

OR

non sine: litotes

Line 4   What is the case and use of *aurarum et silvae?* **objective genitive**

Line 5   What is the case and use of *veris?* **subjective genitive with *adventus* (line 2)**

Line 6   What is the case and use of *adventus?* **nominative subject of *inhorruit* (line 5)**

What is the case and use of *foliis?* **ablative of place where with *inhorruit***

What does *virides* modify? ***lacertae* (line 7)**

What is the case and use of *rubum*? **direct object of *dimovere* (line 7)**

Line 7   The verb *dimovere* is an alternative of what verb? ***dimoverunt***

Line 8   What is the case and use of *corde*? **ablative of means or ablative of place where or ablative of specification with *tremit***

Line 9   What three figures of speech (2 non-AP) are in this line? ***ego te:* juxtaposition; *tigris ut:* postposition/anastrophe; *non . . . tigris ut:* simile**

What is the case and use of *te*? **accusative, direct object of *persequor* (line 10)**

What is the case and use of *tigris*? **nominative in apposition to *ego***

Line 10   What is the case and use of *leo*? **nominative in apposition to *ego***

What verb form is *frangere*, and how is it used grammatically in its context? **an infinitive showing purpose with *persequor***

Lines 9–10   What figure of speech is in these lines? ***non ego te . . . persequor:* hyperbole**

OR

***tigris ut:* simile**

Line 11   What is the case and use of *matrem*? **accusative, direct object of *sequi* (line 12)**

Line 12   What is the translation of *tempestiva*? **"seasonable, ripe, timely, at the right time (for)"**

What word does *tempestiva* modify? **the understood *tu,* subject of *desine,* line 11—sc. Chloe.**

What is the form of *sequi*? **present active infinitive of *sequor***

On what word does *sequi* depend? ***desine* (line 11)**

What is the case and use of *viro*? **dative with adjective *tempestiva***

Multiple Choice Questions *Suggested time: 14 minutes*

Vitas inuleo me similis, Chloe,
quaerenti pavidam montibus aviis
    matrem non sine vano
      aurarum et siluae metu.

5   nam seu mobilibus veris inhorruit
adventus foliertae,
    et corde etis, seu virides rubum
      dimovere lac genibus tremit.

> atqui non ego te tigris ut aspera
> 10 Gaetulusve leo frangere persequor:
> tandem desine matrem
> tempestiva sequi viro.

Ode 1.23

1. In lines 1–4, the fawn is afraid of
   - a. its mother
   - b. the speaker
   - **c. the breezes**
   - d. Chloe

2. The case of *inuleo* (line 1) is determined by
   - a. *vitas* (line 1)
   - b. *me* (line 1)
   - c. *quaerenti* (line 2)
   - **d. *similis* (line 1)**

3. The person who is described as panicky in line 2 is
   - **a. the mother deer**
   - b. the fawn
   - c. the speaker
   - d. Chloe

4. A figure of speech contained in lines 2–3 is
   - **a. chiasmus**
   - b. synchysis
   - c. zeugma
   - d. hysteron proteron

5. The case and number of *veris* (line 5) are
   - **a. genitive singular**
   - b. ablative plural
   - c. accusative plural
   - d. nominative singular

6. The subject of *inhorruit* (line 5) is
   - a. *inuleo* (line 1)
   - b. *Chloe* (line 1)
   - c. *veris* (line 5)
   - **d. *adventus* (line 6)**

7. The form of the word *dimovere* (line 7) is
   - a. present infinitive
   - **b. perfect indicative**
   - c. perfect participle
   - d. present indicative

8. The meaning of *ut* in line 9 is
   - a. that
   - **b. as**
   - c. how
   - d. in order to

9. In line 9, *aspera* modifies
   - a. *ego* (line 9)
   - b. *te* (line 9)
   - **c. *tigris* (line 9)**
   - d. *leo* (line 10)

10. In lines 9–10, the speaker tells Chloe that

    a. she will not escape unharmed

    c. she will avoid tigers and lions

    b. no tiger will chase after her

    d. he will not harm her

11. The case of *viro* (line 12) is determined by

    a. *desine* (line 11)

    c. *tempestiva* (line 12)

    b. *sequi* (line 12)

    d. *tandem* (line 11)

12. In lines 11–12, the speaker tells Chloe that she

    a. should stop following a man

    c. should at last follow her mother

    b. is ready for a man

    d. must not be angry at her mother

Translation *Suggested time: 15 minutes*

Translate as literally as possible.

> Vitas inuleo me similis, Chloe,
> quaerenti pavidam montibus aviis
> matrem non sine vano
> aurarum et siluae metu.
>
> 5   nam seu mobilibus veris inhorruit
> adventus foliis, seu virides rubum
> dimovere lacertae,
> et corde et genibus tremit.

Ode 1.23.1–8

16 chunks. 8 points, 1/2 point each. Round up to nearest whole point.

vitas . . . me	**you avoid/evade/shun me**
similis, Chloe	**Chloe, like/similar**
inuleo . . . quaerenti	**(to) a fawn . . . seeking/looking for**
pavidam . . . matrem	**(its) panicky/frightened/terrified mother**
montibus aviis	**in trackless/untrod/lonely/pathless/remote mountains**
non sine vano . . . metu	**not without vain/empty/useless . . . fear ("with" is not acceptable for *non sine*, which must be translated as a negative)**
aurarum et silvae	**of breezes and (of) the woods/forest**
nam seu . . . seu	**for whether . . . or**
mobilibus . . . foliis	**in the movable/mobile/pliant . . . leaves**
veris	**of spring (must be genitive, must be connected to *adventus*)**
inhorruit adventus	**the arrival/coming (must be connected to *veris*, sc. "of spring")** **bristled/trembled/began to tremble in (must be connected to *foliis*)**
virides . . . lacertae	**green lizards (must be subject of *dimovere*)**
rubum dimovere	**moved apart/separated the brambles/bramble bush**
et . . . et	**both . . . and**
corde . . . genibus	**in/with (its) heart [and] (its) knees**
tremit	**it/she trembles/shudders (subject must be the fawn)**

Short Analysis Questions *Suggested time: 10 minutes.*

Vitas inuleo me similis, Chloe,
quaerenti pavidam montibus aviis
   matrem non sine vano
     aurarum et siluae metu.

5   nam seu mobilibus veris inhorruit
adventus foliis, seu virides rubum
   dimovere lacertae,
     et corde et genibus tremit.

atqui non ego te tigris ut aspera
10   Gaetulusve leo frangere persequor:
   tandem desine matrem
     tempestiva sequi viro.

Ode 1.23

Ten points total.

1. Briefly describe the fawn's fear and its mother's fear in lines 1–4.

   **Two points. One point for description of each one's fear. Do not deduct points for
   unconvincing explanations of motives of fear, for these explanations are not demanded
   by the question. Always grade by awarding credit to what is correct.**

2. Name a figure of speech that occurs in lines 3–4, and write out the Latin word(s) that illustrate
   it.

   **Two points. One point for identifying litotes or chiasmus or hendiadys. One point for citing
   the Latin.**

   litotes: *non sine . . . metu*

   chiasmus: *vano aurarum . . . silvae metu*

   hendiadys: *aurarum et silvae* **can be interpreted as "forest/woodland breezes"**

3. In lines 5–8, the speaker gives two examples meant to show why he thinks that the fawn's emotions are groundless.

   Four points: two for *a* and two for *b*.

   a. Explain how each example, according to the speaker's argument, is an instance of groundless emotion.

   **One point for each of two examples that show the objects of the fawn's fear as harmless
   according to the speaker, i.e.,: the fawn fears the leaves moving/fears the breezes moving
   the leaves/fears the lizards moving the brambles**

b. Cite and translate or paraphrase accurately the Latin that supports your case about each example.

One point for Latin support for each example.

4. What two reasons does the speaker offer Chloe in lines 9–12 for why she should favor him?

Two points. One point for each of two reasons why Chloe should favor the speaker:

a. he (says he) will not hurt her/does not pursue her as a tiger or lion

b. she is at the right age (*tempestiva*) for a man/husband (*viro*) (The speaker's injunction that Chloe cease following her mother does not amount to a reason why she should favor him.)

Essay *Suggested time: 20 minutes*

> Vitas inuleo me similis, Chloe,
> quaerenti pavidam montibus aviis
> matrem non sine vano
>   aurarum et siluae metu.
>
> 5 nam seu mobilibus veris inhorruit
> adventus foliis, seu virides rubum
> dimovere lacertae,
>   et corde et genibus tremit.
>
> atqui non ego te tigris ut aspera
> 10 Gaetulusve leo frangere persequor:
> tandem desine matrem
>   tempestiva sequi viro.

Ode 1.23

In this poem, Horace represents a speaker attempting a persuasive speech. Readers have differed in their views about the character of the speaker. In a **short**, well-organized essay, discuss how Horace creates an impression of the sort of person that the speaker is.

Support your assertions with references to the Latin text **throughout** the poem. All Latin words must be copied or their line numbers provided, AND they must be translated or paraphrased closely enough so that it is clear you understand the Latin. It is your responsibility to convince your reader that you are basing your conclusions on the Latin text and not merely on a general recollection of the passage. Direct your answer to the question; do not merely summarize the passage. Please write your essay on a separate piece of paper.

Students who have mastered the Latin and are original thinkers can do a lot with this open-ended question. Impressions of the speaker's character may range from well-meaning gentleman giving a timid girl advice about growing up to sinister seducer of said girl. Our only evidence for the speaker's character is his words. Fruitful elements of his rhetoric for this purpose include: vivid imagery, much

of it drawn from the animal world, replete with disguised challenges to the validity of Chloe's emotions (e.g., Chloe and her mother are unreasonably afraid, she is silly to be so attached to her mother); manipulation of word order to intimate linkages that are not stated in the propositions of the poem (e.g., *ego te*, line 9; *sequi viro*, line 12); the fallacy of hyperbolic analogy, in which, if the denial of the extreme form of the analogy is granted (e.g., I do not pursue you as a tiger or lion to break you, lines 9–10), it does not follow that a weaker form will not be true; command (e.g., *desine*, line 11). Further observations may rest on such elements of the poem as the content of the speaker's choice of images, which reveal what he is thinking about, his tone, or the order of the points he makes. Although they may rely more on restating the speaker's words than on drawing inferences about his character from them, satisfactory essays must undertake some analysis of how Horace creates an impression of the speaker as a character. The more perceptive an essay's discussion of the implied situation that prompts the speaker's words, the better its grasp of the implied purposes of the speaker, and the more fully this sense is grounded in the Latin text, the better it is.

6 – Excellent, perceptive account of how Horace creates the speaker's character. Liberal, appropriate and accurate use of Latin support, correctly cited; discussion of the entire poem. The student will draw and support inferences about the speaker's character and aims from the surface meaning of his words. Several features of the speaker's character will be discussed.

5 – Good, solid discussion with less full Latin support, and/or not as much insight into how the speaker's words reveal his character. One or two significant elements of the speaker's discourse may go unnoticed. Insight into the speaker's character is not as broad as in an excellent paper; only a couple of traits may be identified and discussed.

4 – Satisfactory, adequate, "bare bones" analysis of how Horace depicts the speaker's character. Latin support is apt and accurate but minimal. Several parts of the passage may go without comment. In general, the paper may tend toward description more than analysis. Only one feature of the speaker's character may receive discussion, but the student draws it out of the Latin by analysis rather than by merely asserting it or merely restating what the speaker says to Chloe.

3 – Superficial, weak discussion, may be rambling, general, or uneven. Unlike a satisfactory essay, a superficial one will not convince you that the student has adequately undertaken any analysis; the paper may amount to a restatement of the Latin. Or, analysis may be attempted but off-base, as, for example, if the student does not analyze how the speaker's character is depicted, but instead discusses an evident fact about the speaker, such as his romantic interest in Chloe. Alternatively, an essay may be judged superficial because it lacks correctly cited and translated/paraphrased Latin support.

2 – Inadequate, vague, faulty discussion of the question. The student may show a major misconception about the passage. Very scanty Latin or even no Latin correctly cited.

1 – The student says only one meaningful thing in response to the question and based on the passage.

0 – The student says nothing correct or meaningful derived from the passage, although something may be guessed at from the wording of the question itself.

Scansion

Scan the following lines and name the meter.   **The meter is fourth Asclepiadean.**

```
      _    _    _ ᴗᴗ _  _ᴗ ᴗ _ ᴗx
5    nam seu mobilibus veris inhorruit
```

```
   _    _   _   ᴗᴗ_   _  ᴗᴗ _  ᴗ x
   adventus foliis, seu virides rubum
```

```
         _  _  _ᴗ ᴗ _   x
      dimovere lacertae,
```

```
            _    _    _   ᴗ ᴗ _   ᴗ x
         et cord(e) et genibus tremit.
                    ᴗ
```

```
   _    _   _   ᴗ ᴗ _  _  ᴗ ᴗ _   ᴗ x
   atqui non ego te tigris ut aspera
```

```
       _ _  _   ᴗ ᴗ_   _   ᴗᴗ _  ᴗ x
10   Gaetulusve leo frangere persequor:
```

```
         _    _      _ᴗ ᴗ  _ x
      tandem desine matrem
```

```
         _    _   _ᴗ ᴗ _  ᴗx
      tempestiva sequi viro.
```

Ode 1.23.5–12

ODE 1.24

Quis desiderio sit pudor aut modus
tam cari capitis? praecipe lugubris
cantus, Melpomene, cui liquidam pater
    vocem cum cithara dedit.

5   ergo Quintilium perpetuus sopor
urget? cui Pudor et Iustitiae soror,
incorrupta Fides nudaque Veritas
    quando ullum inveniet parem?

      multis ille bonis flebilis occidit,
10   nulli flebilior, quam tibi, Vergili.
tu, frustra pius, heu, non ita creditum
    poscis Quintilium deos.

quid, si Threicio blandius Orpheo
auditam moderere arboribus fidem,
15   num vanae redeat sanguis imagini,
    quam virga semel horrida

non lenis precibus fata recludere
nigro compulerit Mercurius gregi?
durum, sed levius fit patientia,
20   quicquid corrigere est nefas.

Short Answer Questions

Line 1	What is the translation of *quis*? **"what"**
	What is the case and use of *desiderio*? **dative of possession**
Line 2	What figure of speech is in this line? *capitis:* **synecdoche**
	What is the case and use of *capitis*? **objective genitive with *desiderio***
	Who is to perform the action of the verb *praecipe*? *Melpomene* **(line 3)**
Lines 1–2	What figure of speech (non-AP) is in these lines? **rhetorical question**
Line 3	What is the case and use of *cantus*? **accusative, direct object of *praecipe***
Line 6	What is the case and use of *cui*? **dative with *parem***
	What is the function of *cui*? **connecting relative pronoun ("linking *qui*")**

Lines 5–6	What two figures of speech are in these lines? *sopor urget:* **metaphor;** *perpetuus* *sopor:* **metaphor for death; enjambment**
Line 8	What is the function of *quando?* **interrogative adverb**
	What is the function of *ullum?* **adjective used as a substantive, i.e., "when will they find anyone equal?"**
	What is the subject of *inveniet?* **the three virtues** *Pudor, Fides,* **and** *Veritas* **The verb is attracted into the singular by proximity to the series of singular subjects.**
	What is the case and use of *parem?* **predicate accusative with** *ullum*
Lines 5–8	What two figures of speech (2 non-AP) are in these lines? **each sentence is a rhetorical question**
Line 9	What is the case and use of *bonis?* **dative of reference with** *flebilis*
	What is its function? **adjective used as a substantive**
	What does *flebilis* modify? *ille,* **i.e., Quintilius**
Line 10	What is the case and use of *nulli?* **dative of reference with** *flebilior*
	What is the case of *Vergili?* **vocative**
Line 11	What does *creditum* modify? By whom and to whom was that person entrusted? *Quintilium* **(line 12); he was entrusted to Vergil by the gods.**
Line 12	What is the case and use of *Quintilium?* **accusative, secondary object denoting thing being asked for**
	What is the case and use of *deos?* **accusative, direct object, denoting person being asked**
Line 13	What is the form of *blandius?* **comparative adverb, "more charmingly"**
	What is the case and use of *Orpheo?* **ablative of comparison**
Line 14	What is the case and use of *arboribus?* **dative of agent after** *auditam*
	What figure of speech is in this line? *arboribus:* **personification**
	How can one tell apart the Latin words for "faith" and "string/lyre?" *Fides, -ei,* **f. faith and** *fides, -is,* **f. string belong to different declensions.**
Lines 14–15	Why are *moderere* and *redeat* subjunctive? **present subjunctive in future less vivid conditional: "if you should play ... surely blood would not return"**
Line 15	What is the case and use of *imagini?* **dative, indirect object of intransitive verb** *redeat*
Line 16	What is the case and use of *virga?* **ablative of means**
	What figure of speech is in this line? *horrida:* **transferred epithet**

Line 17   What is the case and use of *precibus*? **dative with *recludere***

What two figures of speech are in this line? ***non lenis:* litotes; *fata:* metonymy for "gates of Hades"**

Line 18   What is the case and use of *gregi*? **dative of direction/motion with *compulerit***

Line 19   What figure of speech is in this line? **ellipsis of *est***

What is the subject of *fit*? **the clause *quicquid corrigere est nefas* (line 20)**

Multiple Choice Questions *Suggested time: 15 minutes*

> ergo Quintilium perpetuus sopor
> urget? cui Pudor et Iustitiae soror,
> incorrupta Fides nudaque Veritas
>   quando ullum inveniet parem?
>
> 5   multis ille bonis flebilis occidit,
> nulli flebilior, quam tibi, Vergili.
> tu, frustra pius, heu, non ita creditum
>   poscis Quintilium deos.
>
> quid, si Threicio blandius Orpheo
> 10   auditam moderere arboribus fidem,
> num vanae redeat sanguis imagini,
>   quam virga semel horrida
>
> non lenis precibus fata recludere
> nigro compulerit Mercurius gregi?

Ode 1.24.5–18

1. The sister mentioned in line 2 is
    a. **Faith**   b. Modesty
    c. Justice   d. Truth

2. The case of *cui* (line 2) is determined by
    a. *soror* (line 2)   b. *inveniet* (line 4)
    c. ***parem* (line 4)**   d. *Quintilium* (line 1)

3. The tense and mood of *inveniet* (line 4) are
    a. present subjunctive   b. perfect indicative
    c. present indicative   d. **future indicative**

4. From lines 5–6, we learn that

   a. good men mourned no one more than they mourned Vergil

   c. many good men wept because of Vergil's grief

   b. Quintilius died of grief over many good men

   d. no one wept for Quintilius more than Vergil did

5. In line 5, *ille* refers to

   a. *Quintilium* (line 1)

   c. *parem* (line 4)

   b. *Vergili* (line 6)

   d. *nulli* (line 6)

6. The case and number of *flebilis* (line 5) are

   a. accusative plural

   c. genitive singular

   b. nominative singular

   d. dative plural

7. A figure of speech contained in line 5 is

   a. chiasmus

   c. interlocked word order/synchysis

   b. hyperbole

   d. oxymoron

8. From the words *non ita creditum poscis Quintilium* (lines 7–8), we learn that Vergil

   a. lost faith after Quintilius' death

   c. does not demand Quintilius as he did before

   b. wants Quintilius back unreasonably

   d. put his trust in Quintilius in vain

9. The form *moderere* (line 10) is

   a. present infinitive

   c. imperative

   b. imperfect subjunctive

   d. present subjunctive

10. From lines 9–11, we learn that

    a. poetry immortalizes the dead

    c. no music can revive the dead

    b. Quintilius was a greater poet than Orpheus

    d. Orpheus swore an oath to the trees

11. The case of *Orpheo* (line 9) is determined by

    a. *auditam* (line 10)

    c. *moderere* (line 10)

    b. *blandius* (line 9)

    d. *fidem* (line 10)

12. The best translation of line 13 (*lenis . . . recludere*) is

    a. to open up the fates with gentle prayers

    c. to open up the gentle fates with prayers

    b. the fates for gentle prayers to open up

    d. gentle to open up the fates to prayers

13. What did Mercury do to the *nigro . . . gregi* (line 14)?

    a. he opened the fates to it

    b. he compelled it to open up

    c. he drove Quintilius' shade into it

    d. he forced it to heed a virgin's prayers

Translation *Suggested time: 15 minutes*

Translate the passage below as literally as possible.

> ergo Quintilium perpetuus sopor
> urget? cui Pudor et Iustitiae soror,
> incorrupta Fides nudaque Veritas
>   quando ullum inveniet parem?
>
> 5   multis ille bonis flebilis occidit,
> nulli flebilior, quam tibi, Vergili.
> tu, frustra pius, heu, non ita creditum
>   poscis Quintilium deos.

Ode 1.24.5–12

18 chunks. 9 points, 1/2 point each. Round up to nearest whole point.

ergo . . . perpetuus sopor	**therefore/then (does) perpetual/unending sleep**
Quintilium . . . urget?	**press upon/push (upon) Quintilius (must be accusative)**
cui Pudor et	**(translation must make clear connection of "to whom" to "equal") to whom Modesty/Shame and**
Iustitiae soror	**the sister of Justice**
incorrupta Fides	**uncorrupted Faith/Trust**
nudaque Veritas	**and nude/naked Truth**
quando . . . inveniet	**when . . . will . . . find (accept either singular or plural subject)**
ullum . . . parem	**any/anyone equal (*parem* must govern *cui*)**
multis . . . bonis	**to/for/by many good men/people**
ille . . . flebilis	**he/that one/that man worthy to be mourned, worthy of tears, lamentable**
occidit	**has fallen/has died or falls/dies**
nulli flebilior	**more lamentable/more worthy of tears to/for no one/none**
quam tibi, Vergili	**than to/for you Vergil (must be vocative)**
tu . . . heu	**you . . . alas**
frustra pius	**pious/dutiful/devoted in vain/to no purpose (not "frustrated"; may govern *pius* or *poscis*)**
non ita	**not thus/not so/not on this basis**
creditum . . . Quintilium	**entrusted . . . Quintilius (must be object of *poscis*)**
poscis . . . deos	**you demand of/from the gods (must understand the double accusative, i.e., you demand Quintilius of/from the gods)**

Short Analysis Questions *Suggested time: 10 minutes*

> Quis desiderio sit pudor aut modus
> tam cari capitis? praecipe lugubris
> cantus, Melpomene, cui liquidam pater
>   vocem cum cithara dedit.
>
> 5   ergo Quintilium perpetuus sopor
> urget? cui Pudor et Iusitiae soror,
> incorrupta Fides nudaque Veritas
>   quando ullum inveniet parem?
>
> multis ille bonis flebilis occidit,
> 10   nulli flebilior, quam tibi, Vergili.
> tu, frustra pius, heu, non ita creditum
>   poscis Quintilium deos.

Ode 1.24.1–12

Eight points total.

1.   What is the attitude toward Quintilius' death among those who knew him? Cite and translate two Latin words or phrases that illustrate this attitude.

    Three points. One point for attitude: grief, yearning for the one lost, sadness

    One point for each of two supporting Latin words or phrases translated: *desiderio, lugubris, flebilis*

2.   Name two qualities of character that the poem attributes to Quintilius. Cite and translate a Latin word or phrase that illustrates each quality.

    Two points. One point for each of the two qualities with its Latin support translated or accurately paraphrased: modesty/shame, *Pudor*; faith/faithfulnes (incorrupta) *Fides*; truth/truthfulness, (*nuda*) *Veritas*. Do not award credit for answers like "dear" or "mourned for," which correspond to others' feelings about Quintilius, not to qualities of his character.

3.   Name a figure of speech that occurs in lines 5–8 and write out the Latin word(s) that illustrate it.

    One point for matching the figure of speech (metaphor or personification or tricolon or rhetorical question) with illustrative Latin (*perpetuus sopor urget*; *Pudor, Fides, Veritas ergo . . . urget? cui . . . . parem?*)

4.   Identify one criticism that the poet makes of Vergil's reaction to Quintilius' death, and cite and translate or accurately paraphrase the Latin word or phrases that support your point.

    One point for identifying a criticism of Vergil: his piety is to no purpose; he makes the unjustified demand of the gods that Quintilius' life should have been longer than it was fated to be (this point can be expressed in various ways); he mourns or yearns for Quintilius beyond the proper limit.

    One point for Latin support accurately translated or paraphrased: *frustra pius*; *non ita . . . poscis*

Essay *Suggested time: 20 minutes*

Quis desiderio sit pudor aut modus
tam cari capitis? praecipe lugubris
cantus, Melpomene, cui liquidam pater
    vocem cum cithara dedit.

5   ergo Quintilium perpetuus sopor
urget? cui Pudor et Iustitiae soror,
incorrupta Fides nudaque Veritas
    quando ullum inveniet parem?

multis ille bonis flebilis occidit,
10   nulli flebilior, quam tibi, Vergili.
tu, frustra pius, heu, non ita creditum
    poscis Quintilium deos.

quid, si Threicio blandius Orpheo
auditam moderere arboribus fidem,
15   num vanae redeat sanguis imagini,
    quam virga semel horrida

non lenis precibus fata recludere
nigro compulerit Mercurius gregi?
20   durum, sed levius fit patientia,
    quicquid corrigere est nefas.

Ode 1.24

The occasion of this poem is the death of Horace's and Vergil's friend, Quintilius. In a **short** essay, explain what Horace suggests poetry can and cannot do in response to the death of a loved one, and show how he conveys this message.

Support your assertions with references to the Latin text **throughout** the poem. All Latin words must be copied or their line numbers provided, AND they must be translated or paraphrased closely enough so that it is clear you understand the Latin. It is your responsibility to convince your reader that you are basing your conclusions on the Latin text and not merely on a general recollection of the passage. Direct your answer to the question; do not merely summarize the passage. Please write your essay on a separate piece of paper.

The task is four-fold: to articulate what the author shows poetry as doing and as being unable to do in response to the death of a loved one; to show *how* he conveys these "can do" and "cannot do" aspects of poetry. Most students will find it easier to say something about the "cannot do" part of the question, since stanzas four and five, with the example of the myth of Orpheus and Eurydice, suggest through rhetorical questions that poetry cannot bring the dead back to life or change fate. A superior essay needs to go on to analyze what the poem indicates poetry *can* do in the face of a loved one's death. One possible analysis of poetry's capacities is something like this: poetry expresses or teaches us to express grief, it honors or even immortalizes the dead, and it counsels us how to live with grief. Perceptive students will also discuss how the poet gets his points across. For example, they may show

that some of poetry's capacities are suggested via the poem's exemplification of them rather than by explicit assertion: e.g., stanza two honors the virtues of Quintilius, conferring immortality of fame, and lines 19–20 counsel us how to live with grief. Students may pinpoint our yearning for a beloved but irrevocably absent person (*desiderio . . . cari capitis*, lines 1–2) as the poem's understanding of grief, and they may seek to explain how poetry's functions as represented in this ode help us express or face this emotion. Less analytical essays may simply quote these lines and say something about grief. Students may discuss the effect of various features such as mythological allusion, imagery, figures of speech, word choice and word placement, direct address, or shifts in tense. An essay may agree or disagree with the author's implicit assumptions—denying, perhaps, that endurance makes grief for a deeply beloved person easier to bear—but going as it does beyond the question, such an opinion neither improves nor detracts from the essay's score.

6 – Excellent, perceptive, analytical account of what the ode shows poetry as able and as unable to do in the face of grief for the dead, and of how it conveys each of these claims. In broad outline, the whole poem is discussed. That means that the student shows what poetry can do (express grief, praise the dead person, and teach or model how to cope with grief) and what it cannot do (bring the dead to life and/or change fate). The student may also discuss poetry's conferral of immortality through fame. Liberal, appropriate and accurate use of Latin support, correctly cited. The student will draw and support inferences about the speaker's character and aims from the surface meaning of his words. Several features of the speaker's character will be discussed.

5 – Good, solid discussion, not as full, not as detailed on what poetry can do for human grief. Less full Latin support, and/or not as much insight into the mechanisms by which the poem's claims about poetry are conveyed, although some analysis fleshes out major points.

4 – Satisfactory, adequate, even "bare bones" analysis of the poem's claims for poetry. Possibly only one element of what it can do for grief is treated fully. Latin support is apt and accurate but minimal. The student may jump to conclusions about what the poem claims for poetry without showing that most of these conclusions are inferences from what it says about Quintilius, his friends, or about the Orpheus myth. In general, the paper may tend toward description more than analysis.

3 – Superficial, weak discussion, may be rambling, general, or uneven. A superificial paper, unlike a satisfactory one, will not convince you that the student has adequately undertaken any analysis; the paper may amount to a restatement of the Latin. If attempted, analysis may concern only one of the two poles of the question, i.e., what poetry can do or what it cannot do, or a good analysis may address the wrong question, as, for example, if the student analyzes how this poem expresses grief for the death of Quintilius. Alternatively, a superficial essay may lack correctly cited and translated/paraphrased Latin support .

2 – Inadequate, vague, faulty discussion of the question. The student will express some correct information but may betray a major misconception about the poem. Very scanty Latin or even no Latin correctly cited.

1 – The student says only one meaningful thing in response to the question and based on the passage.

0 – The student says nothing correct or meaningful derived from the passage, although something may be guessed at from the wording of the question itself.

Scansion

Scan the following lines and name the meter.   **The meter is third Asclepiadean.**

$$\_\ \_\ \_\ \cup\cup\ \_\ \ \_\ \cup\cup\ \_\ \cup\times$$
multis ille bonis flebilis occidit,

10    $$\_\ \_\ \ \_\ \cup\cup\_\ \ \ \_\ \ \cup\cup\ \_\ \cup\times$$
nulli flebilior, quam tibi, Vergili.

$$\_\ \ \_\ \ \_\ \cup\cup\ \ \ \_\ \ \_\ \cup\cup\ \_\ \cup\times$$
tu, frustra pius, heu, non ita creditum

$$\_\ \ \_\ \ \_\ \cup\cup\_\ \ \cup\times$$
poscis Quintilium deos.

$$\_\ \ \_\ \ \_\cup\cup\ \ \_\ \cup\cup\ \_\ \ \cup\times$$
quid, si Threicio blandius Orpheo

$$\_\ \_\ \_\ \ \cup\ \cup\ \_\ \ \_\ \cup\cup\ \_\ \cup\times$$
auditam moderer(e) arboribus fidem,

15    $$\_\ \ \_\ \ \_\ \cup\ \cup\_\ \ \_\ \cup\ \cup\ \_\cup\times$$
num vanae redeat sanguis imagini,

$$\_\ \ \_\ \ \_\ \cup\ \cup\ \_\ \cup\times$$
quam virga semel horrida

Ode 1.24.9–16

ODE 1.25

Parcius iunctas quatiunt fenestras
iactibus crebris iuvenes protervi,
nec tibi somnos adimunt, amatque
    ianua limen,

5   quae prius multum facilis movebat
cardines. audis minus et minus iam:
'me tuo longas pereunte noctes,
    Lydia, dormis?'

invicem moechos anus adrogantis
10   flebis in solo levis angiportu,
Thracio bacchante magis sub inter-
    lunia vento,

cum tibi flagrans amor et libido,
quae solet matres furiare equorum,
15   saeviet circa iecur ulcerosum,
    non sine questu,

laeta quod pubes hedera virenti
gaudeat pulla magis atque myrto,
aridas frondes hiemis sodali
20   dedicet Hebro.

Short Answer Questions

Line 1   What form is *parcius,* and what does it modify? **comparative adverb modifying *quatiunt* (or *iunctas*)**

What is the subject of *quatiunt?* ***iuvenes* (line 2)**

Line 2   What is the case and use of *iactibus?* **ablative of means with *quatiunt***

What figure of speech is in this line? ***iactibus:* metonymy for thrown stones**

Lines 3–4   What two figures of speech are in these lines? ***amat ianua limen:* personification of the door and metaphor for its remaining closed**

Line 5   What is the antecedent of *quae? **ianua* (line 4)**

Line 7	What is the case and use of *me*? **ablative, substantive in ablative absolute**
	What does *tuo* signify? **a substantive in apposition to *me*, i.e., "your lover," or "yours"**
	What form is *pereunte*, and what does it modify? **present participle ablative singular, from *perire*, modifies *me***
Line 9	What is the case and use of *moechos*? **accusative, direct object of *flebis***
	What is the case and use of *anus*? **nominative in apposition to "you," the subject of *flebis***
	What does *adrogantis* modify? ***moechos***
Line 10	What is the case and use of *levis*? **nominative modifying subject of *flebis***
Line 12	What is the case and use of *vento*? **ablative, substantive in ablative absolute with *bacchante***
Line 13	Translate *cum*. **"when"**
	What figure of speech is in this line? ***flagrans amor:* metaphor**
Line 14	What verb form is *furiare*, and how is it used grammatically in its context? **a complementary infinitive with *solet***
	What is the case and use of *equorum*? **genitive of possession with *matres***
Line 15	What is the tense and the subject of *saeviet*? **future indicative attracted to singular because last member of nominative series, *amor et libido*, is singular**
	What is the case and use of *iecur*? **accusative after preposition *circa***
Lines 14–16	What figure of speech is in these lines? ***(libido) saeviet:* personification**
Line 17	What does *laeta* modify? ***pubes***
	What is the case and use of *hedera*? **ablative with *gaudeat***
Line 19	What is the case and use of *hiemis*? **genitive of possession with *sodali***
	What is the case and use of *sodali*? **dative in apposition to *Hebro***
Line 20	What is the case and use of *Hebro*? **dative, indirect object of *dedicet***

Multiple Choice Questions *Suggested time: 15 minutes*

Parcius iunctas quatiunt fenestras
iactibus crebris iuvenes protervi,
nec tibi somnos adimunt, amatque
    ianua limen,

5   quae prius multum facilis movebat
cardines. audis minus et minus iam:
'me tuo longas pereunte noctes,
    Lydia, dormis?'

    invicem moechos anus adrogantis
10   flebis in solo levis angiportu,
Thracio bacchante magis sub inter-
    lunia vento,

Ode 1.25.1–12

1.   From lines 1–2, we learn that now youths
    a. close and shake the windows   **b. rarely throw stones at the shutters**
    c. seek joined windows   d. come in crowds to the windows

2.   The case of *iactibus* (line 2) is determined by
    a. *quatiunt* (line 1)   b. *crebris* (line 2)
    c. *protervi* (line 2)   d. *parcius* (line 1)

3.   From *amatque ianua limen* (lines 3–4), we may infer that
    a. the doorkeeper loves his position   b. the doorframe fits snugly around the door
    c. light shines on the door   **d. the door rarely opens**

4.   A correct translation of the words *prius . . . cardines* (lines 5–6) is
    a. a very easy hinge was moving   b. at the very beginning was moving easy hinges
    c. formerly used to move its hinges very readily   d. was the first to move its hinges with ease

5.   Lines 7–8 are spoken by Lydia's
    a. lover   b. son
    c. husband   d. servant

6. The experience that is long (line 7) is
   a. the speaker's death
   b. waiting for Lydia to open the door
   c. a night spent with Lydia
   d. Lydia's listening at the door

7. In line 9, *invicem* signals a reversal of roles between
   a. the old woman and adulterers
   b. Lydia and old women
   c. the speaker of lines 7–8 and adulterers
   d. Lydia and her lovers

8. The case and number of *adrogantis* (line 9) are
   a. genitive singular
   b. accusative plural
   c. ablative plural
   d. nominative singular

9. A figure of speech contained in line 10 is
   a. transferred epithet
   b. chiasmus
   c. prolepsis
   d. hendiadys

10. In line 10, *levis* modifies
   a. *moechos* (line 9)
   b. *adrogantis* (line 9)
   c. *angiportu* (line 10)
   d. the subject of *flebis* (line 10)

11. The best translation of *solo* (line 10) is
   a. usual
   b. sunny
   c. lonely
   d. earthy

12. In line 11, *bacchante* describes
   a. a Thracian
   b. Lydia
   c. the wind
   d. the moon

Translation *Suggested time: 15 minutes*

Translate the passage below as literally as possible.

> invicem moechos anus adrogantis
> flebis in solo levis angiportu,
> Thracio bacchante magis sub inter-
> lunia vento,
>
> 5   cum tibi flagrans amor et libido,
> quae solet matres furiare equorum,
> saeviet circa iecur ulcerosum,
> non sine questu,

Ode 1.25.9–16

18 chunks. 9 points total, 1/2 point each. Round up to nearest whole point.

invicem	in turn
moechos . . . adrogantis	arrogant/insolent adulterers (must be direct object of *flebis*)
anus	(as an) old woman
flebis	you will weep over/weep for/lament
in solo	in the lonely
levis	unimportant/fickle/light (must modify subject of *flebis*)
angiportu	alley(way)
Thracio bacchante . . . vento	with the Thracian wind raging/raving (as a bacchante) or as a subordinate clause in contemporaneous tense, e.g., "as/when the Thracian wind rages . . ."
magis	more
sub interlunia	just before/around the time of/under the period(s) between the old moon and the new/moonless skies
cum tibi	when for you/your
flagrans amor	blazing/flaming/hot/passionate love
et libido	and lust/desire
quae solet . . . furiare	which is accustomed to/usually madden(s)/drive(s) mad
matres . . . equorum	mothers of horses/mares
saeviet	will rage/rave/be savage (may be rendered as present if *flebis* was rendered as future)
circa iecur ulcerosum	around (your) ulcerous/full of sores liver
non sine questu	not without (a) complaint/lament

Short Analysis Questions *Suggested time: 10 minutes*

> cum tibi flagrans amor et libido,
> quae solet matres furiare equorum,
> saeviet circa iecur ulcerosum,
>   non sine questu,
>
> 5 laeta quod pubes hedera virenti
> gaudeat pulla magis atque myrto,
> aridas frondes hiemis sodali
>   dedicet Hebro.

Ode 1.25.13–20

Eight points total.

1. To what is Lydia compared in line 2? What does this comparison say about her character?

    Two points. One point for identifying the comparison: Lydia is compared to mares in heat, or mothers of horses in a frenzy of lust. The student must show here or in answer to the second part of the question that the focus of the comparison is the mares' sexual desire. A comment may also be made about Lydia's projected age (cf. *matres equorum*).

    One point for explaining that the comparison shows Lydia's sexual desire to be very strong. The question does not require one to say that mares in heat were reputed to be very lustful, although some students may add this information.

2. In line 3 (*saeviet circa iecur ulcerosum*),

    a. why does mention of the bodily organ, *iecur*, fit this context?

    Two points. One point for identifying *iecur* as the liver and saying that it was believed to be the seat of the emotions.

    b. what is the significance of *ulcerosum* as a description of Lydia?

    One point for defining *ulcerosum* ("full of sores, ulcerous") and saying that this adjective attributes disordered or unhealthy emotions to Lydia.

3. Write out and scan line 3.

    One point for copying out and correctly scanning the line:

    ‾ ◡ ‾ ‾ ◡◡ ‾ ◡ ‾ ×
    saeviet circa iecur ulcerosum

4. Name a figure of speech that appears in line 4, and write out the Latin that illustrates it.

    One point for identifying litotes in the words *non sine questu*.

5. In lines 5–8, the speaker contrasts dry leaves to two other plants. Briefly,

    a. identify these plants (and)

    One point for identifying the plants as (green) ivy and (somber/dark/gray) myrtle.

b. show how the contrast contributes to the speaker's point about Lydia.

One point for stating that the dry leaves represent Lydia, who is too old to be attractive to lovers, and the other plants represent women of younger ages. To receive credit, it is not necessary that the student explain the symbolic difference between ivy and myrtle in the poem (cf. Ancona, *Horace*, 1999, 2nd edition, 2005, *ad loc.*).

Essay *Suggested time: 20 minutes*

Parcius iunctas quatiunt fenestras
iactibus crebris iuvenes protervi,
nec tibi somnos adimunt, amatque
    ianua limen,

5   quae prius multum facilis movebat
cardines. audis minus et minus iam:
'me tuo longas pereunte noctes,
    Lydia, dormis?'

    invicem moechos anus adrogantis
10   flebis in solo levis angiportu,
Thracio bacchante magis sub inter-
    lunia vento,

cum tibi flagrans amor et libido,
quae solet matres furiare equorum,
15   saeviet circa iecur ulcerosum,
    non sine questu,

laeta quod pubes hedera virenti
gaudeat pulla magis atque myrto,
aridas frondes hiemis sodali
20   dedicet Hebro.

Ode 1.25

In this ode, a speaker delivers invective, or verbal abuse, against Lydia. In a short essay, discuss how the speaker uses references to present, past, and future to help convey his invective.

Support your assertions with references to the Latin text **throughout** the poem. All Latin words must be copied or their line numbers provided, AND they must be translated or paraphrased closely enough so that it is clear you understand the Latin. It is your responsibility to convince your reader that you are basing your conclusions on the Latin text and not merely on a general recollection of the passage. Direct your answer to the question; do not merely summarize the passage. Please write your essay on a separate piece of paper.

The question asks the student to show how the poem's three time frames contribute to its element of invective. Superior essays will pick out the poem's references to present, past, and future time to analyze how they function in the speaker's verbal abuse of Lydia. An excellent essay need not, and probably cannot, go into every temporal reference in the poem, but it will range over the whole poem.

Important references to the present are the descriptions in stanzas one and two of Lydia's lessening popularity among young men. The past is signaled by *movebat*, line 5, as well as by two adverbs or adverbial phrases of temporal comparison: *parcius*, and *minus et minus iam*. These parts of the text ascribe to Lydia greater popularity among lovers in the past. In turn, *invicem*, line 9, is an adverb that creates temporal comparison of past, and by extension, of present, with a bleak future that is most clearly denoted by the future tense verbs *flebis* and *saeviet*. The text's description of Lydia's future is enriched by subordinate elements that are contemporaneous with that future: ablative absolute (lines 11–12), relative clause (line 14).

An excellent treatment will analyze all three temporal segments of the poem in a coherent argument that clarifies their function within invective. It will demonstrate mastery of the Latin in adducing appropriate and plentiful support, correctly cited and translated or closely paraphrased. An acceptable essay will go into less depth, offer less Latin support and use it with less mastery, and in general will strike one as "adequate" rather than excellent. Less than satisfactory essays will misconstrue the poem, fail to discuss entire time frames altogether, or contain little or no correct Latin support.

6 – Excellent, perceptive, analytical account of how the ode uses references to all three time frames (present, past and future) to speak against Lydia. In broad outline, the whole poem is discussed. Liberal, appropriate and accurate use of Latin support, correctly cited.

5 – Good, solid discussion but not as full on how the three frames of temporal reference contribute to the invective. The analysis will not be as deep or as well organized as that of an excellent essay. Less full Latin support, but what appears is accurate and appropriate.

4 – Satisfactory, adequate analysis of the three time frames and their effect. The essay may be thinner and tend more toward description than analysis, although some analysis of how the temporal references function must be present. Latin support is apt and accurate but minimal, possibly only one citation for one time frame. Alternatively, a satisfactory essay may present a convincing analysis, with strong Latin support, of two of the temporal frames but do a weak job with the third.

3 – Superficial, weak discussion, may be rambling, general, or uneven. Unlike a satisfactory essay, a superficial one will not convince you that the student has adequately undertaken any analysis; the paper may amount to a restatement of the Latin. If attempted, analysis fails to engage all three time frames, or it may analyze the poem as invective but fail to show how temporal references are an element of this. Alternatively, a superficial paper may present a good essay that lacks correctly cited and translated/paraphrased Latin support.

2 – Inadequate, vague, faulty discussion of the question. The student will express some correct information but may betray a major misconception about the poem. Very scanty Latin support or even no Latin correctly cited.

1 – The student says only one meaningful thing in response to the question and based on the passage.

0 – The student says nothing correct or meaningful derived from the passage, although something may be guessed at from the wording of the question itself.

Scansion

Scan the following lines and name the meter.   **The meter is Sapphic.**

_ ∪ _ _ _ ∪ ∪ _ ∪ _ ×
cum tibi flagrans amor et libido,

_ ∪ _ _ _ ∪ ∪ _ ∪ _ ×
quae solet matres furiar(e) equorum,
‿

_ ∪ _ _ _ ∪ ∪ _ ∪ _ ×
15   saeviet circa iecur ulcerosum,

_ ∪ ∪ _ ×
non sine questu,

_ ∪ _ _ _ ∪ ∪ _ ∪ _ ×
laeta quod pubes hedera virenti

_ ∪ _ _ _ ∪ ∪ _ ∪ _ ×
gaudeat pulla magis atque myrto,

_ ∪ _ _ _ ∪ ∪ _ ∪ _ ×
aridas frondes hiemis sodali

_ ∪ ∪ _ ×
20   dedicet Hebro.

Ode 1.25.13–20

ODE 1.37

Nunc est bibendum, nunc pede libero
pulsanda tellus, nunc Saliaribus
　　ornare pulvinar deorum
　　　　tempus erat dapibus, sodales.

5　antehac nefas depromere Caecubum
cellis avitis, dum Capitolio
　　regina dementis ruinas
　　　　funus et imperio parabat

contaminato cum grege turpium
10　morbo virorum, quidlibet inpotens
　　sperare fortunaque dulci
　　　　ebria; sed minuit furorem

vix una sospes navis ab ignibus,
mentemque lymphatam Mareotico
15　redegit in veros timores
　　　　Caesar ab Italia volantem

remis adurgens, accipiter velut
mollis columbas aut leporem citus
　　venator in campis nivalis
20　　　Haemoniae, daret ut catenis

fatale monstrum, quae generosius
perire quaerens nec muliebriter
　　expavit ensem, nec latentis
　　　　classe cita reparavit oras,

25　ausa et iacentem visere regiam
voltu sereno, fortis et asperas
　　tractare serpentes, ut atrum
　　　　corpore combiberet venenum,

deliberata morte ferocior:
30　saevis Liburnis scilicet invidens
　　privata deduci superbo
　　　　non humilis mulier triumpho.

Short Answer Questions.

Line 1   What is the case and use of *pede libero*? **ablative of means**

Line 3   On what words in the sentence does *ornare* depend? **ornare is an (epexegetical) infinitive depending on tempus erat**

           What is the case and use of *pulvinar*? **accusative, direct object of ornare**

Line 4   What is the case and use of *dapibus*? **ablative of means with ornare**

Lines 1–4   What four figures of speech are in the first stanza? **whole stanza: tricolon crescens/crescendo; bibendum est—pulsanda—tempus erat: asyndeton; nunc ... nunc ... nunc: anaphora; dapibus: hyperbaton (its modifier appeared in line 2); libero pede: transferred epithet (n.b. five options)**

Line 5   What figure of speech is in this line? **nefas: ellipsis (erat omitted)**

           What is the case and use of *nefas*? **predicate nominative with understood impersonal verb erat**

           On what word does *depromere* depend? **depromere is an (epexegetical) infinitive depending on nefas (erat)**

Line 6   What is the case and use of *cellis*? **ablative of separation with depromere**

           What is the case and use of *Capitolio*? **dative of disadvantage with ruinas parabat**

Line 8   What figure of speech (non-AP) is in this line? **funus et: postposition/anastrophe**

           What is the case and use of *funus*? **accusative, direct object of parabat**

           What is the case and use of *imperio*? **dative of disadvantage with funus parabat**

Line 9   What is the case and use of *grege*? **ablative of accompaniment with cum**

Line 10   What is the case and use of *morbo*? **ablative of cause with turpium**

           What is the case and use of *quidlibet*? **accusative, direct object of sperare**

           What does *inpotens* modify? **regina, the subject of parabat**

Line 11   What is the case and use of *fortuna*? **ablative of cause with ebria**

Lines 11–12   What figure of speech is in these lines? **fortuna ... ebria: metaphor**

Line 13   What figure of speech is in this line? **vix una sospes navis: hyperbole**

Line 14   Of what verb is *mentem* the object, and what is the subject of that verb? **mentem is the direct object of redegit; subject of verb is Caesar**

           What is the case and use of *Mareotico*? **ablative of means with lymphatam**

Line 16   What figure of speech is in this line? **volantem: metaphor**

Line 17   What is the case and use of *remis?* **ablative of means with *adurgens***

What figure of speech (non-AP) is in this line? ***accipiter velut:* postposition/ anastrophe**

Line 18   What is the case and use of *mollis?* **accusative, modifying *columbas,* the direct object of *adurgens***

Line 19   What is the case and use of *nivalis?* **genitive singular, modifying *Haemoniae***

Line 20   What is the case and use of *catenis?* **dative, indirect object with *daret monstrum***

Lines 17–20   What figure of speech is in these lines? ***velut:* simile**

Lines 18–20   Of what verb are *accipiter* and *venator* the subjects? **an understood *adurgens***

Line 21   What form is *generosius?* **comparative adverb modifying *perire***

Line 23   What does *latentis* modify? ***oras,* accusative plural**

Line 24   What is the case and use of *classe?* **ablative of means with *reparavit***

Line 26   What is the case and use of *voltu* and what is another spelling of this word? **ablative of manner with *visere;* often spelled *vultu***

What figure of speech (non-AP) is in this line? ***fortis et:* postposition/anastrophe**

Line 29   What is the case and use of *morte?* **ablative absolute with *deliberata***

Line 30   What two figures of speech are in this line? ***saevis Liburnis:* transferred epithet and personification**

Line 31   What is the case and use of *privata?* **nominative in apposition to the subject of the action *invidens***

What figure of speech (non-AP) is in this line? ***deduci superbo:* juxtaposition**

Lines 31–32   What three figures of speech are in these lines? ***non humilis:* litotes; *superbo humilis mulier triumpho:* chiasmus; *superbo triumpho:* transferred epithet or personification**

Multiple Choice Questions *Suggested time: 15 minutes*

fatale monstrum, quae generosius
perire quaerens nec muliebriter
   expavit ensem, nec latentis
     classe cita reparavit oras,

5   ausa et iacentem visere regiam
voltu sereno, fortis et asperas
   tractare serpentes, ut atrum
     corpore combiberet venenum,

> deliberata morte ferocior:
> 10 saevis Liburnis scilicet invidens
> privata deduci superbo
> non humilis mulier triumpho.

Ode 1.37.21–32

1. In line 1, *fatale monstrum* is a reference to
   a. the Minotaur
   c. the Egyptian bull god

   b. Marc Antony
   d. Cleopatra

2. The words *quae . . . ensem* (lines 1–3) are translated
   a. which, generously seeking to die, did not fear a woman's sword
   c. and which the son-in-law, seeking to go through, did not, as a woman would, fear the sword

   b. who, seeking to perish more nobly, neither panicked like a woman at a sword
   d. who, dying with more dignity, did not dread the sword as a woman

3. From lines 3–4, we learn that Cleopatra did not
   a. prepare oars for her fleet
   c. make her fleet ready secretly

   b. repair the prows of her ships
   d. sail to secluded regions

4. The case of *classe* (line 4) is determined by
   a. *cita* (line 4)
   c. *reparavit* (line 4)

   b. *latentis* (line 3)
   d. *oras* (line 4)

5. The form of the word *visere* (line 5) is
   a. present infinitive
   c. present imperative

   b. perfect indicative
   d. present indicative

6. In line 6, *voltu sereno* is an ablative
   a. absolute
   c. of cause

   b. of means
   d. of manner

7. Lines 5–6 state that Cleopatra
   a. saw the queen lying with a serene face

   c. did not shrink from going to her ruined palace

   b. dared to throw queenly looks from her calm face
   d. calmly faced danger while resting in her palace

8. In line 6, *fortis* modifies
   a. *regiam* (line 5)
   c. the person described as *ausa* (line 5)

   b. *serpentes* (line 7)
   d. *voltu* (line 6)

9. In line 7, the word *ut* is translated

 a. with the result that   **b. in order to**

 c. as   d. that

10. A figure of speech found in line 8 is

 a. metaphor   b. zeugma

 c. simile   d. oxymoron

11. The case and number of *deliberata* (line 9) are

 a. accusative plural   b. nominative singular

 c. nominative plural   **d. ablative singular**

12. From line 9, we learn that Cleopatra was ferocious

 a. more than death   b. with the force of death

 c. when she decided to die   d. against death

13. The words *scilicet invidens privata deduci* (lines 10–11) are translated

 a. evidently refusing to be escorted as a private person b. if it is allowed for private things to be brought down

 c. of course envying a private woman being led down d. of course, having been deprived, she was led down unseen

Translation *Suggested time: 15 minutes*

Translate the passage below as literally as possible.

> Nunc est bibendum, nunc pede libero
> pulsanda tellus, nunc Saliaribus
>   ornare pulvinar deorum
>   tempus erat dapibus, sodales.
>
> 5 antehac nefas depromere Caecubum
> cellis avitis, dum Capitolio
>   regina dementis ruinas
>   funus et imperio parabat

Ode 1.37.1–8

18 chunks. 9 points total, 1/2 point each. Round up to nearest whole point.

Nunc . . . nunc . . . nunc	**Now . . . now . . . now (*nunc* must be translated three times)**
est bibendum	**one/we must drink/drinking must be done/it must be drunk**
pede libero	**with/by a free foot**
pulsanda tellus	**the earth must be beaten/struck (repeatedly)**
Saliaribus . . . dapibus	**with/by feasts/banquets of the Salii/priests**

ornare	to adorn/bedeck/deck out/decorate/honor
pulvinar deorum	the (sacred) couch of the gods
tempus erat	it was/it has been time
sodales	companions/fellows
antehac	before/before this/previously
nefas	(it was) a/an abomination/crime (student should supply verb)
depromere Caecubum	to bring down/bring out/produce Caecuban wine
cellis avitis	from ancestral/grandfathers' cells/storerooms/storage chambers (must be ablative)
Capitolio	for/against the Capitoline (must be dative)
dum . . . regina . . . parabat	while the queen was preparing/readying
dementis ruinas	mad/insane collapse/ruin/downfall (may be plural)
funus et	and death/a funeral/destruction (*funus* must be object of *parabat*)
imperio	for/against the empire/power/government/command

Short Analysis Questions *Suggested time: 10 minutes*

remis adurgens, accipiter velut
mollis columbas aut leporem citus
    venator in campis nivalis
        Haemoniae, daret ut catenis

5   fatale monstrum, quae generosius
perire quaerens nec muliebriter
    expavit ensem, nec latentis
        classe cita reparavit oras,

Ode 1.37.17–24

Eight points total.

1. The simile of stanza one involves hunters and their prey.

   a. Write out and translate the Latin words that denote the hunters and the prey.

      One point for the Latin words and translations for the hunter: *accipiter*, "hawk;" (*citus*) ve-*nator*, "(swift) hunter"

      One point for the Latin words and translations for the prey: (*mollis*) *columbas*, "(soft/gentle) doves"; *leporem*, "hare/rabbit."

   b. Which historical personage is represented by the hunters, and which historical personage is represented by the prey?

      One point for matching the hawk and hunter with Octavian/Augustus Caesar and the doves and hare with Cleopatra.

   c. According to the passage, for what reason did the one historical personage pursue the other? Cite and translate or paraphrase the Latin words that support your answer.

      One point for statement with supporting Latin that Augustus wanted to put Cleopatra in chains: *daret ut catenis* (*fatale monstrum*).

2. Line 5 contains a shift in gender between words that refer to the same person.

    a. Citing the Latin, identify and explain this shift.

        One point for identifying the shift from neuter antecedent, *monstrum*, to feminine relative pronoun, quae, and citing the Latin words.

    b. How does this shift help the poet develop his image of the person concerned? Support your statement by referring to the Latin text.

        Two points for explaining how shift helps the poet develop his image of Cleopatra, with supporting evidence from the Latin. Students may say that the image changes from hostile to respectful, from dehumanizing to human, etc.

        (One point for a convincing statement that is not supported from the Latin text).

3. Write out and scan line 8 (*classe . . . oras*).

    One point for copying out and correctly scanning the line:

         _ ∪ ∪_ ∪ ∪ _ ∪ _ ×
    clásse cíta reparávit óras,

Essay *Suggested time: 20 minutes*

> Nunc est bibendum, nunc pede libero
> pulsanda tellus, nunc Saliaribus
>   ornare pulvinar deorum
>   tempus erat dapibus, sodales.
>
> 5   antehac nefas depromere Caecubum
> cellis avitis, dum Capitolio
>   regina dementis ruinas
>   funus et imperio parabat
>
> contaminato cum grege turpium
> 10 morbo virorum, quidlibet inpotens
>   sperare fortunaque dulci
>   ebria; sed minuit furorem
>
> vix una sospes navis ab ignibus,
> mentemque lymphatam Mareotico
> 15   redegit in veros timores
>   Caesar ab Italia volantem
>
> remis adurgens, . . .

Ode 1.37.1–17

The ode from which these lines are excerpted was written in commemoration of the victory of Octa-vian/Augustus Caesar over Cleopatra. In a **short,** well-organized essay, describe the attitude that is expressed in the quoted passage toward this victory, and show how Horace conveys this attitude.

Support your assertions with references to the Latin text **throughout** the passage quoted above. All Latin words must be copied or their line numbers provided, AND they must be translated or paraphrased closely enough so that it is clear you understand the Latin. It is your responsibility to convince your reader that you are basing your conclusions on the Latin text and not merely on a general recollection of the passage. Direct your answer to the question; do not merely summarize the passage. Please write your essay on a separate piece of paper.

Many readers have felt that the tone taken in the text toward Octavian's foe, Cleopatra, and toward his victory over her, shifts in the middle of the ode. This essay question limits itself to the "anti-Cleopatra" half of the poem and asks the student to discuss how that section conveys an attitude toward the victory.

Students must distill their case from the whole passage (lines 1–17) and must show how it conveys the attitude toward the victory that they detect in it. The grader should not look for whether the student correctly identified the passage's attitude, for people may label it differently. The grader should evaluate the student's argument for its perception and analytical quality, its treatment of the passage as a whole, and its Latin support. Many students will characterize the attitude as one of joy or exultation. Some may find qualities like relief or admiration, or they may consider beliefs about the victory as part of attitude. Handling the invective against Cleopatra's character may prove the hardest part of the task for many, for the student has to tie that invective to the passage's attitude toward the victory and not stop at its vilification of Cleopatra the person. Perceptive students will discuss effects by which the passage conveys the attitude. Analysis of propositional content and imagery is always a fruitful direction for the student, as well as discussion of the effects of word choice (e.g., in the abuse of Cleopatra and her followers), word placement, figures like the tricolon crescens/crescendo of the first stanza, even omissions: e.g., by postponing clarification of what the rejoicing is about, Horace creates a mood of exultation even before the intellect knows the reason for it. Limited treatments may not go much beyond saying that the attitude is one of joy and then describing what is said in the passage. Some analysis from beginning, middle and end with at least minimal Latin support should be present in a satisfactory paper. If a student focuses on the passage's attitude toward Cleopatra rather than on its attitude toward the victory, give credit for that which may be said implicitly about the victory.

6 – Excellent, perceptive, analytical account of what attitude the passage expresses about Augustus' victory over Cleopatra and of how it conveys that attitude. In broad outline, the whole poem is discussed. Liberal, appropriate and accurate use of Latin support, correctly cited.

5 – Good, not as full a treatment of all parts of the passage or of the way they exert their effects. The analysis will not be as full or as well organized as that of an excellent essay. Less full Latin support, but what appears is accurate and appropriate.

4 – Satisfactory, adequate identification of the passage's attitude toward the victory and some analysis of how it conveys that attitude, although the essay is thinner than a good or excellent one and tends more toward description. Latin support is apt and accurate but not liberal. Alternatively, a satisfactory essay may present a convincing analysis, with strong Latin support, of parts of the passage but merely touch on other major sections.

3 – Superficial, weak discussion, may be rambling, general, or uneven. Unlike a satisfactory essay, a superficial one will not convince you that the student has adequately undertaken any analysis; the paper may amount to a restatement of the Latin. If attempted, analysis fails to engage the question and veers into another direction, e.g., analysis of the passage's attitude to Cleopatra with almost nothing said about the victory except that people are supposed to drink, or rejoice, or the like. Alternatively, a superficial paper may present a good essay that lacks correctly cited and translated/paraphrased Latin support.

2 – Inadequate, vague, faulty discussion of the question. The student will express some correct information but may betray a major misconception about the poem. Very scanty Latin support or even no Latin correctly cited.

1 – The student says only one meaningful thing in response to the question and based on the passage.

0 – The student says nothing correct or meaningful derived from the passage, although something may be guessed at from the wording of the question itself.

Scansion

Scan the following lines and name the meter. **The meter is Alcaic.**

‾ ‾ ⏑ ‾ ‾ ‾ ⏑ ⏑ ‾ ⏑×
fatale monstrum, quae generosius

⏑ ‾ ⏑ ‾ ‾ ‾ ⏑ ⏑ ‾ ⏑×
perire quaerens nec muliebriter

‾ ‾ ⏑ ‾ ‾ ‾ ⏑ ‾ ×
expavit ensem, nec latentis

‾ ⏑ ⏑ ‾ ⏑ ⏑ ‾ ⏑ ‾ ×
classe cita reparavit oras,

‾ ‾ ⏑ ‾ ‾ ‾ ⏑ ⏑ ‾ ⏑×
25 **aus(a) et iacentem visere regiam**

‾ ‾ ⏑ ‾ ‾ ‾ ⏑ ⏑ ‾ ⏑ ×
voltu sereno, fortis et asperas

‾ ‾ ⏑ ‾ ‾ ‾ ⏑ ‾ ×
tractare serpentes, ut atrum

‾ ⏑ ⏑ ‾ ⏑ ⏑ ‾ ⏑ ‾ ×
corpore combiberet venenum.

Ode 1.37.21–28

ODE 1.38

Persicos odi, puer, apparatus,
displicent nexae philyra coronae;
mitte sectari, rosa quo locorum
    sera moretur.

5   simplici myrto nihil adlabores
sedulus, curo: neque te ministrum
dedecet myrtus, neque me sub arta
    vite bibentem.

Short Answer Questions

Lines 1–2   What figure of speech is in these lines? **asyndeton**

Line 2   What is the case and use of *philyra?* **ablative of means with *nexae***

Line 3   What is the translation of *mitte sectari?* **"stop/leave off chasing (after)"**

    What is the case and use of *locorum?* **partitive genitive with *quo***

Line 5   What is the case and use of *myrto?* **dative with *adlabores***

    What is the case and use of *nihil?* **accusative, direct object of *adlabores* or accusative of respect used adverbially**

Lines 6–7   What two figures of speech are in these lines? ***neque . . . neque:* anaphora; *neque . . . dedecet:* litotes**

Line 7   What does *arta* modify? ***vite* (line 8)**

Line 8   What is the case and use of *vite?* **ablative, object of preposition *sub* (line 7)**

Line 9   What does *bibentem* modify? **modifies the speaker (*me,* line 7)**

Multiple Choice Questions *Suggested time: 13 minutes*

Persicos odi, puer, apparatus,
displicent nexae philyra coronae;
mitte sectari, rosa quo locorum
    sera moretur.

5   simplici myrto nihil adlabores
sedulus, curo: neque te ministrum
dedecet myrtus, neque me sub arta
    vite bibentem.

Ode 1.38

1. Line 1 (*Persicos . . . apparatus*) is translated
   - **a. I hate, boy, Persian magnificence**
   - b. Boy, hate Persian paraphernalia
   - c. I hated Persian pomp, boy
   - d. Be prepared, boy, to hate the Persians

2. The case and number of *apparatus* (line 1) are
   - a. nominative singular
   - **b. accusative plural**
   - c. genitive singular
   - d. vocative singular

3. The adjective *Persicos* is appropriate for use in line 1 because Persia was proverbial for
   - a. archery
   - b. warfare
   - **c. luxury**
   - d. deceit

4. The case of *philyra* (line 2) is determined by
   - a. *coronae* (line 2)
   - **b. *nexae* (line 2)**
   - c. *apparatus* (line 1)
   - d. *displicent* (line 2)

5. The words *rosa . . . moretur* (lines 3–4) are translated
   - a. where the rosy evening passes away
   - b. in what place the evening rose tarries
   - c. by which the last rose of the places is delayed
   - **d. to the place where the late rose lingers**

6. The tense and mood of *moretur* (line 4) are
   - **a. present subjunctive**
   - b. future indicative
   - c. present indicative
   - d. imperfect subjunctive

7. From lines 5–6, we learn that the speaker does not want the *puer* to
   - a. do no work
   - **b. look for more than myrtle**
   - c. stop at simple tasks
   - d. sit simply and work

8. In line 5, *simplici* modifies

    a. the subject of *adlabores* (line 5)   b. *nihil* (line 5)

    c. the subject of *curo* (line 6)   **d. *myrto* (line 5)**

9. A figure of speech contained in lines 6–7 is

    a. synecdoche   b. metaphor

    c. transferred epithet   **d. anaphora**

10. In lines 6–8, the *puer* is envisioned as

    a. decently clothed   b. drinking wine

    c. wearing myrtle   d. beneath a vine

11. From the words *arta vite* (lines 7–8), we may infer that the vine

    a. is artfully entwined on a trellis   **b. has dense leaves**

    c. has numerous limbs   d. grows high overhead

Translation *Suggested time: 15 minutes*

Translate the passage below as literally as possible.

> Persicos odi, puer, apparatus,
> displicent nexae philyra coronae;
> mitte sectari, rosa quo locorum
>   sera moretur.
>
> 5   simplici myrto nihil adlabores
> sedulus, curo: neque te ministrum
> dedecet myrtus, neque me sub arta
>   vite bibentem.

Ode 1.38

18 chunks. 9 points total, 1/2 point each. Round up to nearest whole point.
Note: Lines 5–6 may be construed in more than one way; cf. Ancona, *Horace*, 1999, 2nd edition 2005, *ad loc.*

Persicos . . . apparatus	**Persian paraphernalia/preparations/pomp/magnificence (must be object of *odi*; may be rendered as singular)**
odi, puer	**I hate, boy**
displicent . . . coronae	**garlands/crowns displease/are displeasing**
nexae philyra	**woven/entwined with lime bast/binding material**
mitte sectari	**leave off/banish/do not/send away pursue(ing)/chase(ing)**
quo locorum	**(to) where of places/to what place/in what place**
rosa . . . sera	**the late rose**
moretur	**lingers/delays**
simplici myrto	**to simple myrtle (must be dative)**

nihil	**nothing (if rendered as object of *adlabores*)**
	OR
	nothing/not/not at all (if construed with *curo*)
adlabores	**that you (should) add by labor/add by taking trouble/work hard (at); (*myrto* must be indirect object)**
sedulus	**attentive/diligent or may be rendered adverbially (may be construed with *adlabores* or *curo*)**
curo	**I care/I am concerned**
neque . . . neque	**neither . . . nor**
te ministrum	**you (as the) servant/assistant (must be object of *dedecet*)**
dedecet myrtus	**myrtle is not fitting/ill befits/is not suitable for/is not appropriate to/for**
me . . . bibentem	**me drinking/as I drink (must be object of *dedecet*)**
sub arta vite	**beneath a dense/close-leaved vine**

Short Analysis Questions *Suggested time: 10 minutes*

Persicos odi, puer, apparatus,
displicent nexae philyra coronae;
mitte sectari, rosa quo locorum
    sera moretur.

5   simplici myrto nihil adlabores
sedulus, curo: neque te ministrum
dedecet myrtus, neque me sub arta
    vite bibentem.

Ode 1.38

Eight points total.

1.   Enumerate three things the speaker tells the boy he does not want. Copy and translate the Latin words that denote them.

    Three points.

    One point for each thing the speaker does not want, with supporting Latin:

    Persian sumptuousness/paraphernalia *Persicos apparatus;* garlands woven with lime bast *nexae* ("garlands" alone does not suffice); (the late) rose *rosa* (*sera*)

    OR

    that the boy look for the late rose
    mitte sectari, rosa quo locorum/sera moretur

2.   Identify a figure of speech that is found in the first stanza, and copy the Latin words that illustrate it.

    One point for asyndeton between lines 1 and 2
    OR tricolon crescens/crescendo in whole stanza

3.　a.　Of what plant does the speaker approve?

One point for identifying myrtle as the plant approved by the speaker.

　　b.　What does he tell the boy to do with this plant?

One point for saying that the speaker tells the boy not to (take pains to) add to myrtle/get anything else besides myrtle/tells him only to provide myrtle.

　　c.　What reason does he give for these instructions?

One point for the reason: myrtle is not unbecoming to the speaker or to the boy.

4.　Copy and scan line 2 (*displicent . . . coronae*).

One point for copying out and correctly scanning the line:

$$\text{— ͝ —　— —　͝ ͝ —　͝ — ×}$$
displicent nexae philyra coronae;

Essay *Suggested time: 20 minutes*

Persicos odi, puer, apparatus,
displicent nexae philyra coronae;
mitte sectari, rosa quo locorum
　　sera moretur.

5　simplici myrto nihil adlabores
　　sedulus, curo: neque te ministrum
　　dedecet myrtus, neque me sub arta
　　　vite bibentem.

Ode 1.38

Readers of this poem have made various attempts to identify the principles or values to which the poet commits himself. In a short, well-organized essay, set forth your view about the principles that the ode expresses and show how the poet conveys them.

Support your assertions with references to the Latin text **throughout** the poem. All Latin words must be copied or their line numbers provided, AND they must be translated or paraphrased closely enough so that it is clear you understand the Latin. It is your responsibility to convince your reader that you are basing your conclusions on the Latin text and not merely on a general recollection of the passage. Direct your answer to the question; do not merely summarize the passage.

This question allows the student much latitude in formulating a view of the principles or values to which the implied author commits himself. On its surface, the poem only lays down dicta about decorations for drinking parties: the speaker dislikes elaborate decorations and prefers simple ones like myrtle garlands. Some readers will maintain that the poem's significance is limited to the sympotic setting, while others will detect in the sympotic setting a metaphor for other fields of concern—perhaps as a manifesto for a certain kind of poetry, or as recommending a lifestyle of limiting desire to that which one can enjoy in the present. Whatever the student identifies as principles, the essay, in order to be

judged superior, needs to go beyond saying, "Horace does not like fancy party decorations"; it needs to argue convincingly that his preferences bespeak generalized values that rest on reasons, and it needs to analyze the text to show how it reveals the principles the student thinks it presupposes. For example, a student may support a *carpe diem* claim by arguing that the speaker wants to enjoy what nature affords already at hand, like myrtle twigs and a vine's shade, rather than to wait for products of time-consuming effort, like fancy garlands or a hard-to-find rose, which provide no more pleasure and pass away just the same. A merely satisfactory essay, on the other hand, will be a more pedestrian treatment, less able to perceive layers of significance, perhaps describing what the poet praises and blames and drawing one or two valid inferences about principles.

6 – Excellent, perceptive, analytical discussion about what principles the poem expresses AND of how it conveys them. For a poem this short, every line should be discussed, and the essay should manifest lucid, logical structure, in which the principles are stated and their presence in the poem is argued. Liberal, appropriate, and accurate use of Latin support is correctly cited.

5 – Good, not as full a treatment of every line of the poem or of the way it conveys the principles that the student has identified. The analysis will not be as full or as well organized as that of an excellent essay. Less full Latin support is presented, but what appears is accurate and appropriate.

4 – Satisfactory, adequate identification of the passage's implied principles and some analysis of how it conveys them, although the essay is thinner than a good or excellent one and tends more toward description. Latin support is apt and accurate but not liberal. Alternatively, a satisfactory essay may present a convincing analysis, with strong Latin support, of parts of the poem but merely touch on or even omit a few lines.

3 – Superficial, weak discussion, may be rambling, general, or uneven. Unlike a satisfactory essay, a superficial one will not convince you that the student has adequately undertaken any analysis; the paper may amount to a restatement of the Latin. The student may recount what things the poet says he dislikes and what things he wants and leave the discussion at that, without considering what principles the poet's assertions presuppose. Alternatively, a superficial paper may present a good essay that lacks correctly cited and translated/paraphrased Latin support.

2 – Inadequate, vague, faulty discussion of the question. The student will express some correct information but may betray a major misconception about the poem. Very scanty Latin support is presented or even no Latin correctly cited.

1 – The student says only one meaningful thing in response to the question and based on the passage.

0 – The student says nothing correct or meaningful derived from the passage, although something may be guessed at from the wording of the question itself.

Scansion

Scan the following lines and name the meter. **The meter is Sapphic.**

$$\text{— ∪ — — — ∪∪ — ∪ — ×}$$
Persicos odi, puer, apparatus,

$$\text{— ∪ — — — ∪∪ — ∪ — ×}$$
displicent nexae philyra coronae;

$$\text{— ∪ — — — ∪∪ — ∪ — ×}$$
mitte sectari, rosa quo locorum

$$\text{— ∪ ∪ — ×}$$
sera moretur.

$$\text{— ∪ — — — ∪∪ — ∪ — ×}$$
5   **simplici myrto nihil adlabores**

$$\text{— ∪ — — — ∪ ∪ — ∪ — ×}$$
sedulus, curo: neque te ministrum

$$\text{— ∪ — — — ∪ ∪ — ∪ — ×}$$
dedecet myrtus, neque me sub arta

$$\text{— ∪ ∪ — ×}$$
vite bibentem.

Ode 1.38

ODE 2.3

Aequam memento rebus in arduis
servare mentem, non secus in bonis
   ab insolenti temperatam
      laetitia, moriture Delli,

5   seu maestus omni tempore vixeris,
seu te in remoto gramine per dies
   festos reclinatum bearis
      interiore nota Falerni.

quo pinus ingens albaque populus
10   umbram hospitalem consociare amant
   ramis? quid obliquo laborat
      lympha fugax trepidare rivo?

huc vina et unguenta et nimium brevis
flores amoenae ferre iube rosae,
15   dum res et aetas et sororum
      fila trium patiuntur atra.

cedes coemptis saltibus et domo
villaque, flavos quam Tiberis lavit,
   cedes, et exstructis in altum
20   divitiis potietur heres.

divesne prisco natus ab Inacho,
nil interest, an pauper et infima
   de gente sub divo moreris,
      victima nil miserantis Orci:

25   omnes eodem cogimur, omnium
versatur urna serius ocius
   sors exitura et nos in aeternum
      exilium inpositura cumbae.

Short Answer Questions

Line 2   What verb form is *servare*, and how is it used grammatically in its context?
             complementary infinitive depending on *memento* (line 1)

Lines 1–2   What two figures of speech are in these lines? ***aequam ... mentem:* hyperbaton and extended chiasmus (ABBA)**

Line 4	What is the case and use of *Delli*? **vocative, direct address**
Line 7	What does *reclinatum* modify? **te (line 6)**
Line 8	What figure of speech is in this line? **nota: metonymy for the wine itself or for the vintage**
	What is the case and use of *nota*? **ablative of means with bearis (line 7)**
Lines 9–10	What figure of speech is in these lines? **pinus ... populus ... amant: personification**
Line 11	What is the case and use of *ramis*? **ablative of means with consociare (line 10)**
	What figure of speech is in this line? **(lympha) laborat: personification**
Line 15	What is the case and use of *sororum*? **genitive of possession with fila (line 16)**
Line 16	What does *atra* modify? **fila**
Line 17	What is the case and use of *saltibus*? **ablative of separation with cedes**
	What is the case and use of *domo*? **ablative of separation with cedes**
Line 18	What is the case and use of *villa*? **ablative of separation with cedes**
Line 21	What does *natus* modify? **an understood "you," the subject of moreris (line 23)**
Line 22	What is the subject of *nil interest*? **The subject of nil interest, a verb used_ impersonally, is the clause containing the disjunction divesne ... an pauper ... moreris (lines 21–23)**
Lines 21–22	How are *ne ... an* translated? **"whether ... or"**
Line 24	What is the case and use of *nil*? **accusative, direct object of miserantis or accusative of respect used adverbially**
	What does *miserantis* modify? **Orci**
	What is the case and use of *Orci*? **genitive of possession with victima**
Line 26	What is the subject of *versatur*? **sors (line 27)**
Line 27	What does *exitura* modify? **sors**
	What is the case and use of *nos*? **accusative, direct object of inpositura**
Line 28	What is the case and use of *exilium*? **accusative, object of preposition in (line 27)**
	What does *inpositura* modify? **sors**
	What figure of speech is in this line? **inpositura cumbae: metaphor for death as well as literal skiff of Charon**
Lines 26–28	What figure of speech is in these lines? **omnium versatur urna ... sors: metaphor**

Multiple Choice Questions *Suggested time: 15 minutes*

quo pinus ingens albaque populus
umbram hospitalem consociare amant
ramis? quid obliquo laborat
lympha fugax trepidare rivo?

5   huc vina et unguenta et nimium brevis
flores amoenae ferre iube rosae,
dum res et aetas et sororum
fila trium patiuntur atra.

cedes coemptis saltibus et domo
10 villaque, flavos quam Tiberis lavit,
cedes, et exstructis in altum
divitiis potietur heres.

Ode 2.3.9–20

1. In line 1, *quo* is translated
   - a. by what
   - **b. to what purpose**
   - c. to where
   - d. by which

2. A figure of speech that is contained in line 1 is
   - a. transferred epithet
   - b. hendiadys
   - c. interlocked word order/synchysis
   - **d. chiasmus**

3. From the words *quo . . . ramis* (lines 1–3) we learn that
   - a. public associations gladly care for the sick
   - **b. the pine grows close to the poplar**
   - c. the huge population loves to gather among the pines
   - d. the poplar shades the pine as its guest

4. The case of *ramis* (line 3) is determined by
   - **a. *consociare* (line 2)**
   - b. *amant* (line 2)
   - c. *hospitalem* (line 2)
   - d. *umbram* (line 2)

5. The thing that "labors" in line 3 is a
   - a. fluid in the body
   - b. runaway slave
   - c. drink
   - **d. brook**

6. The items enumerated in line 5 are preparations for a
   - **a. drinking party**
   - b. wedding
   - c. religious festival
   - d. voyage

7. In line 5, *nimium* modifies
    a. *ferre* (line 6)
    c. brevis (line 5)
    b. *iube* (line 6)
    d. *amoenae* (line 6)

8. In line 7, *aetas* is translated
    a. summer
    c. tide
    b. life
    d. heat

9. In line 7, *sororum* refers to the
    a. Muses
    c. Fates
    b. Graces
    d. Hours

10. The case and number of *atra* (line 8) are
    a. nominative plural
    c. accusative plural
    b. ablative singular
    d. nominative singular

11. From lines 9–12 (*cedes . . . heres*), we learn that the addressee will
    a. go bankrupt
    c. bequeath property
    b. surrender
    d. emigrate

12. The words *exstructis . . . potietur* (lines 11–12) are translated
    a. gains control of the wealth built out into the deep
    c. will allow the wealth to be piled up on high
    b. gets possession of the rich structures extending into the sea
    d. will gain possession of the riches piled on high

Translation *Suggested time: 15 minutes*

Translate the passage below as literally as possible.

> Aequam memento rebus in arduis
> servare mentem, non secus in bonis
>   ab insolenti temperatam
>   laetitia, moriture Delli,
>
> 5   seu maestus omni tempore vixeris,
> seu te in remoto gramine per dies
>   festos reclinatum bearis
>   interiore nota Falerni.

Ode 2.3.1–8

18 chunks. 9 points total, 1/2 point each. Round up to nearest whole point.

Aequam . . . mentem	an even/equal/impartial mind/mindset/state of mind
memento	remember/recall (must be imperative)
rebus in arduis	in/among difficult/arduous/steep/difficult affairs/things/situations
servare	to preserve/keep/save
non secus	no/not differently/otherwise
in bonis	in good (ones) (must modify *rebus*)
ab insolenti . . . laetitia	from (not "by") unaccustomed/excessive/immoderate (not "insolent") joy/happiness
temperatam	held back/moderated/regulated/restrained
moriture Delli	(oh) Dellius about to die/who will die (must be future)
seu . . . seu	whether . . . or
maestus . . . vixeris	you shall have lived/will live sad/unhappy/sorrowful
omni tempore	on every occasion/in all time
te . . . reclinatum	yourself (must be reflexive with *bearis*) (having) reclined/reclining/leaning back
in remoto gramine	on/in (a) secluded/remote grass/meadow
per dies festos	during/through festival/festive days
bearis	you shall have made/shall make happy/blessed (object must be *te . . . reclinatum*)
interiore nota	by/with an inner/interior mark/label/vintage
Falerni	of Falernian (wine)

Short Analysis Questions *Suggested time: 10 minutes*

> divesne prisco natus ab Inacho,
> nil interest, an pauper et infima
> de gente sub divo moreris,
> victima nil miserantis Orci:
>
> 5   omnes eodem cogimur, omnium
> versatur urna serius ocius
> sors exitura et nos in aeternum
> exilium inpositura cumbae.

Ode 2.3.21–28

Eight points total.

1. Two sets of personal characteristics are said to "make no difference" (*nil interest,* line 2).

   a. Identify these characteristics and cite the Latin words that refer to them.

   One point for identifying the characteristic, wealth or financial status, and citing *dives* and *pauper.*

   One point for identifying the characteristic, social class or status, and citing *prisco natus ab Inacho* and *infima de gente.*

   b. Why do these characteristics make no difference?

   One point for explaining that these characteristics do not matter in the face of our inevitable death.

2. Write out and scan line 3.

   One point for copying out and correctly scanning the line:

   $$\_\ \_\ \cup\ \_\ \ \_\ \_\ \cup\ \_\ \times$$
   dē gēnte sub dīvō morēris

3. Who is Orcus, and why is this character described as *nil miserantis* (line 4)?

   One point for identifying Orcus as Hades/Pluto/god of the underworld (or, by metonymy, as the underworld or death).

   One point for explaining *nil miserantis* as a statement that death has pity on/reprieves/ excuses no one/no living thing.

4. Lines 6–8 develop an image of the *sors*.

   a. What is a *sors*?

One point for saying that the *sors* is a "lot" that one casts to tell a person's fortune, or for saying that it represents a person's fortune.

   b. What does it represent as it is presented in the image?

One point for saying that when the *sors* comes out of the urn, it represents our allotted span of life coming to its end, and that it represents our (fated) death when it puts us on the skiff into exile.

Essay *Suggested time: 20 minutes*

> Aequam memento rebus in arduis
> servare mentem, non secus in bonis
>   ab insolenti temperatam
>   laetitia, moriture Delli,
>
> 5 seu maestus omni tempore vixeris,
> seu te in remoto gramine per dies
>   festos reclinatum bearis
>   interiore nota Falerni.
>
> quo pinus ingens albaque populus
> 10 umbram hospitalem consociare amant
>   ramis? quid obliquo laborat
>   lympha fugax trepidare rivo?
>
> huc vina et unguenta et nimium brevis
> flores amoenae ferre iube rosae,
> 15   dum res et aetas et sororum
>   fila trium patiuntur atra.

Ode 2.3.1–16

Much of this ode is composed of references to the natural world. In a short, well-organized essay, discuss how Horace's nature references help him develop the advice about life that he gives Dellius.

Support your assertions with references to the Latin text **throughout** the passage. All Latin words must be copied or their line numbers provided, AND they must be translated or paraphrased closely enough so that it is clear you understand the Latin. It is your responsibility to convince your reader that you are basing your conclusions on the Latin text and not merely on a general recollection of the passage. Direct your answer to the question; do not merely summarize the passage. Please write your essay on a separate piece of paper.

Implicit in the question is the requirement that the student say what he/she thinks the poet's advice is: something like "keep your state of mind on an even keel in whatever circumstances you find yourself." Students may draw various other inferences about the advice from the imagery; e.g., that pleasure of quiet enjoyment of nature shows a way to live happily with a calm mind, or that one cannot notice pleasure in the present if the mind is excited or disturbed by imaginings about the future (from stanza three). Details about Dellius' life are not relevant unless the student uses them in answering the question. The student's principal task is to show how the nature references throughout the passage help the poet convey his advice. "Throughout the passage" means that the student should discuss the major nature references: Dellius reclining on the grass enjoying a fine wine, the pine and poplar loving to cast shade, the brook rushing, and the outdoor drinking party, complete with too-short-lived rose blossoms. It also requires students to account for lines 15–16, perhaps by including their content in the poem's statement of advice. An excellent essay develops an argument, uses Latin evidence, and undertakes perceptive analysis of how each image helps convey Horace's advice. A merely satisfactory essay will undertake some analysis of how the nature references relate to the advice, but much of it may simply describe the nature scenes, and its use of Latin support will be correct but minimal.

6 – Excellent, perceptive, analytical discussion about how the passage's nature references relate to the advice. The content of this advice must be stated. All parts of the passage must be discussed. Liberal, appropriate and accurate use of Latin support, is correctly cited.

5 – Good, but not as full a treatment of every image in the poem or of the way the nature references help convey the advice. The analysis will not be as full or as well organized as that of an excellent paper. Latin support is less full, but what appears is accurate and appropriate. Very full and accurate Latin support may pull a merely adequate analysis to this level if most of the passage is discussed.

4 – Satisfactory, adequate identification of the passage's moral advice and some analysis of how the nature references help convey it. The essay is thinner than an excellent or good essay and tends more toward description. Latin support is apt and accurate but not liberal. Alternatively, a satisfactory essay may present a convincing analysis, with strong Latin support, of parts of the poem but merely touch on or even omit certain lines.

3 – Superficial, weak discussion, may be rambling, general, or uneven. Unlike a satisfactory essay, a superficial one will not convince you that the student has adequately undertaken any analysis; the paper may amount to a restatement of the Latin. The student may recount what things the poet says about natural settings, without considering how the lines in question relate to the advice. Alternatively, a superficial paper may present a good essay that lacks correctly cited and translated/paraphrased Latin support.

2 – Inadequate, vague, faulty discussion of the question. The student will express some correct information but may betray a major misconception about the poem. Very scanty Latin support is presented or even no Latin is correctly cited.

1 – The student says only one meaningful thing in response to the question and based on the passage.

0 – The student says nothing correct or meaningful derived from the passage, although something may be guessed at from the wording of the question itself.

Scansion

Scan the following lines and name the meter. **The meter is Alcaic.**

$$\bar{\ }\ \bar{\ }\ \smallsmile\ \bar{\ }\ \bar{\ }\ \mid\ \bar{\ }\ \smallsmile\smallsmile\ \bar{\ }\ \smallsmile\ \times$$

hūc vīn(a) et unguent(a) et nimium brevis

$$\bar{\ }\ \bar{\ }\ \smallsmile\ \bar{\ }\ \mid\ \bar{\ }\ \bar{\ }\ \smallsmile\smallsmile\ \bar{\ }\ \smallsmile\ \times$$

flōres amoenae ferre iube rosae,

$$\bar{\ }\ \bar{\ }\ \smallsmile\ \bar{\ }\ \bar{\ }\ \bar{\ }\ \smallsmile\ \bar{\ }\ \times$$

dūm res et aetas et sororum

$$\bar{\ }\ \smallsmile\ \smallsmile\ \bar{\ }\ \smallsmile\smallsmile\ \bar{\ }\ \smallsmile\ \bar{\ }\ \times$$

fila trium patiuntur atra.

17
$$\bar{\ }\ \bar{\ }\ \smallsmile\ \bar{\ }\ \bar{\ }\ \bar{\ }\ \smallsmile\smallsmile\ \bar{\ }\ \smallsmile\ \times$$

cedes coëmptis saltibus et domo

$$\bar{\ }\ \bar{\ }\ \smallsmile\ \bar{\ }\ \bar{\ }\ \bar{\ }\ \smallsmile\smallsmile\ \bar{\ }\ \smallsmile\ \times$$

villaque, flavos quam Tiberis lavit,

$$\bar{\ }\ \bar{\ }\ \smallsmile\ \bar{\ }\ \bar{\ }\ \bar{\ }\ \smallsmile\ \bar{\ }\ \times$$

cedes, et exstructis in altum

$$\bar{\ }\ \smallsmile\smallsmile\ \bar{\ }\ \smallsmile\smallsmile\ \bar{\ }\ \smallsmile\ \bar{\ }\ \times$$

divitiis potietur heres.

Ode 2.3.13–20

ODE 2.7

O saepe mecum tempus in ultimum
deducte Bruto militiae duce,
   quis te redonavit Quiritem
     dis patriis Italoque caelo,

5   Pompei, meorum prime sodalium,
cum quo morantem saepe diem mero
   fregi coronatus nitentis
     malobathro Syrio capillos?

tecum Philippos et celerem fugam
10   sensi relicta non bene parmula,
   cum fracta virtus et minaces
     turpe solum tetigere mento.

sed me per hostis Mercurius celer
denso paventem sustulit aere,
15   te rursus in bellum resorbens
     unda fretis tulit aestuosis.

ergo obligatam redde Iovi dapem,
longaque fessum militia latus
   depone sub lauru mea, nec
20   parce cadis tibi destinatis.

oblivioso levia Massico
ciboria exple, funde capacibus
   unguenta de conchis. quis udo
     deproperare apio coronas

25   curatve myrto? quem Venus arbitrum
dicet bibendi? non ego sanius
   bacchabor Edonis: recepto
     dulce mihi furere est amico.

Short Answer Questions

Line 2   What is the case and use of *deducte*? **vocative, modifying addressee, *Pompei* (line 5)**

What is the case and use of *militiae*? **objective genitive with *Bruto ... duce***

Line 4	What figure of speech is in this line? **chiasmus: noun adjective adjective noun**
	What is the case and use of *dis?* **dative, indirect object of *redonavit* (line 3)**
Line 5	What is the case and use of *Pompei?* **vocative, direct address**
Line 6	What figure of speech is in this line? *morantem diem:* **personification**
	What is the case and use of *mero?* **ablative of means with *fregi* (line 7)**
Lines 6–7	What figure of speech is in these lines? *diem . . . fregi:* **metaphor**
Lines 7–8	What is the figure of speech in these lines? *nitentis malobathro Syrio capillos:* **chiasmus**
Line 11	What two figures of speech are in this line? *fracta virtus:* **metaphor;** *fracta (est):* **ellipsis**
	What is the case and use of *minaces?* **nominative, adjective acting as substantive, subject of *tetigere* (line 12)**
Line 12	The verb *tetigere* is an alternative of what verb form? *tetigerunt*
	What figure of speech is in this line? *turpe solum:* **transferred epithet**
	What is the case and use of *mento?* **ablative of means**
Line 13	What is the case and use of *me?* **accusative, direct object of *sustulit* (line 14)**
Line 14	What does *paventem* modify? *me* **(line 13)**
	What is the case and use of *aere?* **ablative of means with *sustulit* or ablative of place where**
Line 16	What is the case and use of *fretis?* **ablative of means with *tulit* or ablative of place where**
Lines 14–16	What figure of speech is in these lines? **asyndeton: no conjunction between *sustulit* (line 14) and *tulit* (line 16)**
Line 17	What is the case and use of *Iovi?* **dative, indirect object with *redde***
Line 18	What figure of speech is in this line? *longa fessum militia latus:* **interlocked word order/synchysis/synchesis**
	What is the case and use of *militia?* **ablative of cause with *fessum***
	What is the case and use of *latus?* **accusative, direct object of *depone* (line 19)**
Line 20	What is the figure of speech in this line? *parce cadis:* **metonymy (*cadis* for the wine inside them)**
	What is the case and use of *cadis?* **object of verb governing the dative (*parcere*)**
Line 22	What figure of speech is in this line? **asyndeton**
Lines 21–22	What figure of speech is in these lines? *oblivioso levia Massico ciboria:* **interlocked word order/synchysis**

Line 24   On what other word in the sentence does *deproperare* depend? **curat (line 25)**

What is the case and use of *apio*? **ablative of means with *deproperare coronas***

Line 25   What two words does *-ve* contrast? **apio (line 24) and myrto**

What is the case and use of *myrto*? **ablative of means with *deproperare coronas***

What is the case and use of *arbitrum*? **predicate accusative with *dicet* (line 26)**

Line 26   What is the form of *bibendi*? **genitive gerund, "of drinking"**

What figure of speech is in this line? **non sanius: litotes**

Line 27   What is the case and use of *Edonis*? **ablative of comparison with *sanius* (line 26)**

Line 28   What is the case and use of *mihi*? **dative of reference with *dulce***

What is the subject of *est*? **furere**

What is the case and use of *amico*? **ablative absolute (recepto . . . amico)**

Multiple Choice Questions *Suggested time: 15 minutes*

> Pompei, meorum prime sodalium,
> cum quo morantem saepe diem mero
>   fregi coronatus nitentis
>   malobathro Syrio capillos?
>
> 5   tecum Philippos et celerem fugam
> sensi relicta non bene parmula,
>   cum fracta virtus et minaces
>   turpe solum tetigere mento.
>
> sed me per hostis Mercurius celer
> 10   denso paventem sustulit aere,
>   te rursus in bellum resorbens
>   unda fretis tulit aestuosis.

Ode 2.7.5–16

1.   A figure of speech contained in line 1 is
    a.   hyperbole   **b.   interlocked word order/synchysis**
    c.   transferred epithet   d.   asyndeton

2.   The translation of *quo* (line 2) is
    a.   what   b.   to where
    c.   whom   d.   which

3. From lines 2–3, we learn that Horace and Pompeius used to drink
   a. **during the day**
   b. watered-down wine
   c. together rarely
   d. beginning at dusk

4. In line 3, *coronatus* modifies
   a. *Pompei* (line 1)
   b. *nitentis* (line 3)
   c. *capillos* (line 4)
   d. **the subject of *fregi* (line 3)**

5. The case of *capillos* (line 4) is determined by
   a. *malobathro* (line 4)
   b. ***coronatus* (line 3)**
   c. *nitentis* (line 3)
   d. *fregi* (line 3)

6. The words *celerem . . . parmula* (lines 5–6) are translated
   a. I did not hear the swift flight well when I left my little shield behind
   b. I perceived well the swift flight and the little shield not left behind
   c. **I experienced the swift flight, having basely left my little shield behind**
   d. I did not understand the swift flight well, nor how my little shield was abandoned

7. Lines 7–8 refer to the defeat of the forces of
   a. **Brutus and Cassius**
   b. Antony and Cleopatra
   c. Pompey and the senate
   d. Pompey's sons

8. The translation of *solum* (line 8) is
   a. alone
   b. only
   c. **the ground**
   d. the accustomed

9. The form of the word *tetigere* (line 8) is
   a. present infinitive
   b. **perfect indicative**
   c. present indicative
   d. perfect participle

10. From lines 9–10, we learn that Horace
    a. **escaped battle safely**
    b. was pursued by a god
    c. feared the hostility of Mercury
    d. fled in a fog on the pavement

11. In line 10, *sustulit* is a form of
    a. *fero*
    b. *sustulo*
    c. ***tollo***
    d. *surgo*

12. From lines 11–12, we can infer that Pompeius
    a. never saw Horace again
    b. was shipwrecked
    c. sailed during the summer
    d. fought longer than Horace did

13. The subject of *tulit* (line 12) is
    a. *Mercurius* (line 9)
    b. *hostis* (line 9)
    c. *rursus* (line 11)
    d. *unda* (line 12)

Translation *Suggested time: 15 minutes*

Translate the passage below as literally as possible.

> oblivioso levia Massico
> ciboria exple, funde capacibus
>   unguenta de conchis. quis udo
>   deproperare apio coronas
>
> 5   curatve myrto? quem Venus arbitrum
>   dicet bibendi? non ego sanius
>   bacchabor Edonis: recepto
>   dulce mihi furere est amico.

                                        Ode 2.7.21–28

18 chunks. 9 points total, 1/2 point each. Round up to nearest whole point.

oblivioso . . . Massico	**with forgetful/forgetfulness-inducing Massic (wine)**
levia . . . ciboria	**smooth/polished goblets/drinking cups (must be object of *exple*)**
exple	**fill/fill up**
funde . . . unguenta	**pour perfumes/unguents/ointments**
capacibus . . . de conchis	**from/down from capacious/spacious (conch) shells/seashells/ perfume dishes**
quis	**who (must be interrogative)**
udo . . . apio	**with/from moist/wet/pliant celery/parsley**
deproperare . . . coronas	**to hurry to complete/make in a hurry (must depend on *curat*) garlands/crowns**
curatve myrto	**or takes care/attends/cares with/from myrtle**
quem	**whom (must be interrogative)**
arbitrum . . . bibendi	**as master of drinking/master of ceremonies**
Venus . . . dicet	**will Venus appoint/pronounce/say (is), speak of as (must be future)**
non . . . sanius	**not more sanely/more healthily**
ego . . . bacchabor	**I shall/will rave/rage (as a bacchante)/celebrate the festival of Bacchus**
Edonis	**than the Edoni/Thracians**
recepto. . . amico	**with a/the/my friend received/recovered/regained OR**
	may be translated as a temporal or causal clause
dulce . . . est	**it is sweet**
mihi furere	**for/to me to rave/rage/be crazy/behave wildly**

Short Analysis Questions *Suggested time: 10 minutes*

ergo obligatam redde Iovi dapem,
longaque fessum militia latus
    depone sub lauru mea, nec
        parce cadis tibi destinatis.

5   oblivioso levia Massico
ciboria exple, funde capacibus
    unguenta de conchis. quis udo
        deproperare apio coronas

curatve myrto? . . .

Ode 2.7.17–25

Nine points total.

1. a. Why does the speaker want a banquet?

    One point for saying that the speaker wants a banquet to celebrate Pompeius' return (from the civil wars), or that it will serve to thank the gods for this.

    b. Why does he say it is owed to Jupiter?

    One point for saying that *obligatam* implies the speaker had made a vow to Jupiter for Pompeius' safe return.

2. What are two things the speaker tells the addressee to do in lines 2–4? Write out the Latin word(s) that support your answer.

    One point: Pompeius should rest his weary side (beneath Horace's laurel tree), with corresponding Latin.

    One point: Pompeius should drink/not spare the flasks (set aside for him), with corresponding Latin.

3. Write out and scan line 3.

    One point for writing out and correctly scanning line 3:

    _ _ ∪ _   _ _ ∪_ ×
    depone sub lauru mea, nec

4. What is the significance of the adjective *oblivioso* (line 5) in its context?

    One point for saying that the wine makes drinkers forget.

    One point for finding significance as invitation to Pompeius to forget the wars/sufferings of war (if mentioned, sufferings or the like must be tied to the wars) or as allusion to Octavian's amnesty after civil war

5. a. What does the speaker want in lines 7–9?

   One point for saying the speaker wants (someone to hurry to prepare) garlands (of celery/parsley or myrtle).

   b. For what purpose does he want this?

   One point for saying that garlands will be worn in a drinking party (which will take place for Pompeius).

Essay *Suggested time: 20 minutes*

> O saepe mecum tempus in ultimum
> deducte Bruto militiae duce,
>   quis te redonavit Quiritem
>   dis patriis Italoque caelo,
>
> 5 Pompei, meorum prime sodalium,
> cum quo morantem saepe diem mero
>   fregi coronatus nitentis
>   malobathro Syrio capillos?
>
> tecum Philippos et celerem fugam
> 10 sensi relicta non bene parmula,
>   cum fracta virtus et minaces
>   turpe solum tetigere mento.
>
> . . . .
>
> . . . quem Venus arbitrum
> dicet bibendi? non ego sanius
> 15   bacchabor Edonis: recepto
>   dulce mihi furere est amico.

Ode 2.7.1–12, 25–28

In the above excerpts, Horace rejoices at the return of his friend, Pompeius. In a short, well-organized essay, discuss the ways in which Horace in this passage shows what Pompeius means to him as a friend.

Support your assertions with references to the Latin text **throughout** the quoted passage. All Latin words must be copied or their line numbers provided, AND they must be translated or paraphrased closely enough so that it is clear you understand the Latin. It is your responsibility to convince your reader that you are basing your conclusions on the Latin text and not merely on a general recollection of the passage. Direct your answer to the question; do not merely summarize the passage. Please write your essay on a separate piece of paper.

From the opening *O saepe mecum*, the student can do much with word choice, word placement, imagery, and mythological and historical allusion to discuss the ways in which Horace creates a sense of how precious to him is his friend, Pompeius. Major elements of this creation include: narrative elements in the picture of how far back their friendship goes, and how much they went through together; rich use of adjectives and pronouns; vocabulary that evokes their common homeland (esp. lines 3–4); description of the celebration that will ensue over Pompeius' return; joyful hyperbole. Competent essays will range from the analytically perceptive and well-supported to those that offer limited analysis and rely more on description. Less-than-satisfactory essays betray themselves by misunderstanding the passage and/or its occasion, failing to offer correct Latin support, and/or failing to analyze at all how Horace produces the effect asked for in the question.

6 – Excellent, perceptive, analytical account of the nature of Horace's friendship with Pompeius and how he represents it. In broad outline, the whole passage is discussed, and the student seeks to make an argument from Horace's poetic technique as well as from the implied narrative content. Liberal, appropriate, and accurate use of Latin support, correctly cited.

5 – Good, but not as analytical or as organized a job of showing how Horace depicts the significance for him of his friendship with Pompeius. A few parts of the passage may be passed over. Latin support is less full than an excellent essay, but what appears is accurate and appropriate. Very full and accurate Latin support can raise a merely adequate analysis to this level if most of the passage is discussed.

4 – Satisfactory, adequate analysis of Horace's representation of what Pompeius means to him as a friend. The essay may be thinner and tend more toward description than analysis, although some analysis must be present. For example, it may talk about what Horace did and will do with Pompeius but draw few inferences from these lines. Latin support is accurate but less extensive than in an excellent or good essay. Alternatively, a merely satisfactory essay may present a convincing analysis, with strong Latin support, of Horace's depiction of the friendship but fail to treat beginning, middle and end of the passage.

3 – Superficial, weak discussion, may be rambling, general, or uneven. Unlike a 4, a 3 will not convince you that the student has adequately undertaken any analysis; the paper may amount to a restatement of the Latin. If attempted, analysis engages only part of the passage (perhaps only the past or the present). Alternatively, a 3 may be awarded to a good essay that lacks correctly cited and translated/paraphrased Latin support.

2 – Inadequate, vague, faulty discussion of the question. The student will express some correct information but may betray a major misconception about the poem. Very scanty Latin support or even no Latin correctly cited.

1 – The student says only one meaningful thing in response to the question and based on the passage.

0 – The student says nothing correct or meaningful derived from the passage, although something may be guessed at from the wording of the question itself.

Scansion

Scan the following lines and name the meter. **The meter is Alcaic.**

```
       _   _   ∪ _     _  ∪ ∪ _∪×
5    Pompei, meorum prime sodalium,
```

```
       _    _  ∪ _  _     _  ∪ ∪_    ∪ ×
     cum quo morantem saepe diem mero
```

```
        _ _ ∪ _ _ _   ∪ _  ×
       fregi coronatus nitentis
```

```
          _ ∪ ∪  _ ∪∪_ ∪ _ ×
        malobathro Syrio capillos?
```

```
       _  _   ∪ _  _  _  ∪∪ _   ∪ ×
     tecum Philippos et celerem fugam
```

```
       _  _ ∪ _  _  _  ∪ ∪ _  ∪×
10   sensi relicta non bene parmula,
```

```
       _     _  ∪ _  _  _  ∪ _ ×
     cum fracta virtus et minaces
```

```
        _  ∪ ∪ _   ∪∪ _ ∪   _ ×
       turpe solum tetigere mento.
```

Ode 2.7.5–12

ODE 2.10

Rectius vives, Licini, neque altum
semper urgendo, neque—dum procellas
cautus horrescis—nimium premendo
    litus iniquum.

5   auream quisquis mediocritatem
diligit, tutus caret obsoleti
sordibus tecti, caret invidenda
    sobrius aula.

saepius ventis agitatur ingens
10   pinus et celsae graviore casu
decidunt turres feriuntque summos
    fulgura montis.

sperat infestis, metuit secundis
alteram sortem bene praeparatum
15   pectus. informis hiemes reducit
    Iuppiter, idem

submovet. non, si male nunc, et olim
sic erit: quondam cithara tacentem
suscitat Musam, neque semper arcum
20   tendit Apollo.

rebus angustis animosus atque
fortis appare: sapienter idem
contrahes vento nimium secundo
    turgida vela.

Short Answer Questions

Line 1   What tense is *vives?* **future**

Line 2   What is the case and use of *urgendo,* and what is its object? **gerund, ablative of means with *vives,* object is *altum* (line 1)**

Line 3   What is the case and use of *premendo,* and what is its object? **gerund, ablative of means with *vives,* object is *litus* (line 4)**

Line 7   What is the case and use of *sordibus*?   **ablative with *caret*, which governs ablative**

               What is the case and use of *tecti*?   **genitive of possession with *sordibus***

               What are the case, use, and literal translation of *invidenda*?   **ablative gerundive, modifying *aula* (line 8), "which ought to be envied, to be envied"**

Line 9   What is the case and use of *ventis*?   **ablative of means with *agitatur***

Line 10   What is the case and use of *graviore casu*?   **ablative of manner**

Line 11   What is the subject of *feriunt*?   ***fulgura* (line 12)**

Lines 11–12   What is the translation of *summos montis*?   **"the tops of mountains/mountain tops, highest mountains"**

Lines 9–12   What figure of speech is in these lines?   **allegory of how the prominent are cast down and the humble escape damage**

Line 13   What two figures of speech are in this line?   ***sperat . . . secundis:* interlocked word order/synchysis/synthesis, asyndeton**

Line 15   What does *informis* modify?   ***hiemes***

Lines 13–15   What figure of speech is in these lines?   ***sperat . . . metuit . . . pectus:* synecdoche**

Line 16   What are the case, use, and translation of *idem*?   **nominative pronoun, subject of *submovet* (line 17), refers to *Iuppiter*, translation: either "the same one" or "likewise, he"**

Line 17   What is the object of *submovet*?   ***hiemes***

Line 18   What is the subject of *erit*?   ***erit* is used impersonally with understood subject "things in general" or "it"**

               What is the case and use of *cithara*?   **ablative of means with *suscitat***

Line 19   What is the subject of *suscitat*?   **Apollo**

Line 22   What is the case and use of *fortis*?   **nominative, modifies understood subject of *appare***

               What is the form of *appare*?   **present second person singular imperative**

               What is the case and use of *idem*?   **nominative pronoun, modifies subject of *contrahes***

Line 23   What is the object of *contrahes*?   ***vela* (line 24)**

               What is the case and use of *vento*?   **ablative of attendant circumstance with *contrahes* or ablative of means or ablative of cause with *turgida***

Lines 23–24   What figure of speech is in these lines?   **metaphor**

Multiple Choice Questions *Suggested time: 15 minutes*

auream quisquis mediocritatem
diligit, tutus caret obsoleti
sordibus tecti, caret invidenda
    sobrius aula.

5   saepius ventis agitatur ingens
pinus et celsae graviore casu
decidunt turres feriuntque summos
    fulgura montis.

sperat infestis, metuit secundis
10   alteram sortem bene praeparatum
pectus. informis hiemes reducit
    Iuppiter, idem

submovet. . . .

Ode 2.10.5–17

1. The words *quisquis mediocritatem diligit* (lines 1–2) are translated

    a. whatever mediocrity loves   b. whoever chooses the mean

    c. who selects the middle road   **d. whoever esteems moderation**

2. In line 1, *auream* symbolizes

    a. breezes   b. air

    c. excellence   d. listening

3. The words *caret . . . aula* (lines 3–4) warn against

    a. excessive sobriety   b. feeling envious

    c. the wine jar   **d. a sumptuous residence**

4. In the imagery of lines 5–8, danger threatens things that are too

    a. weak   b. heavy

    c. tall   d. massive

5. In line 6, *celsae* modifies

    a. *turres* (line 7)   b. *decidunt* (line 7)

    c. *montis* (line 8)   d. *graviore* (line 6)

6. The case of *casu* (line 6) is determined by
   a. *graviore* (line 6)
   b. *decidunt* (line 7)
   c. *celsae* (line 6)
   d. *turres* (line 7)

7. The translation of *feriunt* (line 7) is
   a. strike
   b. bear
   c. drive wild
   d. bring

8. The case and number of *montis* (line 8) are
   a. genitive singular
   b. accusative plural
   c. ablative plural
   d. nominative plural

9. A figure of speech found in line 9 is
   a. asyndeton
   b. oxymoron
   c. personification
   d. chiasmus

10. In lines 9–11, the poet advises his listener to
    a. hope amidst favorable circumstances, fear amidst hostile ones
    b. hope and fear in moderation
    c. prepare for fate to repeat itself
    d. expect circumstances to undergo reversal

11. In line 11, *informis* modifies
    a. *Iuppiter* (line 12)
    b. *hiemes* (line 11)
    c. *reducit* (line 11)
    d. *idem* (line 12)

12. From lines 11–13, we learn that Jupiter
    a. has no visible form
    b. alters climate
    c. changes weather
    d. rules everything

Translation *Suggested time: 15 minutes*

Translate the passage below as literally as possible.

> Rectius vives, Licini, neque altum
> semper urgendo, neque—dum procellas
> cautus horrescis—nimium premendo
>   litus iniquum.
>
> 5   auream quisquis mediocritatem
> diligit, tutus caret obsoleti
> sordibus tecti, caret invidenda
>   sobrius aula.

Ode 2.10.1–8

16 chunks. 8 points total, 1/2 point each. Round up to nearest whole point.

Rectius	**more rightly/more properly/more correctly**
vives, Licini	**you will live Licinius**
neque . . . neque	**neither . . . nor**
altum	**the deep/deep water/open sea (must be object of *urgendo*)**
semper urgendo	**by always pressing upon/pushing (into)/heading into/making for**
dum procellas	**while/as long as squalls/gales/storms (must be object of *horrescis*)**
cautus horrescis	**(you) cautious/cautiously you shudder at/tremble at/bristle at**
nimium premendo	**by pressing/hugging/staying close to too much/excessively**
litus iniquum	**the uneven/treacherous/unfavorable shore/coast**
auream . . . mediocritatem	**golden mean/moderation/middle way**
quisquis . . . diligit	**whoever esteems/loves/holds dear**
tutus caret	**safe/safely lacks/is free from/is without**
sordibus	**filth/dirt/squalor/baseness**
obsoleti . . . tecti	**of a worn out/shabby/ordinary house/roof/building**
caret . . . sobrius	**lacks/is free from/is without sober/sensible/moderate (or rendered adverbially)**
invidenda . . . aula	**which ought to be envied/to be envied court/palace/hall/noble residence**

Short Analysis Questions *Suggested time: 10 minutes*

> . . . non, si male nunc, et olim
> sic erit: quondam cithara tacentem
> suscitat Musam, neque semper arcum
>   tendit Apollo.
>
> 5   rebus angustis animosus atque
> fortis appare: sapienter idem
> contrahes vento nimium secundo
>   turgida vela.

Ode 2.10.17–24

Eight points total.

1. What contrast does the poet make with the words *non, si male nunc, et olim sic erit* (lines 1–2)? Cite and translate the Latin words that support your answer.

    One point for explaining that if events are going badly now (*male nunc*), they will not always be so (*non . . . olim sic*) at another time. One point for Latin translation.

2. a. What actions are attributed to Apollo in lines 2–4?

    Two points.

    One point for Apollo awakening the silent Muse with his lyre/inspiring poetry

    One point for Apollo not shooting/stretching the bow

    OR

    One point for saying that at other times Apollo does shoot the bow

    b. How do these actions reinforce the theme of this ode?

    One point for relating this image to theme: i.e., one should act with expectation that fortune will change OR one should pursue a middle/moderate course in varying circumstances.

3. Explain the contrast drawn in the second stanza between two modes of action. Cite and translate or paraphrase the supporting Latin words.

    Three points.

    One point for contrasting brave appearance in difficult circumstances with caution in favorable circumstances.

    One point for supporting Latin for brave appearance.

    One point for supporting Latin for caution during success (or for translation of key words of furled sails metaphor).

    OR

    Two points total for a contrast with supporting Latin between appearing brave and taking in/furling sails, i.e., for failing to explain the "sails" metaphor.

4. Copy and scan line 6.

One point for copying and correctly scanning line 6:

$$\bar{~} \cup \bar{~} \quad \bar{~} \quad \bar{~} \quad \cup \cup \bar{~} \quad \cup \quad \bar{~} \times$$
fortis appare: sapienter idem

Essay *Suggested time: 20 minutes*

> saepius ventis agitatur ingens
> pinus et celsae graviore casu
> decidunt turres feriuntque summos
>   fulgura montis.
>
> 5   sperat infestis, metuit secundis
> alteram sortem bene praeparatum
> pectus. informis hiemes reducit
>   Iuppiter, idem
>
> submovet. non, si male nunc, et olim
> 10   sic erit: quondam cithara tacentem
> suscitat Musam, neque semper arcum
>   tendit Apollo.
>
> rebus angustis animosus atque
> fortis appare: sapienter idem
> 15   contrahes vento nimium secundo
>   turgida vela.

Ode 2.10.9–24

The ode from which this passage is taken has been criticized for elaborating only one point: that a person should be cautious in success and resolute in adversity. In a short, well-organized essay, discuss the techniques by which Horace in this passage tries to sustain the reader's interest as he develops this point.

Support your assertions with references to the Latin text **throughout** the passage. All Latin words must be copied or their line numbers provided, AND they must be translated or paraphrased closely enough so that it is clear you understand the Latin. It is your responsibility to convince your reader that you are basing your conclusions on the Latin text and not merely on a general recollection of the passage. Direct your answer to the question; do not merely summarize the passage. Please write your essay on a separate piece of paper.

Students are asked to show how Horace tries to sustain the reader's interest as he develops the point that one should be cautious in success and resolute in adversity. The prompt states this point in order to restrict the task of this 20-minute essay to discussing how Horace's poetic technique operates to sustain interest. Students may analyze, but are not limited to, Horace's rich imagery, his juxtaposition

of generalizing claims or mandates with concrete images (e.g., last stanza), word choice, word placement, sound effects, allusions to myth or other writers, and figures of speech. Perceptive students will reveal how Horace turns a maxim into a poem—whether or not they deem him successful at sustaining interest. Merely satisfactory treatments will display less insight in connecting the writing to the poem's propositional content, in analyzing the writing, and in adducing evidence from the Latin text.

6 – Excellent, clear statement of the main point made in the poem combined with perceptive, analytical discussion of the techniques by which this point is developed in an interesting way. Time does not allow every line to be treated, but the student should deal with the poem as a whole. Liberal, appropriate and accurate use of Latin support, correctly cited.

5 – Good, although not as strong at relating Horace's language to the main point of the poem or of showing how his language creates interesting effects. Less full Latin support, but what appears is accurate and appropriate.

4 – Satisfactory, adequate statement of the poem's main point and some analysis of how the poet tries to develop it in an interesting way. The essay is thinner than an excellent or good essay and tends more toward description. Latin support is apt and accurate but not liberal. Alternatively, a satisfactory essay may present a convincing analysis, with strong Latin support, of parts of the poem but merely touch on or even omit significant portions.

3 – Superficial, weak discussion, may be rambling, general, or uneven. Unlike a satisfactory essay, a superficial one will not convince you that the student has adequately undertaken any analysis; the paper may amount to a restatement of the Latin. The student may talk about scattered literary devices without considering how they relate to the main point of the poem. Alternatively, a superficial paper may offer a good essay but lack correctly cited and translated/paraphrased Latin support.

2 – Inadequate, vague, faulty discussion of the question. The student will express some correct information but may betray a major misconception about the poem. Very scanty Latin support or even no Latin correctly cited.

1 – The student says only one meaningful thing in response to the question and based on the passage.

0 – The student says nothing correct or meaningful derived from the passage, although something may be guessed at from the wording of the question itself.

Scansion

Scan the following lines and name the meter.   **The meter is Sapphic.**

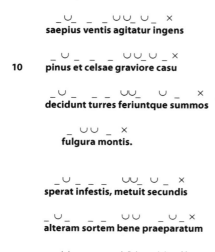

_ ◡ _ _ _ ◡◡_ ◡ _ ×
saepius ventis agitatur ingens

10
_ ◡ _ _ _ ◡◡_◡ _ ×
pinus et celsae graviore casu

_ ◡ _ _ _ ◡◡_ ◡ _ ×
decidunt turres feriuntque summos

_ ◡◡ _ ×
fulgura montis.

_ ◡ _ _ _ ◡◡_ ◡ _ ×
sperat infestis, metuit secundis

_ ◡ _ _ _ ◡◡ _ ◡ _ ×
alteram sortem bene praeparatum

15
_ ◡ _ _ _ ◡◡ _ ◡ _ ×
pectus. informis hiemes reducit

_ ◡◡ _ ×
Iuppiter, idem

Ode 2.10.9–16

ODE 2.14

Eheu fugaces, Postume, Postume,
labuntur anni, nec pietas moram
   rugis et instanti senectae
      adferet indomitaeque morti,

5   non, si trecenis, quotquot eunt dies,
amice, places inlacrimabilem
   Plutona tauris, qui ter amplum
      Geryonen Tityonque tristi

conpescit unda, scilicet omnibus,
10   quicumque terrae munere vescimur,
   enaviganda, sive reges,
      sive inopes erimus coloni.

frustra cruento Marte carebimus
fractisque rauci fluctibus Hadriae,
15   frustra per autumnos nocentem
      corporibus metuemus Austrum:

visendus ater flumine languido
Cocytos errans et Danai genus
   infame damnatusque longi
20   Sisyphus Aeolides laboris.

linquenda tellus et domus et placens
uxor, neque harum, quas colis, arborum
   te praeter invisas cupressos
      ulla brevem dominum sequetur,

25   absumet heres Caecuba dignior
servata centum clavibus et mero
   tinguet pavimentum superbo,
      pontificum potiore cenis.

Short Answer Questions

Line 1   What figure of speech (non-AP) is in this line? **pathos in repetition of *Postume, Postume***

What does *fugaces* modify? ***anni***

Line 3	What is the case and use of *rugis?* **dative, indirect object with *adferet* (line 4)**
Line 5	What figure of speech is in this line? ***trecenis:* hyperbole**
	What does *trecenis* modify? ***tauris***
Line 6	What is the case and use of *amice?* **vocative, direct address**
	What form is *places,* and why is it used? **present subjunctive in mixed conditional sentence with future *adferet*: "will bring to, . . . not if you should placate . . . "**
Line 7	What is the case and use of *tauris?* **ablative of means with *places***
	What does *ter* modify? ***amplum (Geryonen)***
Line 8	What two figures of speech are in this line? ***tristi:* transferred epithet and personification**
Line 9	What two figures of speech are in this line? ***conpescit unda:* metaphor; *unda:* synecdoche**
	What is the case and use of *unda?* **ablative of means**
Line 10	What figure of speech is in this line? ***terrae munere:* metonymy**
	What is the case and use of *terrae?* **subjective genitive with *munere***
Line 11	What is the case and use of *reges?* **predicate nominative**
Line 12	What is the case and use of *coloni?* **predicate nominative**
Line 13	What is the case and use of *Marte?* **ablative with *carebimus,* which governs ablative**
Line 14	What two figures of speech are in this line? **interlocked word order/synchysis/synchesis; synecdoche (*Hadriae* for sea in general)**
	What is the case and use of *fluctibus?* **ablative with *carebimus***
Line 15	What does *nocentem* modify? ***Austrum* (line 16)**
Lines 13–16	What figure of speech is in these lines? ***frustra . . . frustra:* anaphora**
Line 17	What is the case and use of *flumine?* **ablative of means with *errans***
Line 18	What is the case and use of *genus?* **nominative, coordinate with *Cocytos* as subjects of *visendus (est)* (line 17)**
Lines 17–18	What two figures of speech are in these lines? ***visendus . . . errans:* extended chiasmus (AABBAA); ellipsis of *est***
Line 19	What does *infame* modify? ***genus***
Lines 19–20	What figure of speech is in these lines? ***longi . . . laboris:* chiasmus**
Line 21	What figure of speech is in this line? **ellipsis of *est***
	What does *linquenda* modify? ***tellus***

Line 22   What is the antecedent of *quas*?   **arborum (note that relative pronoun may be placed before antecedent)**

What is the case and use of *arborum*?   **partitive genitive with *neque . . . ulla***

Lines 21–22   What figure of speech is in these lines?   **tricolon crescens/crescendo**

Line 23   What is the case and use of *te*?   **accusative, direct object of *sequetur***

Line 24   What is the case and use of *ulla*?   **nominative, adjective used as substantive, subject of *sequetur***

What is meant by *brevem dominum*?   **brevem signifies "short-lived master" or "master for a short time"**

What is the case and use of *dominum*?   **accusative, direct object of *sequetur***

Line 25   What is the case and use of *Caecuba*?   **accusative, direct object of *absumet***

Line 26   What two figures of speech are in this line?   ***centum clavibus:* hyperbole and metonymy**

What is the case and use of *clavibus*?   **ablative of means with *servata***

What is the case and use of *mero*?   **ablative of means with *tinguet***

Line 27   What two figures of speech are in this line?   ***superbo:* personification and transferred epithet**

Line 28   What is the case and use of *pontificum*?   **genitive of possession or subjective genitive with *cenis***

What does *potiore* modify?   ***mero***

What is the case and use of *cenis*?   **ablative of comparison**

Multiple Choice Questions *Suggested time: 15 minutes*

Eheu fugaces, Postume, Postume,
labuntur anni, nec pietas moram
    rugis et instanti senectae
        adferet indomitaeque morti,

5   non, si trecenis, quotquot eunt dies,
amice, places inlacrimabilem
    Plutona tauris, qui ter amplum
        Geryonen Tityonque tristi

>   conpescit unda, scilicet omnibus,
> 10   quicumque terrae munere vescimur,
>   enaviganda, sive reges,
>   sive inopes erimus coloni.

Ode 2.14.1–12

1. What element of tone is established in lines 1–4?
   - a. irony
   - b. tragedy
   - **c. pathos**
   - d. sarcasm

2. The words *fugaces . . . labuntur anni* (lines 1–2) are translated
   - a. fugitives of the year slip away
   - b. you will flee, the years glide by
   - c. the fleeing years labor
   - **d. the years slide by fleeing**

3. According to the words *nec . . . adferet* (lines 2–4), piety will not bring
   - a. an easy death
   - **b. a delay of aging**
   - c. a regretful old age
   - d. death to wrinkles and old age

4. A figure of speech contained in line 3 is
   - **a. hendiadys**
   - b. transferred epithet
   - c. synecdoche
   - d. chiasmus

5. The case of *morti* (line 4) is determined by
   - **a. *adferet* (line 4)**
   - b. *indomitae* (line 4)
   - c. *senectae* (line 3)
   - d. *moram* (line 2)

6. From lines 5–7, we learn that Pluto
   - a. demands sacrifices of bulls
   - b. delays death for those who sacrifice
   - **c. is not won over by tears**
   - d. is friendly to Postumus

7. In line 7, *qui* refers to
   - **a. *Plutona* (line 7)**
   - b. the subject of *places* (line 6)
   - c. *tauris* (line 7)
   - d. *amice* (line 6)

8. Geryon and Tityos (line 8) were
   - a. friends
   - b. philosophers
   - c. tyrants
   - **d. monsters**

9. In line 8, *tristi* modifies
   - a. *Geryonen* (line 8)
   - b. *Tityon* (line 8)
   - **c. *unda* (line 9)**
   - d. *qui* (line 7)

10. In line 9, *unda* is a reference to
    - a. the sea
    - **b. the River Styx**
    - c. reflection in the water
    - d. tears

11. The words *quicumque . . . vescimur* (line 10) are translated
    - a. whoever feed on the gift of the earth
    - b. however we perform our duty for the earth
    - c. whoever we are, fed by the service of the earth
    - **d. whoever we are who feed on the gift of the earth**

12. Lines 11–12 reinforce the point that
    - a. the future is an open book
    - **b. death awaits all equally**
    - c. the simple life is the happiest
    - d. life is short

Translation *Suggested time: 15 minutes*

Translate the passage below as literally as possible.

> frustra cruento Marte carebimus
> fractisque rauci fluctibus Hadriae,
>   frustra per autumnos nocentem
>   corporibus metuemus Austrum:
>
> 5   visendus ater flumine languido
> Cocytos errans et Danai genus
>   infame damnatusque longi
>   Sisyphus Aeolides laboris.

Ode 2.14.13–20

18 chunks. 9 points total, 1/2 point each. Round up to nearest whole point.

frustra . . . frustra	**in vain/vainly/to no purpose (twice)**
cruento Marte	**bloody/cruel Mars/war must be governed by *carebimus***
carebimus	**we shall/will lack/be without/be free from**
fractisque . . . fluctibus	**and the broken waves/disturbances (must be governed by *carebimus*)**
rauci . . . Hadriae	**of the raucous/strident Adriatic**
per autumnos	**through/during autumn/s, fall/s**
nocentem . . . Austrum	**the harmful/harming/injuring South Wind/Auster**
corporibus	**(our) bodies (must be governed by governed by *nocentem*)**
metuemus	**we shall/will fear**
visendus	**must be visited/looked at**
ater . . . Cocytos	**black/dark Cocytus/a river in Hades**
flumine languido	**with its languid/sluggish/slow stream/river**
errans	**wandering**
et Danai	**and of Danaus**

genus infame	**the infamous/disreputable race/offspring**
damnatusque	**and condemned/damned**
longi . . . laboris	**to ("of" acceptable only if clearly genitive of penalty) long labor/ work/effort**
Sisyphus Aeolides	**Sisyphus son/descendent of Aeolus**

Short Analysis Questions *Suggested time: 10 minutes*

frustra cruento Marte carebimus
fractisque rauci fluctibus Hadriae,
   frustra per autumnos nocentem
      corporibus metuemus Austrum:

5   visendus ater flumine languido
Cocytos errans et Danai genus
   infame damnatusque longi
      Sisyphus Aeolides laboris.

Ode 2.14.13–20

Eight points total.

1. Lines 1–4 say that we shall do certain things in vain *(frustra)*.

   a. What are these things?

   Three points.

   **One point for identifying each of three actions that we shall/will do in vain:
   avoid war *(cruento Marte carebimus)*
   abstain from dangerous voyages *(fractisque rauci fluctibus Hadriae carebimus)*
   fear or take precautions against the unhealthy/harmful South Wind (lines 3–4)**

   b. Why shall our performance of them be in vain?

   **One point for explaining that these are strategies to avoid death, and they are in vain
   because each person must die.**

2. What is *Cocytos* (line 6), and why is its mention appropriate in this context?

   One point for identifying Cocytos as a river in Hades.

   **One point for saying why it is appropriate: to say one must go to see it *(visendus [est])*
   means/is synecdoche or metaphor for saying one must die.**

3. Copy and scan line 7.

   One point for copying and correctly scanning line 7:

   ‾ ‾ ⏑ ‾ ‾ ‾ ⏑ ‾ ×
   infame damnatusque longi

4.   Name a figure of speech found in lines 7–8, and write out the Latin word(s) that illustrate it.

One point for identifying figure of speech with corresponding Latin:
chiasmus: *longi Sisyphus Aeolides laboris*
litotes/meiosis (non-AP): *longi* for *sempiterni/aeterni*
alliteration of the letter "l"
hyperbaton: *longi . . . laboris*

Essay *Suggested time: 20 minutes*

frustra cruento Marte carebimus
fractisque rauci fluctibus Hadriae,
    frustra per autumnos nocentem
        corporibus metuemus Austrum:

5   visendus ater flumine languido
Cocytos errans et Danai genus
    infame damnatusque longi
        Sisyphus Aeolides laboris.

linquenda tellus et domus et placens
10 uxor, neque harum, quas colis, arborum
    te praeter invisas cupressos
        ulla brevem dominum sequetur,

absumet heres Caecuba dignior
servata centum clavibus et mero
15   tinguet pavimentum superbo,
        pontificum potiore cenis.

Ode 2.14.13–28

In the passage above, Horace develops the theme that human beings cannot escape death. In a short, well-organized essay, discuss how he uses imagery to help him develop this theme in this passage.

Support your assertions with references to the Latin text **throughout** the passage. All Latin words must be copied or their line numbers provided, AND they must be translated or paraphrased closely enough so that it is clear you understand the Latin. It is your responsibility to convince your reader that you are basing your conclusions on the Latin text and not merely on a general recollection of the passage. Direct your answer to the question; do not merely summarize the passage. Please write your essay on a separate piece of paper.

Although this ode treats other themes as well (e.g., inexorability of time), the question asks the student to discuss how Horace uses imagery to help him develop the theme that human beings cannot escape death. Superior essays will treat the whole passage, discuss the effect of the imagery upon the theme's expression in an analytical way, and make appropriate and liberal use of the Latin text, correctly cited and translated or closely paraphrased, to support the analysis. Essays that are merely satisfactory will leave out key sections of the poem, rely more on description and restatement of the

text than on analysis, and make less extensive and less accurate use of the Latin. Students may fail to make a logical distinction between the inevitability of death (i.e., a human cannot escape it) and its universality (i.e., all humans die), which is implicit in its inevitability. For that reason, award credit for any statement that recognizes that humans cannot avoid death. Essays that fail to reach a satisfactory level will betray misconception of the poem, offer little or no Latin support, fail to direct analysis to the question, or offer no analysis at all. Very poor essays may say only one or two correct things that cannot be derived from the question itself.

6 – Excellent, perceptive, analytical discussion of the way imagery develops the point that humans cannot escape death. The student should deal with the passage as a whole. Liberal, appropriate and accurate use of Latin support, correctly cited.

5 – Good, not as strong at analyzing how Horace's imagery helps develop the main point of the passage. Less full Latin support, but what appears is accurate and appropriate.

4 – Satisfactory, adequate analysis of how the passage's imagery helps convey the point that humans cannot escape death. The essay is thinner than an excellent or good essay and tends more toward description. Latin support is apt and accurate but not liberal. Alternatively, a satisfactory essay may present a convincing analysis, with strong Latin support, of parts of the poem but merely touch on or even omit significant portions.

3 – Superficial, weak discussion, may be rambling, general, or uneven. Unlike a satisfactory essay, a superficial one will not convince you that the student has adequately undertaken any analysis; the paper may amount to a restatement of the Latin. The student may talk about scattered literary devices without considering how they relate to the main point of the poem. Alternatively, a superficial paper may offer a good essay but lack correctly cited and translated/paraphrased Latin support.

2 – Inadequate, vague, faulty discussion of the question. The student will express some correct information but may betray a major misconception about the poem. Very scanty Latin support or even no Latin correctly cited.

1 – The student says only one meaningful thing in response to the question and based on the passage.

0 – The student says nothing correct or meaningful derived from the passage, although something may be guessed at from the wording of the question itself.

Scansion

Scan the following lines and name the meter.   **The meter is Alcaic.**

5   non, si trecenis, quotquot eunt dies,

      amice, places inlacrimabilem

         Plutona tauris, qui ter amplum

         Geryonen Tityonque tristi

      conpescit unda, scilicet omnibus,

10   quicumque terrae munere vescimur,

         enaviganda, sive reges,

         siv(e) inopes erimus coloni.

Ode 2.14.5–12

ODE 3.1

Odi profanum volgus et arceo.
favete linguis: carmina non prius
    audita Musarum sacerdos
        virginibus puerisque canto.

5   regum timendorum in proprios greges,
reges in ipsos imperium est Iovis,
    clari Giganteo triumpho,
        cuncta supercilio moventis.

est, ut viro vir latius ordinet
10   arbusta sulcis, hic generosior
    descendat in campum petitor,
        moribus hic meliorque fama

contendat, illi turba clientium
sit maior: aequa lege Necessitas
15   sortitur insignis et imos,
        omne capax movet urna nomen.

destrictus ensis cui super impia
cervice pendet, non Siculae dapes
    dulcem elaborabunt saporem,
20   non avium citharaeque cantus

somnum reducent: somnus agrestium
lenis virorum non humilis domos
    fastidit umbrosamque ripam,
        non Zephyris agitata Tempe.

25   desiderantem quod satis est neque
tumultuosum sollicitat mare,
    nec saevus Arcturi cadentis,
        impetus aut orientis Haedi,

non verberatae grandine vineae
30   fundusque mendax, arbore nunc aquas
    culpante, nunc torrentia agros
        sidera, nunc hiemes iniquas.

contracta pisces aequora sentiunt
iactis in altum molibus: huc frequens
35   caementa demittit redemptor
            cum famulis dominusque terrae

fastidiosus, sed Timor et Minae
scandunt eodem, quo dominus, neque
      decedit aerata triremi et
40   post equitem sedet atra Cura.

quodsi dolentem nec Phrygius lapis,
nec purpurarum sidere clarior
      delenit usus, nec Falerna
            vitis Achaemeniumque costum,

45   cur invidendis postibus et novo
sublime ritu moliar atrium?
      cur valle permutem Sabina
            divitias operosiores?

Short Answer Questions

Line 1   What is the direct object of *arceo*? **profanum volgus**

Line 2   What is the case and use of *carmina*? **accusative, direct object of *canto* (line 4)**

Line 3   What is the case and use of *sacerdos*? **nominative, in apposition to subject of *canto* (line 4)**

Line 4   What is the case and use of *virginibus puerisque*? **dative, indirect object of *canto***

Line 5   What is the translation of *timendorum*? **"to be feared, (who) must be feared, dreaded"**

Lines 5–6   What figure of speech is in these lines? **asyndeton**

Line 7   What is the case and use of *triumpho*? **ablative of cause with *clari***

Line 8   What is the grammatical function of *cuncta*? **an accusative neuter plural adjective used as a substantive, i.e., "all things," direct object of *moventis***

Line 9   What is the best translation of *est* in its context? **"it is the case," "it is true"**

             What is the case and use of *viro*? **ablative of comparison with *latius***

             What is the form *latius*? **comparative adverb, "more widely"**

             What figure of speech is in this line? **viro vir: polyptoton**

Line 13   What is the case and use of *turba?* **nominative, subject of *sit* (line 14)**

Line 14   What is the case and use of *lege?* **ablative of manner**

Lines 9–14   In what attribute is each of the four men described in lines 9–14 superior? **the *vir* in line 9 is rich/owns much (farm)land or orchards; *hic* in line 10 is of more noble birth than other political candidates; *hic* in line 12 is of better character and reputation than other candidates; *ille* in line 13 has more clients/is more influential than other candidates**

Line 16   What does the urn symbolize? **fate**

Line 17   What is the antecedent of *cui?* **an understood *ei,* governed by *elaborabunt* (line 19)**

Line 18   What is the case and use of *cervice?* **ablative with preposition *super* (line 17)**

Line 20   What is the case and use of *avium citharaeque?* **subjective genitive with *cantus***

Line 21   What figure of speech is in this line? ***somnum ... somnus:* asyndeton**

Line 22   What is the case and use of *virorum?* **genitive of possession with *domos***

Lines 22–23   What figure of speech is in these lines? ***somnus ... fastidit:* personification**

Line 24   Of what is *Tempe* the object? **direct object of *fastidit* (line 23)**

Line 26   What is the direct object of *sollicitat? **desiderantem* (line 25), a participle used as a substantive**

Line 28   What is the case and use of *impetus?* **nominative, subject of *sollicitat* (line 26)**

Line 29   What is the case and use of *grandine?* **ablative of means with *verberatae***

Line 31   What is the case and use of *agros?* **accusative, direct object of *torrentia***

Lines 30–32   What three figures of speech are in these lines? ***nunc ... nunc ... nunc:* anaphora; *fundusque mendax, arbore ... culpante:* personification; asyndeton; *aquas ... agros ... hiemes:* tricolon**

Line 33   What is the case and use of *pisces?* **nominative, subject of *sentiunt* (line 33)**

            What is the case and use of *aequora?* **accusative, direct object of *sentiunt***

Line 34   What is the case and use of *molibus?* **ablative absolute with *iactis***

Lines 36–37   What two figures of speech are in these lines? ***fastidiosus:* enjambment; *Timor et Minae:* personification**

Line 39   What is the subject of *decedit? **Cura* (line 40)**

            What is the case and use of *triremi?* **ablative of separation with *decedit***

Line 40   What is the figure of speech in this line? ***sedet ... Cura:* personification**

Line 41   What is the function of *dolentem?* **participle used substantively, direct object of *delenit* (line 43)**

Line 42	What is the case and use of *purpurarum?* **objective genitive with *usus* (line 43)**
	What is the case and use of *sidere?* **ablative of comparison with *clarior***
Line 44	What is the case and use of *vitis* and *costum?* **nominative, subjects of *delenit* (line 43)**
Line 45	What is the case and use of *postibus?* **ablative of means or description with *moliar* (line 46)**
Line 46	What is the case and use of *ritu?* **ablative of manner**
Lines 45–46	What two figures of speech (one non-AP) are in these lines? ***postibus et ... ritu moliar:* zeugma; *novo sublime ritu atrium:* interlocked word order/synchysis/ synchesis; rhetorical question**

Multiple Choice Questions *Suggested time: 15 minutes*

destrictus ensis cui super impia
cervice pendet, non Siculae dapes
   dulcem elaborabunt saporem,
      non avium citharaeque cantus

5 somnum reducent: somnus agrestium
lenis virorum non humilis domos
   fastidit umbrosamque ripam,
      non Zephyris agitata Tempe.

desiderantem quod satis est neque
10 tumultuosum sollicitat mare,
   nec saevus Arcturi cadentis,
      impetus aut orientis Haedi, . . .

Ode 3.1.17–28

1. Lines 1–5 allude to the story of the
   a. Apple of Discord   b. Primeval Flood
   c. Pirates and Julius Caesar   **d. Sword of Damocles**

2. The case of *cui* (line 1) is determined by
   a. *pendet* (line 2)   b. *ensis* (line 1)
   c. *destrictus* (line 1)   d. *super* (line 1)

3. From lines 1–5, we learn that the fearful rich person
   a. is kept awake by birds singing   **b. does not enjoy banquets**
   c. is not virtuous   d. has lost his weapons

4. The case and number of *cantus* (line 4) are
   a. accusative plural
   b. nominative plural
   c. nominative singular
   d. genitive singular

5. The word closest in meaning to *citharae* (line 4) is
   a. *lyrae*
   b. *tibiae*
   c. *tubae*
   d. *cicadae*

6. The tense and mood of *reducent* (line 5) are
   a. present indicative
   b. present subjunctive
   c. perfect indicative
   d. future indicative

7. In line 6, *lenis* modifies
   a. *Zephyris* (line 8)
   b. *domos* (line 6)
   c. *humilis* (line 6)
   d. *somnus* (line 5)

8. A figure of speech found in lines 5–7 is
   a. personification
   b. hyperbole
   c. anaphora
   d. hendiadys

9. In line 8, *Zephyris* is ablative of
   a. personal agent
   b. separation
   c. means
   d. place where

10. In line 9, *desiderantem* modifies
    a. *tumultuosum* (line 10)
    b. an understood *hominem*
    c. *satis* (line 9)
    d. *mare* (line 10)

11. From lines 9–12, we learn that changes in weather do not worry the person who
    a. lives by the shady river bank
    b. desires what is enough
    c. is not savage
    d. stays on his farm

12. The imagery in lines 11–12 concerns
    a. seas
    b. barbarian tribes
    c. stars
    d. rivers

Translation *Suggested time: 15 minutes*

Translate the passage below as literally as possible.

> est, ut viro vir latius ordinet
> arbusta sulcis, hic generosior
>   descendat in campum petitor,
>   moribus hic meliorque fama
>
> 5   contendat, illi turba clientium
> sit maior: aequa lege Necessitas
>   sortitur insignis et imos,
>   omne capax movet urna nomen.

Ode 3.1.9–16

18 chunks. 9 points total, 1/2 point each. Round up to nearest whole point.

est, ut	**it is the case/true, that**
viro vir	**(one) man . . . than (another) man**
latius ordinet	**more widely sets in order/arranges/lines up**
	OR may set in order (so with subsequent subjunctives)
arbusta sulcis	**trees/woods in furrows/trenches**
hic . . . petitor	**this candidate/seeker OR this one as a candidate**
generosior descendat	**descends/comes down (as) more noble/nobly born**
in campum	**into the field/plain/Campus (may be proper name)**
moribus . . . -que fama	**in character and reputation/fame**
hic melior	**this (one) better**
contendat	**competes/contends/vies (for office)**
illi	**for that (one) (must be dative singular)**
turba clientium	**the crowd of clients**
sit maior	**is larger/bigger**
aequa lege	**by/with (an) equal/impartial/even/fair law/rule/terms**
Necessitas sortitur	**Necessity chooses (by lot)/casts lots over**
insignis et imos	**(the) distinguished and (the) lowest (ones/candidates)**
omne . . . nomen	**every name (must be object of *movet*)**
capax movet urna	**the capacious/spacious/capable urn moves**

Short Analysis Questions *Suggested time: 10 minutes*

Odi profanum volgus et arceo.
favete linguis: carmina non prius
   audita Musarum sacerdos
     virginibus puerisque canto.

5   regum timendorum in proprios greges,
    reges in ipsos imperium est Iovis,
      clari Giganteo triumpho,
        cuncta supercilio moventis.

                                    Ode 3.1.1–8

Nine points total.

1.   What are three things Horace says about himself in lines 2–4? Write out the Latin words which contain his references to each thing.

   Three points.

   One point for each of up to three things Horace says about himself, with supporting Latin.
   Students may cite:
   Horace writes/sings new songs/a new kind of poetry (*carmina non prius audita*)
   Horace is a priest of the Muses (*Musarum sacerdos*)
   Horace sings his poems to the youth (*virginibus puerisque canto*)

2.   What are three reasons Horace gives in lines 5–8 for us to believe in the greatness of the god Jupiter? Write out the Latin words in which Horace states each attribute of greatness.

   Three points.

   One point for each of up to three reasons for Jupiter's greatness, with supporting Latin.
   Students may cite:
   Jupiter rules over kings (line 6)
   Jupiter triumphed over the Giants (line 7)
   Jupiter controls the world/moves all with his eyebrow/nod (line 8)

3   a.   Copy and scan lines 6–7.

   Two points.

   One point for copying out and correctly scanning each of lines 6 and 7:

   ‾ ‾ ᵕ ‾ ‾ ‾ ᵕᵕ‾ ᵕ ×
   reges in ipsos imperiumst Iovis (students may mark *imperium est* as elision of *-um*)

   ‾ ‾ ᵕ ‾ ‾‾ ᵕ‾ ×
   clari Giganteo triumpho

   b.   Name the meter.

   One point for naming the meter as Alcaic.

Essay *Suggested time: 20 minutes*

```
      contracta pisces aequora sentiunt
      iactis in altum molibus: huc frequens
          caementa demittit redemptor
              cum famulis dominusque terrae

  5   fastidiosus, sed Timor et Minae
      scandunt eodem, quo dominus, neque
          decedit aerata triremi et
              post equitem sedet atra Cura.

      quodsi dolentem nec Phrygius lapis,
 10   nec purpurarum sidere clarior
          delenit usus, nec Falerna
              vitis Achaemeniumque costum,

      cur invidendis postibus et novo
      sublime ritu moliar atrium?
 15       cur valle permutem Sabina
              divitias operosiores?
```

Ode 3.1.33–48

In these lines Horace reflects on the question of how wealth contributes to happiness. In a **short,** well-organized essay, set forth your interpretation of Horace's view and show how he expresses it in the passage.

Support your assertions with references to the Latin text **throughout** the quoted passage. All Latin words must be copied or their line numbers provided, AND they must be translated or paraphrased closely enough so that it is clear you understand the Latin. It is your responsibility to convince your reader that you are basing your conclusions on the Latin text and not merely on a general recollection of the passage. Direct your answer to the question; do not merely summarize the passage. Please write your essay on a separate piece of paper.

The student is asked to do two things: to explain Horace's views about how wealth contributes to happiness, and to show how Horace develops his views on that question throughout the passage. Horace relies heavily on words with emotional connotations: fear, threats, anxiety (stanza 2), grieving (line 9), and envy (line 13). He incorporates these into an elaborate texture of imagery. Students should explain how the images illustrate the way wealth contributes to happiness—or as often, hinders our pursuit of it. They must also accurately translate or closely paraphrase the Latin support for each point they make. A bare-bones discussion of the imagery and other poetic elements, combined with a statement of how wealth impacts on happiness, supported from the Latin text, can earn a 4. To earn 5 or 6, the student must analyze the connection between the elements of Horace's poetic technique and Horace's reflections on wealth's impact on the pursuit of happiness. Essays that do not analyze fall in the 3 range or lower.

6 – A fully-developed essay which discusses Horace's views on wealth and happiness, and how they are developed throughout the passage. The student makes ample reference to specific aspects of the

Latin text to support his analysis and his position. Latin references are properly cited. Even though there may be occasional mistakes, the discussion is coherent and of high quality.

5 – A strong essay. Although the piece has good analysis, it is not so fully developed nor so supported with references to the text as a 6 paper. Latin references are properly cited. The essay reflects familiarity with the poem. A few parts of the passage may receive thin treatment.

4 – A competent response. There may be uneven development. Although limited in quantity, the essay includes accurate and relevant references in responding to the topic. The discussion may be more descriptive than analytical. Some parts of the passage may be glossed over or omitted.

3 – A limited response. The Latin support is weak and/or inappropriate. Latin references are not properly cited. The answer is descriptive and does not reach the level of analysis. In some 3 papers, the student demonstrates an understanding of the poem but cites no Latin to support his answer.

2 – Some understanding of the poem, but the essay is general and/or vague. The discussion is flawed. The Latin cited demonstrates very limited comprehension.

1 – An incoherent response. While it does contain some relevant information, no substantive argument is presented. The student demonstrates no understanding of the poem.

0 – A response that is off-topic, completely incorrect, or irrelevant. Responses that merely restate the question are also a 0.

Scansion

Scan the following lines and name the meter.   **The meter is Alcaic.**

```
     _ _   ∪ _  _     _   ∪ ∪_   ∪ ×
5   regum timendor(um) in proprios greges,


     _ _ ∪ _  _  _  ∪∪_        ∪ ×
    reges in ipsos imperium (e)st Iovis,


        _ _ ∪ _  _ _  ∪_     ×
       clari Giganteo triumpho,


         _   ∪ ∪ _  ∪∪_   ∪ _  ×
        cuncta supercilio moventis.


      _   _  ∪_  _  _∪∪  _  ∪ ×
     est, ut viro vir latius ordinet


     _  _  ∪  _  _   _  ∪ ∪ _∪×
10  arbusta sulcis, hic generosior


       _  _  ∪ _  _   _  ∪ _ ×
      descendat in campum petitor,


        _ ∪ ∪  _   ∪∪_  ∪  _  ×
       moribus hic meliorque fama
```

Ode 3.1.5–12

ODE 3.9

Donec gratus eram tibi,
    nec quisquam potior brachia candidae
cervici iuvenis dabat,
    Persarum vigui rege beatior.

5   'donec non alia magis
    arsisti, neque erat Lydia post Chloen,
multi Lydia nominis
    Romana vigui clarior Ilia.'

me nunc Thressa Chloe regit,
10   dulcis docta modos et citharae sciens,
pro qua non metuam mori,
    si parcent animae fata superstiti.

'me torret face mutua
    Thurini Calais filius Ornyti,
15   pro quo bis patiar mori,
    si parcent puero fata superstiti.'

quid si prisca redit Venus
    diductosque iugo cogit aeneo,
si flava excutitur Chloe,
20   reiectaeque patet ianua Lydiae?

'quamquam sidere pulchrior
    ille est, tu levior cortice et inprobo
iracundior Hadria,
    tecum vivere amem, tecum obeam libens.'

Short Answer Questions

Line 1   What is the case and use of *tibi*? **dative with adjective *gratus,* which governs the dative**

Line 2   What is the function of *quisquam*? ***quisquam* here functions as an indefinite adjective modifying *iuvenis* (line 3)**

              What is the case and use of *brachia*? **accusative, direct object of *dabat* (line 3)**

Line 3   What is the case and use of *cervici*? **dative, indirect object of *dabat***

Line 4   What is the case and use of *rege*? **ablative of comparison with *beatior***

Line 6	What figure of speech is in this line? *arsisti:* **metaphor**
Line 9	What is the case and use of *me*? **accusative, direct object of** *regit*
Line 10	What figure of speech is in this line? *dulcis docta modos:* **alliteration**
Line 12	What is the case and use of *fata*? **nominative, subject of** *parcent*
Line 13	What is the case and use of *face*? **ablative of means with** *torret*
	What figure of speech is in this line? *torret face:* **metaphor**
Line 14	What figure of speech is in this line? *Thurini Calais filius Ornyti:* **chiasmus**
Lines 15–16	What figure of speech is in these lines? **alliteration of "p"**
Line 17	What figure of speech is in this line? *prisca Venus:* **metonymy**
Line 18	What is the case and use of *diductos*? **accusative, adjective used as substantive, direct object of** *cogit*
	What figure of speech is in this line? *iugo aeneo cogit:* **metaphor**
Line 21	What is the case and use of *sidere*? **ablative of comparison with** *pulchrior*
Line 22	What three figures of speech are in this line? *est, tu:* **asyndeton;** *tu levior:* **ellipsis;** *levior cortice:* **metaphor**
	What is the case and use of *cortice*? **ablative of comparison with** *levior*
Line 24	What two figures of speech are in this line? *tecum ... tecum:* **anaphora;** *amem, tecum:* **asyndeton**

Multiple Choice Questions *Suggested time: 15 minutes*

'donec non alia magis
    arsisti, neque erat Lydia post Chloen,
multi Lydia nominis
    Romana vigui clarior Ilia.'

5   me nunc Thressa Chloe regit,
       dulcis docta modos et citharae sciens,
    pro qua non metuam mori,
       si parcent animae fata superstiti.

'me torret face mutua
10   Thurini Calais filius Ornyti,
    pro quo bis patiar mori,
       si parcent puero fata superstiti.'

Ode 3.9.5–16

1.   A figure of speech found in lines 1–2 is
    a. asyndeton
    b. tmesis
    c. metonymy
    d. enjambment

2.   The case and number of *alia* (line 1) are
    a. nominative plural
    b. nominative singular
    c. ablative singular
    d. accusative plural

3.   The best translation of *donec* (line 1) is
    a. as long as
    b. and I do not give
    c. until
    d. gift

4.   In line 3, *multi* . . . refers to
    a. many names
    b. being well known
    c. many famous people
    d. a long line of ancestors

5.   From lines 1–4, we learn that in the past, Lydia was
    a. much talked about
    b. second to Chloe
    c. burning with love
    d. also called Ilia

6.   In line 5, *me* refers to
    a. Lydia
    b. Chloe
    c. the Thracian woman
    d. Lydia's lover

7. The case and number of *modos* (line 6) are determined by
   a. **docta (line 6)**
   b. *dulcis* (line 6)
   c. *sciens* (line 6)
   d. *regit* (line 5)

8. The antecedent of *qua* (line 7) is
   a. *citharae* (line 6)
   b. **Chloe (line 5)**
   c. *docta* (line 6)
   d. *me* (line 5)

9. Line 8, *si . . . superstiti,* is translated
   a. if the survivors spare the soul's fate
   b. if the souls spare the fates of the survivor
   c. if they spare the surviving fates of her life
   d. **if the fates spare her life surviving**

10. The form *mori* (line 7) is
    a. genitive singular
    b. imperative singular
    c. **present infinitive**
    d. nominative plural

11. The speaker of lines 9–12 says that her love for her beloved is
    a. unrequited
    b. eternal
    c. undeserved
    d. **returned equally**

12. The best translation of *patiar* (line 11) is
    a. **I will endure**
    b. let me suffer
    c. I am allowed
    d. I will be allowed

13. A figure of speech found in line 11 is
    a. asyndeton
    b. hysteron proteron
    c. **hyperbole**
    d. ellipsis

14. In line 12, *puero* denotes the same person as
    a. *me* (line 9)
    b. **filius (line 10)**
    c. *Ornyti* (line 10)
    d. the subject of *patiar* (line 11)

Translation *Suggested time: 15 minutes*

Translate the passage below as literally as possible.

> quid si prisca redit Venus
> > diductosque iugo cogit aeneo,
> si flava excutitur Chloe,
> > reiectaeque patet ianua Lydiae?
>
> 5 'quamquam sidere pulchrior
> > ille est, tu levior cortice et inprobo
> iracundior Hadria,
> > tecum vivere amem, tecum obeam libens.'

Ode 3.9.17–24

18 chunks. 9 points, 1/2 point each. Round up to nearest whole point.

quid si	**what if**
prisca redit Venus	**former/ancient love/Venus returns/comes back**
diductos	**those separated/split (the separated ones must be clear as a substantive and direct object)**
-que . . . cogit	**and drives together/compels/forces**
iugo . . . aeneo	**under/by/with a bronze yoke/bond**
si flava	**if blond/yellow (haired)/golden**
excutitur Chloe	**Chloe is shaken off/driven out/banished**
reiectae . . . Lydiae	**to/for rejected Lydia (must be dative)**
-que patet ianua	**and the door lies/is open**
quamquam sidere	**although than a star**
pulchrior ille est	**he/that one is more beautiful**
tu levior	**you (are) more fickle/lighter/unimportant**
cortice	**than cork/bark**
et . . . iracundior	**and more irritable/angry/hot-tempered**
inprobo . . . Hadria	**than the immoderate/unruly/dishonest Adriatic**
tecum . . . tecum	**with you . . . with you**
vivere amem	**I would love to live**
obeam libens	**I would willing(ly) die/go to meet (death)**

Short Analysis Questions *Suggested time: 10 minutes*

> Donec gratus eram tibi,
>> nec quisquam potior brachia candidae
> cervici iuvenis dabat,
>> Persarum vigui rege beatior.

Ode 3.9.1–4

Nine points total.

1. What do the adjectives in this passage suggest about the feelings that the speaker had during the time about which he is speaking now? Refer specifically to four Latin adjectives.

    Eight points.

    One point each for citing up to four adjectives from:
    gratus – pleasing; *(nec) quisquam* - (and not) any; *potior* - more able, more powerful, preferable; *candidae* - bright, radiant, white, gleaming; *beatior* - more blessed, happier, more fortunate

    One point each for explaining how the adjective shows speaker's feelings.

    Possible, sample answers:
    (gratus) happy to perceive himself as successful in pleasing the girl, eager to make an effort to please her; *(quisquam)* happy to feel he was uniquely prized by her; *(potior)* happy and proud to perceive himself as uniquely capable; *(candidae)* desire for the beautiful girl, awe of her beauty; *(beatior)* happy, feeling uniquely fortunate, can't believe his good fortune

2. Name a figure of speech that occurs in line 4. Write out the Latin words that illustrate it.

    One point for identifying hyperbole in the words *Persarum . . . rege beatior*

    OR

    One point for synecdoche of Persian king for happy, rich, or powerful man

Essay *Suggested time: 20 minutes*

> Donec gratus eram tibi,
>> nec quisquam potior brachia candidae
> cervici iuvenis dabat,
>> Persarum vigui rege beatior.
>
> 5 'donec non alia magis
>> arsisti, neque erat Lydia post Chloen,
> multi Lydia nominis
>> Romana vigui clarior Ilia.'

me nunc Thressa Chloe regit,
10   dulcis docta modos et citharae sciens,
pro qua non metuam mori,
    si parcent animae fata superstiti.

'me torret face mutua
    Thurini Calais filius Ornyti,
15   pro quo bis patiar mori,
    si parcent puero fata superstiti.'

quid si prisca redit Venus
    diductosque iugo cogit aeneo,
si flava excutitur Chloe,
20   reiectaeque patet ianua Lydiae?

'quamquam sidere pulchrior
    ille est, tu levior cortice et inprobo
iracundior Hadria,
    tecum vivere amem, tecum obeam libens.'

Ode 3.9.1–24

In this ode, Horace uses time as a structuring element of the lovers' conversation about their relationship. In a **short,** well-organized essay, discuss how their reflection on the past and present influences the lovers' feelings about a future together.

Support your assertions with references to the Latin text **throughout** the poem. All Latin words must be copied or their line numbers provided, AND they must be translated or paraphrased closely enough so that it is clear you understand the Latin. It is your responsibility to convince your reader that you are basing your conclusions on the Latin text and not merely on a general recollection of the passage. Direct your answer to the question; do not merely summarize the passage. Please write your essay on a separate piece of paper.

The student is asked to show how the lovers' reflections on the past and present of their relationship influence their feelings about a shared future. Essays may point out, for example, that the youth's word choices show he was happy with Lydia and hopes to be happy with her again, or that Lydia's past experience has taught her to know the youth's fickle and irascible character and therefore be realistic about loving him (lines 21–23). Some students may add that the way the speakers talk about Chloe and Calais show that their commitments to them are not strong. Others may point out that the competitive and comparative nature of their language suggests that the speaker and Lydia are not suited to a shared future. Merely acceptable answers will offer some analysis of how past, present, and future structure the dialogue, but they may rely more on description than on showing how the speakers' reflections relate to their words in stanzas five and six. Less-than-acceptable essays will fail to cope with the three time frames altogether and/or fail to offer accurate Latin support.

6 – A fully-developed essay, which discusses how the characters' reflections on the past and present stages of their relationship influence what they say about its future. The student makes ample reference to specific aspects of the Latin text to support his analysis and his position. Latin references are properly cited. Even though there may be occasional mistakes, the discussion is coherent and of high quality.

5 – A strong essay. Although the piece has good analysis, it is not as fully developed nor as supported with references to the text as a 6 paper. Latin references are properly cited. The essay reflects familiarity with the poem. A few parts of the passage may receive thin treatment.

4 – A competent response. There may be uneven development of time frames. Although limited in quantity, the essay includes accurate and relevant references in responding to the topic. The discussion may rely more on describing what each character says about time frames than on showing the influence of their reflections on their willingness for a future reconciliation. Some parts of the passage may be glossed over or omitted.

3 – A limited response. The Latin support is weak and/or inappropriate. Latin references are not properly cited. The answer is descriptive and does not reach the level of analysis. In some 3 papers, the student demonstrates an understanding of the poem but cites no Latin to support his or her answer.

2 – Some understanding of the poem, but the essay is general and/or vague. The discussion is flawed. The Latin cited demonstrates very limited comprehension.

1 – An incoherent response. While it does contain some relevant information, no substantive argument is presented. The student demonstrates no understanding of the poem.

0 – A response that is off-topic, completely incorrect, or irrelevant. Responses that merely restate the question are also a 0.

Scansion

Scan the following lines and name the meter.   **The meter is second Asclepiadean.**

<pre>
_   _   _ ∪ ∪ _   ∪ ×
Donec gratus eram tibi,
</pre>

<pre>
_   _   _   ∪ ∪_   _ ∪∪ _ ∪ ×
nec quisquam potior brachia candidae
</pre>

<pre>
_ _ _ ∪ ∪ _   ∪ ×
cervici iuvenis dabat,
</pre>

<pre>
_ _ _   ∪ ∪_ _ ∪ ∪_∪×
Persarum vigui rege beatior.
</pre>

<pre>
        _ _ _ ∪∪_ ∪ ×
5   'donec non alia magis
</pre>

<pre>
_ _ _ ∪   ∪ _ _ ∪∪ _   ∪×
arsisti, nequ(e) erat Lydia post Chloen,
                ∪
</pre>

<pre>
_ _ _ ∪∪ _ ∪×
multi Lydia nominis
</pre>

<pre>
_ _ _ ∪ ∪_ _ ∪∪ _∪×
Romana vigui clarior Ilia.'
</pre>

Ode 3.9.1–8

ODE 3.13

O fons Bandusiae splendidior vitro,
dulci digne mero non sine floribus,
    cras donaberis haedo,
        cui frons turgida cornibus

5   primis et Venerem et proelia destinat,
frustra: nam gelidos inficiet tibi
    rubro sanguine rivos
        lascivi suboles gregis.

te flagrantis atrox hora Caniculae
10   nescit tangere, tu frigus amabile
    fessis vomere tauris
        praebes et pecori vago.

fies nobilium tu quoque fontium
me dicente cavis inpositam ilicem
15   saxis, unde loquaces
        lymphae desiliunt tuae.

Short Answer Questions

Line 1   What is the case and use of *fons*?   **vocative, direct address**

What is the case and use of *vitro*?   **ablative of comparison with *splendidior***

Line 2   What figure of speech is in this line?   ***dulci digne:* alliteration**

Line 3   What is the case and use of *haedo*?   **ablative of means with *donaberis***

Line 4   What is the antecedent of *cui*?   ***haedo* (line 3)**

What is the case and use of *cornibus*?   **ablative of means or ablative of cause with *turgida***

Line 5   What two figures of speech are in this line?   ***Venerem:* metonymy; *Venerem et proelia* may be taken as hendiadys (but cf. note in Ancona, *Horace,* 1999, 2nd edition, 2005, *ad loc.*)**

Line 6   What is the subject of *inficiet*?   ***suboles* (line 8)**

What is the case and use of *tibi*?   **dative of reference**

Line 7   What is the case and use of *sanguine*?   **ablative of means with *inficiet* (line 6)**

Lines 6–7	How does the word order of *gelidos . . . rivos* help to create an image? **The words *rubro sanguine* are surrounded by the pair *gelidos rivos* as the blood would be surrounded by clearer water.**
Line 8	What is the case and use of *lascivi*? **genitive singular adjective modifying *gregis***
Line 9	What is the case and use of *te*? **accusative, direct object of *tangere* (line 10)**
Line 11	What is the case and use of *vomere*? **ablative of cause with *fessis***
Line 12	What is the case and use of *pecori*? **dative, indirect object of *praebes***
Line 13	What is the translation of *fies*? **"you will become"**
Lines 14–15	What two figures of speech (one non-AP) are in these lines? **assonance of "i"; *cavis inpositam ilicem saxis*: chiasmus**

Multiple Choice Questions *Suggested time: 15 minutes*

te flagrantis atrox hora Caniculae
nescit tangere, tu frigus amabile
    fessis vomere tauris
        praebes et pecori vago.

5   fies nobilium tu quoque fontium
me dicente cavis inpositam ilicem
    saxis, unde loquaces
        lymphae desiliunt tuae.

Ode 3.13.9–16

1. From lines 1–2, we learn that the Bandusian spring
   - a. grows warmer at the savage season
   - b. is avoided by fierce dogs
   - c. does not know to touch the blazing hour
   - **d. is not affected in summer**

2. *Caniculae* (line 1) refers to a
   - a. nymph
   - **b. star**
   - c. village
   - d. brook

3. The case of *frigus* (line 2) is determined by
   - a. *vomere* (line 3)
   - b. *amabile* (line 2)
   - c. *fessis* (line 3)
   - **d. *praebes* (line 4)**

4. The *tauris* referred to in line 3
   - a. carry water
   - **b. pull the plow**
   - c. protect the herd
   - d. fight love battles

5. The subject of *praebes* (line 4) is
   a. the spring
   c. Canicula
   b. the reader
   d. the herdsman

6. The case and number of *pecori* (line 4) are
   a. genitive singular
   c. ablative singular
   b. nominative plural
   d. dative singular

7. The tense and mood of *fies* (line 5) are
   a. present indicative
   c. future indicative
   b. present subjunctive
   d. imperfect subjunctive

8. In lines 5–6, the poet pledges to
   a. make the spring famous
   c. sacrifice a kid
   b. plant a tree at the spring
   d. draw inspiration from the spring

9. The case of *saxis* (line 7) is determined by
   a. *cavis* (line 6)
   c. *ilicem* (line 6)
   b. *inpositam* (line 6)
   d. *dicente* (line 6)

10. In line 7, *loquaces* modifies
    a. *tuae* (line 8)
    c. *lymphae* (line 8)
    b. *desiliunt* (line 8)
    d. *unde* (line 7)

11. From lines 6–8, we learn that the spring
    a. stands above an ilex tree
    c. proceeds from hollow rocks
    b. leaps out from a hollow tree
    d. flows quietly

12. A figure of speech found in lines 7–8 is
    a. alliteration
    c. oxymoron
    b. transferred epithet
    d. hyperbaton

Translation *Suggested time: 15 minutes*

Translate the passage below as literally as possible.

> **O fons Bandusiae splendidior vitro,**
> **dulci digne mero non sine floribus,**
> **cras donaberis haedo,**
> **cui frons turgida cornibus**

5 primis et Venerem et proelia destinat,
  frustra: nam gelidos inficiet tibi
   rubro sanguine rivos
    lascivi suboles gregis.

Ode 3.13.1–8

18 chunks. 9 points total, 1/2 point each. Round up to nearest whole point.

O fons Bandusiae	**O spring/source/fountain of Bandusia**
splendidior vitro	**more bright/glittering/splendid than glass**
dulci . . . mero	**of sweet (pure) wine (must be construed with *digne*)**
digne	**worthy/deserving (must be vocative)**
non sine floribus	**not without flowers**
cras donaberis	**tomorrow you will be presented/endowed/rewarded**
haedo, cui	**with a kid (must be ablative) to/for whom/which/whose**
frons turgida	**forehead/brow swollen/turgid**
cornibus primis	**with first horns**
et . . . et	**both . . . and**
Venerem . . . proelia	**Venus/love . . . battles (must be objects of *destinat*)**
destinat, frustra	**destines/intends/determines in vain/to no purpose**
nam . . . inficiet	**for . . . will dye/imbue/stain/infect/taint**
tibi	**for you/your**
gelidos . . . rivos	**cold/icy/chilled . . . streams (not "rivers"; must be object of *inficiet*)**
rubro sanguine	**with red blood**
lascivi . . . gregis	**of the frisky/playful/wanton/lascivious . . . flock/herd**
suboles	**(the) offspring (must be subject of *inficiet*)**

Short Analysis Questions *Suggested time: 10 minutes*

  te flagrantis atrox hora Caniculae
  nescit tangere, tu frigus amabile
   fessis vomere tauris
    praebes et pecori vago.

5 fies nobilium tu quoque fontium
  me dicente cavis inpositam ilicem
   saxis, unde loquaces
    lymphae desiliunt tuae.

Ode 3.13.9-16

Eight points total.

1. Name a figure of speech in lines 1–2 and write out the Latin words that illustrate it.

  **One point for naming the figure and providing the Latin words
  personification: *atrox hora . . . nescit***

  OR

chiasmus: *flagrantis atrox hora Caniculae*

OR

transferred epithet: *atrox* from *Caniculae* to *hora*

OR

asyndeton: *nescit tangere, tu frigus*

2. In lines 1–2,

a. explain what *Caniculae* is.

One point for identifying *Caniculae* as the Dog Star or Sirius.

b. identify and translate *atrox hora Caniculae.*

One point for identifying *atrox hora Caniculae* as a time of very hot weather.

One point for translating *atrox hora Caniculae.*

c. explain the significance of *te . . . nescit tangere* in this context.

Two points for explaining "does not know how to touch you" as the inability to dry up the spring or flow of cool water.

One point if the meaning of the Latin is not made clear.

3. Name two beneficiaries of the spring's action in lines 2–4 and translate the supporting Latin.

Two points.

One point for each indirect object: (tired) bulls, *fessis tauris*; (wandering) herd animals, *pecori vago*.

Essay *Suggested time: 20 minutes*

O fons Bandusiae splendidior vitro,
dulci digne mero non sine floribus,
    cras donaberis haedo,
        cui frons turgida cornibus

5   primis et Venerem et proelia destinat,
frustra: nam gelidos inficiet tibi
    rubro sanguine rivos
        lascivi suboles gregis.

    te flagrantis atrox hora Caniculae
10   nescit tangere, tu frigus amabile
    fessis vomere tauris
        praebes et pecori vago.

fies nobilium tu quoque fontium
me dicente cavis inpositam ilicem
15   saxis, unde loquaces
lymphae desiliunt tuae.

Ode 3.13

One of the features that make Horace's poetry so memorable is its juxtaposition of contrasting qualities or expectations. In a brief, well-organized essay, show how Horace exploits contrasts to enhance
the effect of the poem.

Support your assertions with references to the Latin text **throughout** the poem. All Latin words
must be copied or their line numbers provided, AND they must be translated or paraphrased closely
enough so that it is clear you understand the Latin. It is your responsibility to convince your reader
that you are basing your conclusions on the Latin text and not merely on a general recollection of the
passage. Direct your answer to the question; do not merely summarize the passage. Please write your
essay on a separate piece of paper.

**This question asks the student to analyze Horace's poetic technique. There are more contrasts than a
student can discuss in twenty minutes. Nevertheless, superior essays will do justice to the whole poem.
Examples of contrasts that a student may develop include: a spring's gush to glass' smoothness (line
1); the kid's expected future and his actual fate (lines 4–6); red, hot blood in cold, clear streams (lines
6–7); heat and cold in stanza three; etc. Superior essays will not only identify contrasts and show mastery of the Latin words that contain them; they will also discuss their effect. Merely adequate essays
will discuss a narrower array of contrasts, will supply less well-rendered Latin support, and will be less
successful at showing what the contrast accomplishes. Less-than-adequate essays will fail to discuss
contrasts, will discuss only a few in one part of the poem, and/or will offer faulty or no Latin support.**

**6 – A fully-developed analysis of how Horace uses contrasts to enhance the effect of the poem. A
genuine attempt is made to account for this feature throughout the poem. The student makes ample
reference to specific aspects of the Latin text to support his analysis and his position. Latin references
are properly cited. Even though there may be occasional mistakes, the discussion is coherent and of
high quality.**

**5 – A strong essay. Although the piece has good analysis, it is not as fully developed nor as supported
with references to the text as a 6 paper. There may be some major contrasts that go unnoticed, or the
effect of some contrasts may not be analyzed. Latin references are properly cited but may be fewer
or less masterful than those of a 6. The essay reflects familiarity with the poem.**

**4 – A competent response. There may be uneven development. Although limited in quantity, the
essay includes accurate and relevant references in responding to the topic. The discussion may limit
itself more to describing the contrasts than analyzing their effects. Significant parts of the passage
may be glossed over or omitted.**

**3 – A limited response. The Latin support is weak and/or inappropriate, or Latin references are not
properly cited. The answer is descriptive and does not reach the level of analysis, or only one or two
contrasts are noted. In some 3 papers, the student demonstrates an understanding of the poem and
writes a good essay but cites no Latin to support his answer.**

2 – Some understanding of the poem, but the essay is general and/or vague. The discussion is flawed; for example, words may be translated but no contrast detected. The Latin cited demonstrates very limited comprehension.

1 – An incoherent response. While it does contain some relevant information, no substantive argument is presented. The student demonstrates no understanding of the poem.

0 – A response that is off-topic, completely incorrect, or irrelevant. Responses that merely restate the question are also a 0.

Scansion

Scan the following lines and name the meter.   **The meter is fourth Asclepiadean.**

```
       _  _  _  U U _  _ U  U _ U ×
      te flagrantis atrox hora Caniculae
```

```
      _  _  _   UU  _  _ U U _ U×
10    nescit tangere, tu frigus amabile
```

```
       _  _  _  UU  _ ×
      fessis vomere tauris
```

```
          _  _  _  U U _ U ×
         praebes et pecori vago.
```

```
      _ _   _  UU_  _   U  U _  U×
     fies nobilium tu quoque fontium
```

```
      _  _ _  U U _ _ UU      _ U ×
     me dicente cavis inposit(am) ilicem
                              ⌣
```

```
       _  _  _  U U  _ ×
15    saxis, unde loquaces
```

```
      _      _  _UU_    U ×
     lymphae desiliunt tuae.
```

Ode 3.13.9–16

ODE 3.30

Exegi monumentum aere perennius
regalique situ pyramidum altius,

quod non imber edax, non Aquilo inpotens
possit diruere aut innumerabilis

5   annorum series et fuga temporum.
non omnis moriar, multaque pars mei

vitabit Libitinam: usque ego postera
crescam laude recens, dum Capitolium

scandet cum tacita virgine pontifex.
10   dicar, qua violens obstrepit Aufidus

et qua pauper aquae Daunus agrestium
regnavit populorum, ex humili potens

princeps Aeolium carmen ad Italos
deduxisse modos. sume superbiam

15   quaesitam meritis et mihi Delphica
lauro cinge volens, Melpomene, comam.

Short Answer Questions

Line 1   What is the case and use of *aere*? **ablative of comparison with *perennius***

What does *perennius* modify? **monumentum**

Line 2   What is the case and use of *situ*? **ablative of comparison with *altius***

What is the case and use of *pyramidum*? **possessive genitive or subjective genitive with *situ***

Line 3   What is the antecedent of *quod*? **monumentum (line 1)**

Name three figures of speech in this line. ***non . . . non:* anaphora; *edax, non:* asyndeton; *Aquilo inpotens:* personification**

Line 4   What is (are) the subject(s) of *possit*? **subject of *possit* is multiple: *imber, Aquilo* (line 3), *series* and *fuga* (line 5), with verb attracted into singular**

Line 5	What two figures of speech are in this line? *annorum series . . . fuga temporum:* **chiasmus;** *fuga temporum:* **personification**
	What is the case and use of *temporum?* **subjective genitive**
Lines 3–5	What figure of speech is in these lines? *imber . . . Aquilo . . . series et fuga:* **tricolon crescens/crescendo. The third element of the tricolon is bipartite;** *series* **and** *fuga* **express the same idea and are joined by "*et.*"**
Line 8	What is the case and use of *laude?* **ablative of means or ablative of cause with *recens***
Line 9	What is the case and use of *virgine?* **ablative of accompaniment**
Line 11	What is the case and use of *aquae?* **genitive of reference with *pauper***
Line 12	What is the case and use of *populorum?* **Greek genitive with verb *regnavit***
Line 13	What is the case and use of *carmen?* **accusative, direct object of *deduxisse* (line 14)**
Line 14	On what verb does *deduxisse* depend? *dicar* **(line 10)**
Lines 13–14	What three figures of speech are in these lines? *carmen . . . deduxisse:* **metaphor; alliteration of "s";** *sume superbiam:* **metaphor**
Line 15	What is the case and use of *mihi?* **dative of reference**
Line 16	What is the case and use of *lauro?* **ablative of means with *cinge***
	What is the case and use of *comam?* **accusative, direct object of *cinge***

Multiple Choice Questions *Suggested time: 15 minutes*

Exegi monumentum aere perennius
regalique situ pyramidum altius,

quod non imber edax, non Aquilo inpotens
possit diruere aut innumerabilis

5   **annorum series et fuga temporum.**
non omnis moriar, multaque pars mei

vitabit Libitinam: usque ego postera
crescam laude recens, dum Capitolium

scandet cum tacita virgine pontifex.
10   **dicar, qua violens obstrepit Aufidus**

et qua pauper aquae Daunus agrestium
regnavit populorum, . . .

Ode 3.30.1–12

1. The *monumentum* that Horace describes in lines 1–5 is
   a. a building
   b. a statue
   c. poetry
   d. a farm

2. In line 1, *exegi* is translated
   a. I have completed
   b. I have driven out
   c. I have exacted
   d. I have reduced

3. The case of *regali* (line 2) is determined by
   a. *situ* (line 2)
   b. *exegi* (line 1)
   c. *aere* (line 1)
   d. *perennius* (line 1)

4. In line 2, *altius* modifies
   a. *perennius* (line 1)
   b. *situ* (line 2)
   c. *exegi* (line 1)
   d. *monumentum* (line 1)

5. A figure of speech found in line 3 is
   a. oxymoron
   b. personification
   c. hendiadys
   d. litotes

6. The word *diruere* (line 4) is
   a. present passive indicative
   b. present active infinitive
   c. present active imperative
   d. perfect active indicative

7. The characteristic that Horace does **not** attribute to the pyramids in lines 2–4 is
   a. height
   b. sacredness
   c. fame
   d. royal origin

8. From the words *non omnis . . . Libitinam* (lines 6–7), we learn that Horace believes that
   a. not everyone will die
   b. he will not delay on earth
   c. part of him will survive his death
   d. he will not die

9. The case and number of *postera* (line 7) are
   a. accusative plural
   b. nominative singular
   c. nominative plural
   d. ablative singular

10. The words *dum . . . pontifex* (lines 8–9) refer to a
    a. religious ceremony
    b. wedding procession
    c. poetic contest
    d. senatorial assembly

11. In line 10, *qua* is translated
    a. by which
    c. which
    b. insofar as
    d. where

12. From lines 10–12, we learn that Horace will be spoken of
    a. as a violent man
    c. by Daunus
    b. by rural people
    d. as living in a dry countryside

Translation *Suggested time: 15 minutes*

Translate the passage below as literally as possible.

> Exegi monumentum aere perennius
> regalique situ pyramidum altius,
>
> quod non imber edax, non Aquilo inpotens
> possit diruere aut innumerabilis
>
> 5   annorum series et fuga temporum.
> non omnis moriar, multaque pars mei
>
> vitabit Libitinam: . . .

Ode 3.30.1–7

16 chunks. 8 points, 1/2 point each. Round up to nearest whole point.

Exegi monumentum	**I have completed/executed a monument/memorial**
aere perennius	**more enduring/long-lasting/lasting through years than bronze**
-que . . . altius	**and higher**
regali . . . situ	**than the royal/regal site/deterioration/decay/neglect**
pyramidum	**of the pyramids**
quod	**which (NOT "because")**
non . . . non	**not . . . not/neither . . . nor**
imber edax	**devouring/greedy/destructive rain/shower(s)**
Aquilo inpotens	**wild/violent/powerless/weak North Wind/Aquilo**
possit diruere	**could/would be able to uproot/demolish/overthrow/destroy**
aut innumerabilis	**or the innumerable/countless/numberless**
annorum series	**series/sequence/succession of years**
et fuga temporum.	**and (the) flight of time(s)**
non omnis moriar	**I shall/will not all/entire(ly) die**
multaque pars mei	**and a great/much part/portion of me/of myself**
vitabit Libitinam	**will/shall avoid/shun Libitina/the goddess of funerals/funeral/death**

Short Analysis Questions *Suggested time: 10 minutes*

dicar, qua violens obstrepit Aufidus

et qua pauper aquae Daunus agrestium
regnavit populorum, ex humili potens

princeps Aeolium carmen ad Italos
5   deduxisse modos. sume superbiam

quaesitam meritis et mihi Delphica
lauro cinge volens, Melpomene, comam.

Ode 3.30.10–16

Eight points total.

1. a. To what part of Italy does Horace refer in lines 1–3?

   One point for stating that Horace refers to Southern Italy or Apulia or the region near his birthplace, Venusia.

   b. What is the significance of his references to this part of Italy?

   One point for stating that lines 1–3 indicate Horace will be famous in the region where he grew up/was born.

3. To what poetic accomplishment does Horace refer with the words *ex humili . . . modos* (lines 3–5)? Write out and translate the Latin support for your conclusion.

   Three points.

   One point for identifying Horace's poetic accomplishment in lines 3–5 as his being the first to have adapted Aeolic or Greek poetry to Italian or Latin forms/modes.

   One point for citing the Latin: *princeps Aeolium carmen ad Italos deduxisse modos.*

   One point for translating: first to have brought Aeolian/Aeolic/Greek song/ poetry to Italian modes/poetry/rhythms

3. a. Who is Melpomene?

   One point for identifying Melpomene as a muse (of tragedy).

   b. What are two things she is asked to do (lines 5–7)? Cite the Latin support for each.

   One point for stating she takes on the pride acquired by merits and citing the Latin.

   One point for stating she encircles Horace's hair with (Delphic) laurel and citing the Latin.

Essay *Suggested time: 20 minutes*

Exegi monumentum aere perennius
regalique situ pyramidum altius,

quod non imber edax, non Aquilo inpotens
possit diruere aut innumerabilis

5   annorum series et fuga temporum.
non omnis moriar, multaque pars mei

vitabit Libitinam: usque ego postera
crescam laude recens, dum Capitolium

scandet cum tacita virgine pontifex.
10   dicar, qua violens obstrepit Aufidus

et qua pauper aquae Daunus agrestium
regnavit populorum, ex humili potens

princeps Aeolium carmen ad Italos
deduxisse modos. sume superbiam

15   quaesitam meritis et mihi Delphica
lauro cinge volens, Melpomene, comam.

Ode 3.30

In this ode, Horace reflects on his finished three books of *Odes*. In a brief, well-organized essay, show how Horace uses references to time to talk about his poetic accomplishments. You may discuss, but are not limited to, verb tenses, imagery, or mythological and historical references.

Support your assertions with references to the Latin text **throughout** the poem. All Latin words must be copied or their line numbers provided, AND they must be translated or paraphrased closely enough so that it is clear you understand the Latin. It is your responsibility to convince your reader that you are basing your conclusions on the Latin text and not merely on a general recollection of the passage. Direct your answer to the question; do not merely summarize the passage. Please write your essay on a separate piece of paper.

The student is asked to discuss how Horace uses references to time to talk about his poetic accomplishments. Superior essays will identify temporal references from throughout the poem. They will show how each reference helps Horace reflect on his poetic accomplishments. They will offer liberal and appropriate Latin support, correctly cited and translated, for the points they make. Merely satisfactory essays will omit some parts of the poem, present fewer temporal references, rely more on description than analysis, and/or offer fewer and/or less well-rendered pieces of Latin support.

Students can say many things about how Horace's temporal references help present his poetic accomplishments. A student may make such points as: (1) Horace's selection of perfect tense in *exegi* (line 1) underscores the finality of his poetic accomplishment, for he has completed his work, and it will remain into the future; (2) by reference to the *Aeolium carmen* (line 13), Horace takes credit as the

first to adapt the poetry of his predecessors, Alcaeus and Sappho, to Latin verse. Essays worth a 6 or 5 will not merely identify temporal references such as these, but they will analyze how Horace uses them to present his poetic accomplishments.

6 – A fully-developed essay, which analyzes how Horace's references to time help him talk about his poetic accomplishments. The analysis ranges over the whole poem. The student makes ample reference to specific aspects of the Latin text to support his analysis and his position. Latin references are properly cited. Even though there may be occasional mistakes, the discussion is coherent and of high quality.

5 – A strong essay. Although the piece has good analysis, it is not as fully developed nor as supported with references to the text as a 6 paper. Latin references are properly cited. The essay reflects familiarity with the poem. A few parts of the poem may receive thin treatment.

4 – A competent response. There may be uneven development of time frames. Although limited in quantity, the essay includes accurate and relevant references in responding to the topic. The discussion may rely more on identifying and describing temporal references than on showing how they help present Horace's poetic accomplishments. Some parts of the poem may be glossed over or omitted. Latin support is accurate but not extensive.

3 – A limited response. The Latin support is weak and/or inappropriate. Latin references are not properly cited. The answer is descriptive and does not reach the level of analysis. In some 3 papers, the student demonstrates an understanding of the poem but cites no Latin to support his answer.

2 – Some understanding of the poem, but the essay is general and/or vague. The discussion is flawed. The Latin cited demonstrates very limited comprehension.

1 – An incoherent response. While it does contain some relevant information, no substantive argument is presented. The student demonstrates no understanding of the poem.

0 – A response that is off-topic, completely incorrect, or irrelevant. Responses that merely restate the question are also a 0.

Scansion

Scan the following lines and name the meter.   **The meter is first or lesser Asclepiadean.**

Exegi monument(um) aere perennius

regalique situ pyramid(um) altius,

quod non imber edax, non Aquil(o) inpotens

possit diruer(e) aut innumerabilis

5   annorum series et fuga temporum.

non omnis moriar, multaque pars mei

vitabit Libitin(am): usqu(e) ego postera

crescam laude recens, dum Capitolium

Ode 3.30.1–8

ODE 4.7

Diffugere nives, redeunt iam gramina campis
    arboribusque comae,
mutat terra vices et decrescentia ripas
    flumina praetereunt,

5   Gratia cum Nymphis geminisque sororibus audet
    ducere nuda choros.
immortalia ne speres, monet annus et almum
    quae rapit hora diem.

frigora mitescunt Zephyris, ver proterit aestas
10   interitura, simul
pomifer autumnus fruges effuderit, et mox
    bruma recurrit iners.

damna tamen celeres reparant caelestia lunae:
    nos ubi decidimus,
15   quo pater Aeneas, quo Tullus dives et Ancus,
    pulvis et umbra sumus.

quis scit, an adiciant hodiernae crastina summae
    tempora di superi?
cuncta manus avidas fugient heredis, amico
20   quae dederis animo.

cum semel occideris, et de te splendida Minos
    fecerit arbitria,
non, Torquate, genus, non te facundia, non te
    restituet pietas:

25   infernis neque enim tenebris Diana pudicum
    liberat Hippolytum,
nec Lethaea valet Theseus abrumpere caro
    vincula Pirithoo.

Short Answer Questions

Line 1   What is the case and use of *campis*? **dative of direction/motion**

The verb *diffugere* is an alternative form of what verb? ***diffugerunt***

Lines 1–2	What three figures of speech are in these lines? *diffugere nives:* **personification;** *nives, redeunt:* **asyndeton;** *gramina . . . comae:* **chiasmus**
Line 3	What is the case and use of *vices?* **accusative, direct object of** *mutat*
	What is the case and use of *ripas?* **accusative, direct object of** *praetereunt* **(line 4)**
Line 4	What is the case and use of *flumina?* **nominative, subject of** *praetereunt*
Line 5	What is the case and use of *sororibus?* **ablative of accompaniment after** *cum*
Line 6	What figure of speech is in this line? *nuda:* **hyperbaton**
Line 7	What is the case and use of *immortalia?* **accusative adjective as substantive, direct object of** *speres*
	What figure of speech is in this line? *monet annus:* **personification**
Lines 7–8	What four figures of speech (one non-AP) are in these lines? *almum quae . . . hora:* **postposition/anastrophe;** *rapit hora:* **personfication;** *rapit . . . diem:* **metaphor;** *almum . . . diem:* **hyperbaton**
Line 9	What is the case and use of *Zephyris?* **ablative of means with** *mitescunt*
	What is the case and use of *ver?* **accusative, direct object of** *proterit*
Lines 9–10	What figure of speech is in these lines? *interitura:* **enjambment**
Line 11	What is the tense of *effuderit?* **future perfect**
	What is the case and use of *fruges?* **accusative, direct object of** *effuderit*
Line 12	What two figures of speech are in this line? *bruma . . . iners:* **personification;** *recurrit iners:* **oxymoron**
Line 13	What is the case and use of *damna?* **accusative, direct object of** *reparant*
	What is the case and use of *celeres?* **nominative, adjective modifying** *lunae,* **subject**
	What is the figure of speech in this line? *damna celeres caelestia lunae:* **interlocked word order/synchysis/synchesis**
Line 14	What figure of speech (non-AP) is in this line? *nos ubi:* **anastrophe/postposition**
Line 15	What figure of speech is in this line? *quo . . . quo:* **anaphora**
Line 17	What is the case and use of *summae?* **dative, indirect object of** *adiciant*
Line 18	What is the case and use of *tempora?* **accusative, direct object of** *adiciant* **(line 17)**
Line 19	What is the case and use of *cuncta?* **nominative, adjective acting as substantive, subject of** *fugient*
	What three figures of speech are in this line? *manus avidas:* **personification and transferred epithet;** *manus . . . fugient heredis:* **hands, synecdoche for heir**
Line 20	What is the tense of *dederis?* **future perfect**

Lines 23–24   What five figures of speech are in these lines? **non ... non ... non: anaphora and asyndeton; Torquate: apostrophe; te restituet: personification; non ... pietas: tricolon**

Line 25   What is the case and use of *tenebris*? **ablative of separation**

Line 27   What is the object of *abrumpere*? **vincula (line 28)**

Multiple Choice Questions *Suggested time: 15 minutes*

Diffugere nives, redeunt iam gramina campis
    arboribusque comae,
mutat terra vices et decrescentia ripas
    flumina praetereunt,

5   Gratia cum Nymphis geminisque sororibus audet
    ducere nuda choros.
immortalia ne speres, monet annus et almum
    quae rapit hora diem.

frigora mitescunt Zephyris, ver proterit aestas
10   interitura, simul
pomifer autumnus fruges effuderit, et mox
    bruma recurrit iners.

Ode 4.7.1–12

1.   In line 1, *diffugere* is
    a.   present active infinitive
    b.   perfect active indicative
    c.   present passive imperative
    d.   future passive indicative

2.   The case of *campis* (line 1) is determined by
    a.   *gramina* (line 1)
    b.   *arboribus* (line 2)
    c.   *iam* (line 1)
    d.   redeunt (line 1)

3.   The words *decrescentia ripas flumina praetereunt* (lines 3–4) are translated
    a.   cresting rivers pass beyond their banks
    b.   crested banks surround rivers
    c.   decreasing rivers go past their banks
    d.   rivers pass by, diminishing their banks

4.   From lines 1–4, we may infer that the poem is set in
    a.   late winter
    b.   early spring
    c.   late spring
    d.   summer

5. The *geminis sororibus* (line 5) are
   a. Fates
   b. Nymphs
   c. Castor and Pollux
   d. Graces

6. A figure of speech found in lines 5–6 is
   a. asyndeton
   b. hysteron proteron
   c. prolepsis
   d. hyperbaton

7. In line 7, *almum* modifies
   a. *diem* (line 8)
   b. *rapit* (line 8)
   c. *monet* (line 7)
   d. *quae* (line 8)

8. The antecedent of *quae* (line 8) is
   a. *annus* (line 7)
   b. *almum* (line 7)
   c. *immortalia* (line 7)
   d. *hora* (line 8)

9. In line 7, *ne* introduces a (an)
   a. purpose clause
   b. conditional clause
   c. indirect command
   d. result clause

10. In line 9, *Zephyris* are
    a. horses
    b. winds
    c. nymphs
    d. seasons

11. In line 10, *simul* is translated
    a. at the same time
    b. once for all
    c. simultaneously
    d. as soon as

12. In line 11, *effuderit* is
    a. future perfect indicative
    b. perfect subjunctive
    c. present indicative
    d. future indicative

13. Lines 9–12 emphasize the _____ of the seasons' change.
    a. inevitability
    b. mildness
    c. rapidity
    d. harmony

Translation *Suggested time: 15 minutes*

Translate the passage below as literally as possible.

> cum semel occideris, et de te splendida Minos
> > fecerit arbitria,
> non, Torquate, genus, non te facundia, non te
> > restituet pietas:
>
> 5   infernis neque enim tenebris Diana pudicum
> > liberat Hippolytum,
> nec Lethaea valet Theseus abrumpere caro
> > vincula Pirithoo.

Ode 4.7 21–28

18 chunks. 9 points total, 1/2 point each. Round up to nearest whole point.

cum semel	**when once/once and for all**
occideris	**you fall/die (accept present, future or future perfect)**
et de te	**and about/concerning you**
Minos fecerit	**Minos makes (accept present, future, or future perfect)**
splendida . . . arbitria	**bright/glittering/illustrious/splendid judgments**
non, Torquate, genus	**not, Torquatus, (your) birth/race/stock**
non . . . facundia	**not eloquence**
te . . . te	**you . . . you (must be translated twice, must be direct object of** *restituet***)**
non . . . pietas	**not piety/duty/devotion**
restituet	**will restore/revive (must be future)**
neque enim	**for neither/ for in fact . . . not**
infernis . . . tenebris	**from infernal darkness/darkness below/darkness of the lower world**
Diana . . . liberat	**(does) Diana free/liberate**
pudicum . . . Hippolytum,	**chaste/modest/honorable Hippolytus**
nec . . . valet Theseus	**nor/and . . . not Theseus is strong enough to/has strength to**
Lethaea . . . vincula	**the Lethaean/of Lethe bonds/chains**
abrumpere	**to break off/away/apart**
caro . . . Pirithoo	**for/from dear/beloved Pirithous**

Short Analysis Questions *Suggested time: 10 minutes*

> damna tamen celeres reparant caelestia lunae:
> nos ubi decidimus,
> quo pater Aeneas, quo Tullus dives et Ancus,
> pulvis et umbra sumus.
>
> 5 quis scit, an adiciant hodiernae crastina summae
> tempora di superi?
> cuncta manus avidas fugient heredis, amico
> quae dederis animo.

Ode 4.7.13–20

Eight points total.

1. a. What are the losses (*damna*) of which Horace speaks in line 1?

   One point for explaining the "celestial losses" as the moon's apparent decrease in size when it wanes.

   b. How are these losses repaired?

   One point for explaining that it repairs these losses by waxing again as the month draws on.

2. a. To what place does Horace refer by the word *quo* (line 3)?

   One point for explaining *quo* as a reference to the underworld or death.

   b. Copy and translate two pieces of evidence from the Latin that support your answer.

   One point for each piece of Latin evidence: reference to at least one dead hero of line 3

   AND

   ***pulvis et umbra sumus,* "we are ash and (a) shade," (line 4).**

3. Identify a figure of speech that appears in lines 5–6, and copy the Latin words that illustrate it.

   One point for identifying figure of speech with Latin support:
   interlocked word order/synchysis/synchesis: *hodiernae crastina summae tempora*

   OR

   rhetorical question (non-AP): *quis scit . . . di superi?*

4. a. According to lines 7–8, what action will prevent an heir from coming into possession of certain parts of one's wealth?

   One point for saying that giving one's assets to oneself, i.e., using them oneself, keeps them from one's heir.

   b. Copy and translate the Latin words that support your answer.

   One point for supporting Latin: *amico quae dederis animo.*

Essay *Suggested time: 20 minutes*

> Diffugere nives, redeunt iam gramina campis
>   arboribusque comae,
> mutat terra vices et decrescentia ripas
>   flumina praetereunt,
>
> 5   Gratia cum Nymphis geminisque sororibus audet
>   ducere nuda choros.
> immortalia ne speres, monet annus et almum
>   quae rapit hora diem.
>
> frigora mitescunt Zephyris, ver proterit aestas
> 10   interitura, simul
> pomifer autumnus fruges effuderit, et mox
>   bruma recurrit iners.
>
> damna tamen celeres reparant caelestia lunae:
>   nos ubi decidimus,
> 15   quo pater Aeneas, quo Tullus dives et Ancus,
>   pulvis et umbra sumus.
>
> quis scit, an adiciant hodiernae crastina summae
>   tempora di superi?
> cuncta manus avidas fugient heredis, amico
> 20   quae dederis animo.
>
> cum semel occideris, et de te splendida Minos
>   fecerit arbitria,
> non, Torquate, genus, non te facundia, non te
>   restituet pietas:
>
> 25   infernis neque enim tenebris Diana pudicum
>   liberat Hippolytum,
> nec Lethaea valet Theseus abrumpere caro
>   vincula Pirithoo.

Ode 4.7

Horace's imagery in this ode depicts two kinds of change: change that renews itself and change that reaches an end and stops. In a **short,** well-organized essay, discuss how Horace's images of cyclical change and irreversible change help him to comment on the human condition.

Support your assertions with Latin references from **throughout** the poem. All Latin words must be copied or their line numbers provided, AND they must be translated or paraphrased closely enough so that it is clear you understand the Latin. It is your responsibility to convince your reader that you are basing your conclusions on the Latin text and not merely on a general recollection of the passage. Direct your answer to the question; do not merely summarize the passage. Please write your essay on a separate piece of paper.

This question asks the student to analyze images of two kinds of change: cyclical change and unidirectional, irreversible change. Analysis must show how the imagery of these two kinds of change contributes to Horace's reflections on the human condition (e.g., life and death, and/or friendship). A student may identify the poles of the contrast, for example, as natural phenomena that renew themselves (seasons, heavenly bodies in orbit), and the lives of humans, which end irrevocably in death. Although the poem is too long for students to tackle every image, a top-flight essay will do a reasonable job of discussing the imagery in the poem as a whole (beginning, middle and end). Latin support will be generous and accurately translated or paraphrased. Merely acceptable papers may discuss a minimal number of images or omit significant sections of the poem, may rely more on description than on analysis of how the images help Horace reflect on the human condition, and/or may offer sparse Latin support.

Some students may point out a contrast between mortals, whose lives change irrevocably, and the immortals, who do not change (Graces, Hours, gods, *immortalia*, Diana). Students are not asked to contrast entities as such, however, and such discussion contributes to their scores only insofar as it illuminates the contrast between imagery of cyclical change and imagery of irreversible change.

6 – A fully-developed essay which discusses how Horace's imagery of cyclical change AND his imagery of irreversible change help him comment on the human condition. The student makes ample reference to specific aspects of the Latin text to support his analysis and his position. Latin references are properly cited. Even though there may be occasional mistakes, the discussion is coherent and of high quality.

5 – A strong essay. Although the piece has good analysis, it is not as fully developed nor as supported with references to the text as a 6 paper. Latin references are properly cited. The essay reflects familiarity with the poem. A few parts of the passage may receive thin treatment.

4 – A competent response. There may be uneven development of the two complexes of change imagery. Although limited in quantity, the essay includes accurate and relevant references in responding to the topic. The discussion may rely more on describing what changes are represented than on connecting their representation to Horace's reflections on the human condition. Some parts of the passage may be glossed over or omitted.

3 – A limited response. The Latin support is weak and/or inappropriate. Latin references are not properly cited. The answer is descriptive and does not reach the level of analysis. In some 3 papers, the student demonstrates an understanding of the poem but cites no Latin to support his answer.

2 – Some understanding of the poem, but the essay is general and/or vague. The discussion is flawed. The Latin cited demonstrates very limited comprehension.

1 – An incoherent response. While it does contain some relevant information, no substantive argument is presented. The student demonstrates no understanding of the poem.

0 – A response that is off-topic, completely incorrect, or irrelevant. Responses that merely restate the question are also a 0.

Scansion

Scan the following lines and name the meter. **The meter is first Archilochian.**

         _ _ _ ∪ ∪ _ ∪ ∪_   _   _ ∪ ∪ _   ×
Diffugere nives, redeunt iam gramina campis

      _   ∪∪ _   ∪ ∪ ×
arboribusque comae,

    _ _   _ ∪ ∪_ _   _ _   _ ∪∪ _ ×
mutat terra vices et decrescentia ripas

      _ ∪ ∪   _ ∪ ∪×
flumina praetereunt,

Ode 4.7.1–4

STUDENT WORKBOOK APPENDIX

PRACTICE MULTIPLE CHOICE EXERCISES AND ANSWER KEY

PASSAGE A

Suggested time: 15 minutes per excerpt

Cicero describes the Fabricii brothers.

C. et L. Fabricii fratres gemini fuerunt ex municipio Aletrinati, homines inter
se cum forma tum moribus similes, municipum autem suorum dissimillimi,
in quibus quantus splendor sit, quam prope aequabilis, quam constans et moderata
ratio vitae, nemo vestrum, ut mea fert opinio, ignorat. His Fabriciis semper est usus
5   Oppianicus familiarissime. Iam hoc fere scitis omnes, quantam vim habeat ad
coniungendas amicitias studiorum ac naturae similitudo. Cum illi ita viverent ut
nullum quaestum esse turpem arbitrarentur, cum omnis ab eis fraus, omnes insidiae
circumscriptionesque adulescentium nascerentur, cumque essent vitiis atque
improbitate omnibus noti, studiose, ut dixi, ad eorum familiaritatem multis iam
10   ante annis Oppianicus se applicarat.

municipium, -i, n., *municipality, town*
cum . . . tum, *both. . . . and*
Aletrinas, m./f., of **Aletrium,** *a town c.50 miles southeast of Rome*
municeps, -ipis, m., *fellow townsman*
aequabilis, -e, *consistent*
Oppianicus, *the name of a citizen of another town*
studium, -i, n., *interest, pursuit*
quaestus, -us, m., *profit*
arbitror, -ari, -atus sum, *think, deem, suppose*
turpis, -e, *base, disgraceful*
circumscriptio, -ionis, f., *cheating, swindling*
vitium, -i, n., *vice, crime*
improbitas, -tatis, f., *dishonesty*
studiose, *earnestly, carefully*

1.   From lines 1–2, we learn that the Fabricii brothers had similar

    a. occupations   b. characters

    c. houses   d. deaths

2.   In line 3, *sit* is subjunctive because it appears in a clause of

    a. purpose   b. result

    c. indirect command   d. indirect question

3. The best translation of *ratio vitae* (line 4) is
    a. manner of life
    b. ratio of living
    c. rations for life
    d. reasonable life

4. The case and number of *vestrum* (line 4) are
    a. accusative singular
    b. nominative singular
    c. genitive plural
    d. vocative singular

5. The case of *Fabriciis* (line 4) is determined by
    a. *His* (line 4)
    b. *est usus* (line 4)
    c. *Oppianicus* (line 5)
    d. *familiarissime* (line 5)

6. In lines 5–6, everyone is said to know how
    a. friendship contributes to human nature
    b. friendship creates similar interests
    c. nature affects friendship more than interests do
    d. similar qualities help form friendships

7. In line 6, *illi* refers to
    a. an understood "you"
    b. Oppianicus
    c. the Fabricii brothers
    d. interests

8. In lines 6–8, Cicero says that the Fabricii brothers
    a. think monetary profit a disgraceful motive
    b. were the victims of fraud
    c. lived in disgrace
    d. cheated many people

9. In line 9, *improbitate* is ablative of
    a. cause
    b. manner
    c. means
    d. description

10. The tense and mood of *applicarat* (line 10) are
    a. present subjunctive
    b. imperfect subjunctive
    c. present indicative
    d. pluperfect indicative

11. From lines 9–10, we learn that Oppianicus
    a. worked for a long time to cultivate the friendship of the Fabricii
    b. tried for many years to avoid the Fabricii
    c. was long known to all for his dishonesty
    d. had long since become a member of the Fabricii family

12. Cicero's attitude toward the Fabricii brothers is one of
    a. respect
    b. disapproval
    c. indifference
    d. admiration

PASSAGE B

The hero Peleus finds the goddess Thetis on the seashore.

>   Est sinus Haemoniae curvos falcatus in arcus:
>   bracchia procurrunt, ubi, si foret altior unda,
>   portus erat (summis inductum est aequor harenis);
>   litus habet solidum, quod nec vestigia servet
> 5   nec remoretur iter, nec opertum pendeat alga.
>   Myrtea silva subest bicoloribus obsita bacis
>   et specus in medio (natura factus an arte,
>   ambiguum, magis arte tamen), quo saepe venire
>   frenato delphine sedens, Theti, nuda solebas.
> 10   Illic te Peleus, ut somno vincta iacebas,
>   occupat: et quoniam precibus temptata repugnas,
>   vim parat innectens ambobus colla lacertis.

Haemonia, -ae, f. *Thessaly* (a region of northern Greece)
falcatus, -a, -um, *curved, sickle-shaped*
remoror, -ari, -atus sum, *to detain, hinder*
operio, -ire, -ii, *opertusm, to cover*
alga, -ae, f. *seaweed*
myrteus, -a, -um, *of myrtle bushes*
obsitus, -a, -um, *overgrown, covered*
baca, -ae, f. *berry*
specus, -us, m. *cave*
freno, -are, -avi, -atum, *to bridle, curb*
repugno, -are, -avi, -atum, *to fight back against, oppose*
innecto, -ere, -nexui, -nexum, *to entwine*
collum, -i, n. *neck*
lacertus, -i, m. *arm*

1. From lines 1–2, we learn that
   a. Thetis wore a billowing hunting dress
   b. Thetis' arms extended from her flowing garment
   c. the beach was suitable for archery practice
   d. the shoreline formed a bay

2. The meaning of the words *si foret altior unda, portus erat* (lines 2–3) is
   a. if the water were deeper, there would be a port
   b. if the waves were higher, there would be a port
   c. if the wave would be deeper, there was a port
   d. if the water were higher, there was a port

3. Lines 4–5 tell us that
    a. soft sand covers the beach
    c. it is easy to walk on the shore
    b. Thetis' footsteps remain in the sand
    d. the footing does not serve the pedestrian

4. In line 5, *remoretur* is subjunctive in a(n)
    a. relative clause of characteristic
    c. relative clause of purpose
    b. indirect question
    d. jussive clause

5. In line 5, *opertum* describes
    a. *pendeat* (line 5)
    c. *solidum* (line 4)
    b. *litus* (line 4)
    d. *iter* (line 5)

6. Lines 6–8 suggest that people may have
    a. fashioned a cave in the rock
    c. painted the cave's walls
    b. planted myrtle to mark the cave
    d. harvested berries

7. A figure of speech that appears in lines 7–8 is
    a. chiasmus
    c. synecdoche
    b. hendiadys
    d. ellipsis

8. The speaker of the words *Theti, nuda solebas* (line 9) is
    a. Thetis
    c. the poet
    b. Peleus
    d. the dolphin

9. In line 10, *vincta* is a form of
    a. *vivo*
    c. *vincio*
    b. *vinco*
    d. *viso*

10. When Peleus saw Thetis, Thetis was
    a. riding on a dolphin
    c. taking the bridle off the dolphin
    b. sitting on the shore
    d. sleeping on the shore

11. The case and number of *colla* (line 12) are
    a. nominative singular
    c. accusative plural
    b. nominative plural
    d. ablative singular

12. The case of *lacertis* (line 12) is determined by
    a. *ambobus* (line 12)
    c. *colla* (line 12)
    b. *innectens* (line 12)
    d. *parat* (line 12)

13. The metrical pattern of the first four feet of line 7 (*et specus* . . . .) is
    a. dactyl-dactyl-spondee-spondee
    c. dactyl-spondee-spondee-spondee
    b. spondee-spondee-dactyl-dactyl
    d. dactyl-dactyl-spondee-dactyl

PASSAGE C

The Trojans journey over the sea.

Postquam altum tenuere rates nec iam amplius ullae
apparent terrae, caelum undique et undique pontus,
tum mihi caeruleus supra caput astitit imber
noctem hiememque ferens, et inhorruit unda tenebris.
5   continuo venti volvunt mare magnaque surgunt
aequora, dispersi iactamur gurgite vasto;
involvere diem nimbi et nox umida caelum
abstulit, ingeminant abruptis nubibus ignes.
excutimur cursu et caecis erramus in undis.
10 ipse diem noctemque negat discernere caelo
nec meminisse viae media Palinurus in unda.

caeruleus, -a, -um, *dark blue*
asto, -are, astiti, *to stand nearby*
continuo, *immediately*
involvo, -ere, involvi, involutum, *to envelop*
excutio, -ere, excussi, excussum, *to shake out, throw off*

1. From lines 1–4, we learn that rain appeared for Aeneas
   a. during the middle of winter
   b. in open sea
   c. in sight of land
   d. after it had detained the ships

2. A figure of speech in line 1 (*Postquam . . . ullae*) is
   a. hyperbole
   b. chiasmus
   c. tmesis
   d. metonymy

3. The metrical pattern of the first four feet of line 1 is
   a. spondee-dactyl-dactyl-spondee
   b. dactyl-dactyl-dactyl-spondee
   c. spondee-dactyl-dactyl-dactyl
   d. dactyl-spondee-dactyl-spondee

4. The case of *mihi* (line 3) is determined by
   a. *tum* (line 3)
   b. *supra* (line 3)
   c. *caeruleus* (line 3)
   d. *astitit* (line 3)

5. The word closest in meaning to *unda* (line 4) is
   a. *nimbus*
   b. *aqua*
   c. *fluctus*
   d. *hiems*

6. From line 4 we learn that
   a. the wave recoiled from the darkness
   b. the storm brought darkness
   c. the Trojans were sailing at night
   d. the rain bristled at the waves

7. The best translation of *iactamur* (line 6) is
   a. we hurl ourselves
   b. we are tossed
   c. we boast
   d. we cast

8. The form *involvere* (line 7) is
   a. present active infinitive
   b. present passive imperative
   c. future passive indicative
   d. perfect active indicative

9. The words *nox umida caelum abstulit* (lines 7–8) tell us that the
   a. storm obscured the sky
   b. sky was moist during the night
   c. night escaped with the sky
   d. humid sky retained sunlight

10. The subject of *negat* (line 10) is
    a. the storm
    b. Aeneas
    c. an understood *nox*
    d. Palinurus

11. The passage states that the ship's location was
    a. discerned by the stars
    b. unknown
    c. discerned by lightning flashes
    d. in a whirlpool

12. The case and number of *media* (line 11) are
    a. nominative singular
    b. accusative plural
    c. nominative plural
    d. ablative singular

13. The case of *viae* (line 11) is determined by
    a. *meminisse* (line 11)
    b. *unda* (line 11)
    c. *media* (line 11)
    d. *Palinurus* (line 11)

PASSAGE D

Catullus addresses his farm.

O funde noster seu Sabine seu Tiburs
(nam te esse Tiburtem autumant, quibus non est
cordi Catullum laedere; at quibus cordi est,
quovis Sabinum pignore esse contendunt),
5   sed seu Sabine sive verius Tiburs,
fui libenter in tua suburbana
villa, malamque pectore expuli tussim,
non inmerenti quam mihi meus venter,
dum sumptuosas appeto, dedit, cenas.
10   Nam, Sestianus dum volo esse conviva,
orationem in Antium petitorem
plenam veneni et pestilentiae legi.
Hic me gravido frigida et frequens tussis
quassavit usque, dum in tuum sinum fugi,
15   et me recuravi otioque et urtica.
Quare refectus maximas tibi grates
ago, meum quod non es ulta peccatum.

fundus, -i, m. *farm*
Sabinus, -a, -um, *Sabine* (of a modest hill district outside Rome)
Tiburs, -tis, *Tiburtine* (of modern Tivoli, a high-class district outside Rome)
autumo, -are, -avi, -atum, *to claim, assert*
quivis, quaevis, quodvis, *any one that you want, any at all*
pignus, pignoris, n. *pledge*
tussis, tussis, f. *cough*
inmerens, -ntis, *undeserving*
venter, ventris, m. *stomach*
sumptuosus, -a, -um, *expensive, luxurious*
petitor, -oris, m. *candidate for political office*
gravido, -dinis, f. *head cold*
quasso, -are, -avi, -atum, *to shake*
usque, *continually*
urtica, -ae, f. *nettle* (a weed often made into a medicinal tea)
ulciscor, -isci, ultus sum, *to punish, avenge*
peccatum, -i, n. *sin*

1.   The word *quibus* (line 2) refers to

    a. *funde* (line 1)   b. *Sabine* (line 1)

    c. *Tiburtem* (line 2)   d. the subject of *autumant* (line 2)

2. In line 3, the case of *cordi* is
   a. dative
   b. nominative
   c. genitive
   d. ablative

3. According to lines 2–4, Catullus is annoyed when people say that his farm
   a. is not fertile
   b. does not belong to him
   c. is Sabine
   d. is Tiburtine

4. The discussion of the farm in lines 1–5 is primarily concerned with
   a. whether or not it is convenient to Rome
   b. whether or not it is fashionable
   c. the beauty of its setting
   d. the size of its fields

5. In lines 1–6, the phrase in which Catullus tells how he felt about staying in the country is
   a. *te esse Tiburtem autumant* (line 2)
   b. *Catullum laedere* (line 3)
   c. *quovis . . . pignore esse contendunt* (line 4)
   d. *fui libenter in tua suburbana villa* (lines 6–7)

6. In line 7, *malam(que)* refers to
   a. Catullus' cough
   b. Catullus' indigestion
   c. the villa that Catullus had inherited
   d. a woman whom Catullus had forced to leave his villa

7. A figure of speech that appears in line 8 is
   a. asyndeton
   b. hyperbole
   c. litotes
   d. metonymy

8. The direct object of *dedit* (line 9) is
   a. *pectore* (line 7)
   b. *quam* (line 8)
   c. *venter* (line 8)
   d. *cenas* (line 9)

9. From line 10, we learn that
   a. Sestius wanted to come to Catullus' dinner party
   b. Catullus lived with Sestius for a while
   c. Catullus flew off to Sestius' house
   d. Sestius was hosting a dinner party

10. In lines 7–12 , Catullus describes the negative effect of Sestius' speech on him. Which of the following is another writer of whose work Catullus does not approve?
   a. Calvus
   b. Cinna
   c. Volusius
   d. Caecilius

11. In line 14, *dum* is translated
   a. although
   b. then
   c. until
   d. as long as

12. From lines 10–15, we can infer that

    a. the speech made Catullus sick

    b. a coughing fit made Catullus leave his farm

    c. Catullus was exiled because of politics

    d. Catullus suffered from chills because of the plague

13. In lines 16–17, we learn that Catullus

    a. is grateful to the farm for his recovery

    b. is guilty of having offended Antius

    c. thanks his friend for his help

    d. regrets his earlier behavior towards Sestius

ANSWER KEY

Passage A

1—b	2—d	3—a
4—c	5—b	6—d
7—c	8—d	9—a
10—d	11—a	12—b

Passage B

1—d	2—a	3—c
4—a	5—b	6—a
7—d	8—c	9—c
10—d	11—c	12—b
13—a		

Passage C

1—b	2—d	3—a
4—d	5—b	6—b
7—b	8—d	9—a
10—d	11—b	12—d
13—a		

Passage D

1—d	2—a	3—c
4—b	5—d	6—a
7—c	8—b	9—d
10—c	11—c	12—a
13—a		

TEACHER'S MANUAL APPENDICES

APPENDIX A
SAMPLE STUDENT ESSAYS ODE 1.5

Essay question, Horace *Ode 1.5*. Suggested time: 20 minutes.

Imagery of weather and seafaring are major elements of 1.5. In a short essay, discuss how the speaker uses this imagery to talk about Pyrrha's treatment of men and about the men's reactions to her treatment of them.

First sample

The complex relationship between lovers is often unpredictable and unstable. Thus, the speaker in Horace's *Ode 1.5* very appropriately uses images of weather and seafaring to describe the way Pyrrha treats men. As Pyrrha changes her treatment from clear, sunny skies to dark, stormy seas, the unsuspecting men lament their change in fortune. Yet the speaker suggests that when the storm is over, the survivor is the stronger for it.

The speaker presents Pyrrha's treatment of her present lover, a slender boy (gracilis . . . puer, line 1) and inexperienced (insolens, "unaccustomed," line 8), as a change from favor to violent conflict or even rejection. He depicts this change by the images of fair weather and a sudden storm. At first, flavam . . . comam, "blonde hair (line 4) amidst multa . . . rosa, "many a rose" (line 1) suggest fair, spring weather. Even Pyrrha herself is described as te . . . aurea, "golden you" (line 9), lovely and sweet to her new-found lover in the season of love. The golden sunshine, however, carries "aurae / fallacis," "deceitful breeze" (11–12), a hint of the storm that is brewing. The speaker's choice of fallacis suggests that Pyrrha, too, is deceitful in giving no hint that she will stormily turn on the boy. The sudden aspera / nigris aequora ventis, "seas harsh with black winds" (7–8) demonstrate her rapid destruction of all the boy's hopes for true love. In this way, we infer, Pyrrha breaks off the relationship.

The boy and anyone else who will see Pyrrha as charming (nites, "you gleam," line 13), are unfortunate (miseri, line 12), if they have no experience of her ways (intemptata, "untried," line 13). At first credulus, "trusting" (line 9), the boy enjoys Pyrrha's golden love and hopes, unknowing, sperat, nescius (11), that the relationship will always be so. When the storm hits, the inexperienced boy fidem mutatosque deos flebit, "will lament his faith and the changed gods" (5–6) and emirabitur insolens, "will wonder, unaccustomed" (8) at the storm. The synchysis and the implied transferred epithet (really the clouds are black) call attention to the violent and surprising mix-up of elements of the storm, just as Pyrrha's anger will be violent and surprising. Postponement of "unaccustomed," insolens, after the verb emphasizes this adjective and suggests that, even after the storm has broken (in the previous lines), the boy can't understand it.

Pyrrha's stormy temperament is a hard blow to the young, bewildered lover. Yet the speaker suggests that, however painful his own experience of Pyrrha may have been, he himself has undergone a transformation from inexperienced boy to weathered survivor. With uvida vestimenta, "wet clothes," 14–16, he has come out with experience and has turned it into his own offering potenti / . . . maris deo, "to the powerful god of the sea," 15–16. The image is of a survivor of a shipwreck, who dedicates the clothes in which he survived as a thank offering to the god who saved him. The favor he has gained with the god suggests that the shipwreck of his love affair has given him wisdom about romantic relationships in general.

By the grading scheme of this book, the authors would award a 6 to the essay.

Second sample

The complex relationship between lovers is often unpredictable and unstable. Thus, the speaker in Horace's *Ode 1.5* very appropriately uses images of weather and seafaring to describe Pyrrha's relationship with men. As Pyrrha changes her treatment from clear, sunny skies to dark, stormy seas, the unsuspecting men lament their change in fortune. Yet the speaker suggests that when the storm is over, the survivor is the stronger for the experience.

The speaker presents Pyrrha's treatment of men as a change from fair weather to sudden storm. At first, the images of blonde hair amidst many roses suggest fair, spring weather. Even Pyrrha herself is described as te . . . aurea, "you are golden" (line 9), lovely and sweet to her new-found lover in the season of love. The golden sunshine, however, carries aurae / fallacis," "deceitful breeze" (11–12), a hint of the storm that is brewing. The sudden aspera / nigris aequora ventis, "difficult seas with black winds" (7–8) demonstrate her rapid destruction of all the men's hopes for true love. In this way, Pyrrha breaks off the relationship.

The men, on the other side of Pyrrha's storm, undergo a transformation from inexperienced boys to weathered men. At first credulus, "trusting" (line 9), each of Pyrrha's lovers enjoys her golden love and "hopes, unknowing" that the relationship will always be so. When the storm hits, the inexperienced boy fidem mutatosque deos flebit and emirabitur insolens at the storm. However, the speaker shows that the men will survive. Although with uvida vestimenta, "wet clothes," 14–16, he has come out with the experience and has turned it into his own offering potenti / . . . maris deo, "to the powerful god of the sea," 15–16.

Pyrrha's stormy temperament is a hard blow to her lovers. Yet the speaker suggests that, however painful this experience may have been, he has grown stronger from it. Indeed, he has gained knowledge of Pyrrha and her ways, and he now has some favor with the god of the sea, suggesting that the relationship has given him a better understanding of relationships in general. Pyrrha, on the other hand, is intemptata, "untested" (13), and may always remain stuck in her unhappy storm.

The authors would award the essay a 5. It offers less analysis, less Latin support correctly cited, shows less mastery of the Latin, and does not account for some important parts of the passage.

Third sample

Horace in this poem uses images of weather and seafaring to describe the way Pyrrha treats men. As Pyrrha changes her treatment from clear, sunny skies to dark, stormy seas, the unsuspecting men lament their change in fortune. Yet the speaker suggests that when the storm is over, the survivor is the stronger for the experience.

The speaker presents Pyrrha's treatment of men as a change from fair weather to sudden storm. At first, she unties her blonde hair amidst many roses in fair, spring weather. Pyrrha is te . . . aurea, "you are golden" (line 9), lovely and sweet to her new-found lover in the season of love. The golden sunshine, however, carries aurae / fallacis," "deceitful breeze" (11–12), a hint of the storm that is brewing. The sudden, difficult seas with black winds demonstrate her rapid destruction of all the men's hopes for true love. In this way, Pyrrha breaks off the relationship. Each of Pyrrha's lovers enjoys her golden love and hopes that the relationship will always be so. When the storm hits, the inexperienced boy fidem mutatosque deos flebit and emirabitur insolens at the storm. However, the speaker shows that the men will survive. Although with uvida vestimenta, "wet clothes," 14–16, he has come out with the experience and has turned it into his own offering potenti / . . . maris deo, "to the powerful god of the sea," 15–16. However painful this experience may have been, he has gained knowledge of Pyrrha and her ways.

The authors would award the essay a 4. It is more descriptive than analytical, offers minimal, correct Latin support, and leaves out some relevant parts of the passage.

Fourth sample

Pyrrha at first has blonde hair amidst many roses. Pyrrha is described as te . . . aurea, "you are golden" (line 9). They are happy and pleased in their cave, grato . . . antro. The golden sunshine, however, carries "aurae / fallacis," "deceitful breeze" (11–12), a hint of the storm that is brewing. The sudden harsh black seas with winds demonstrate her rapid destruction of all the men's hopes for true love. In this way, Pyrrha breaks off the relationship.

The men undergo a transformation from inexperienced boys to weathered men. Each of Pyrrha's lovers enjoys her golden love and "hopes, unknowing" that the relationship will always be so. When the storm hits, the inexperienced boy fidem mutatosque deos flebit and emirabitur insolens at the storm. However, the speaker shows that the men will survive. Although with uvida vestimenta, "dripping clothes," 14–16, he has come out with the experience and has turned it into his own offering potenti / . . . maris deo, "to the god of the powerful sea," 15–16. He is happy because Neptune saved him. He knows not to be tricked by Pyrrha again.

The authors would award the essay a 3. It offers a superficial treatment of the question. Latin support is scanty, sometimes irrelevant, and not well translated.

Fifth sample

Pyrrha likes to untie her blonde hair, and she is surrounded by a large rose bush. She is described as te . . . aurea, "you are golden" (line 9). Pyrrha is a master of perfumes (antro) and odors (odoribus), which her lover brings her. She wants him to relax, but he urges her (urget) and weeps (flebit) because she is bored by the simple life (simplex) of "carpe diem." He does not know that a storm is brewing. The sudden aspera / nigris aequora ventis, "difficult seas with black winds" (7–8) symbolize her rapid destruction of his hopes for true love. In this way, Pyrrha breaks off the relationship.

The man, on the other hand, will survive. Although with uvida vestimenta, he has come out with the experience. Pyrrha, on the other hand, is intemptata, and may always remain stuck in her unhappy storm.

The authors would award the essay a 2. It is vague and faulty, offering only pieces of correct information but betraying no understanding of how to apply the question to the poem. There are only a few pieces of Latin support correctly translated and cited.

Sixth sample

Pyrrha likes to untie her blonde hair, and she is surrounded by a large rose bush. She is described as te . . . aurea, "you are golden" (line 9). Pyrrha is a master of perfumes (antro), which her lover brings her. She wants him to relax, but he urges her (urget) to love the simple life of "carpe diem." When a storm comes (aequora), he does not know what to do. He sails out to sea in his little boat but then goes too close to the shore and is wrecked. The little boat symbolizes Charon's skiff that takes you to the Underworld. That is where souls have to lay down their clothes (uvida vestimenta). The moral of the poem is, we all have to die, so SEIZE THE DAY and spend it with a beautiful girl.

The authors would award a 1 to the essay. Almost nothing correct thing is said and supported that is relevant to the question.

Seventh sample

Pyrrha treats men like storms and the sea. She "urges" (urget, line 2) them to give her fine things like perfumes. She cried, flebit, because her lover does not love the simple life of "carpe diem." When a storm comes (aequora), she does not know what to do. Then she turns around and acts nice again, just like the sky turning color. By the end of the poem, Horace indicates (indicat, line 14) that she will grow old like everyone else. That will be the end of the relationship.

The authors would award a 0 to the essay. Nothing is correct that is supported from the Latin, relevant to the question, and that cannot simply be derived from the prompt of the question itself. Random Latin words correctly translated by themselves do not amount to correct material in the context of the question.

APPENDIX B
SAMPLE STUDENT ESSAYS ODE 2.3

The following are actual student essays written in response to the long essay question on *Ode 2.3*. Students took the test in class and spent roughly 20 minutes—the time suggested—on this question. The authors concur with the classroom teacher on the grading.

First sample

In *Ode 2.3*, Horace provides his addressee, Dellius, with a paraenesis of living in accord with the "golden mean," so to speak, and enjoying the days while they last, themes common to his other odes. By referring to many objects connotated with nature, Horace successfully develops these ideas about life.

The first stanza lays out Horace's proposition. He calls Dellius "moriture" (line 4) or "about to die," reminding Dellius of the fate that is destined for all humankind. Horace also writes, "aequam . . . laetitia" (lines 1–4), or "Remember to keep an equal mind in hard times, not otherwise a (mind) tempered from insolent happiness in good times." This advice is reminiscent of the "aurea mediocritas" (golden mean) of *Ode 2.10*.

With the proposition having been laid out, Horace proceeds with his allusions to nature in the second stanza. He provides two contrasting images: "whether you will have lived wretchedly for all time" (line 5) or recline through festive days (holidays) on remote grass (lines 6–7). The reference to "gramine" is interesting since grass is considered to be rare in the Mediterranean. Thus "remote grass on holidays" effectively conveys the value of such an experience. Of course, as he often does with sympoticon poems, Horace slips in a reference to wine in line 8, "with the inner sign of Falernian (wine)," further emphasizing the worth of this enjoyable experience, which only exists in the present life.

The third stanza poses two rhetorical questions, both of which have to do with nature. Firstly, Horace asks, "for whom do the huge pine tree and the white poplar tree love to unite a hospitable shade with their branches?" (lines 9–10). This rhetorical question is rich, with a schema Horatianum (the trees) and amatory vocabulary ("amant" and "consociare"). The trees are, in effect, engaged in human behavior, uniting in love. Like trees, Dellius must also appreciate the joys of life. Horace then asks, "Why does the fleeing stream work to hurry in a zigzagged stream?" (lines 11–12). Like the imagery invoked by the trees, the stream carries itself in a manner which can be related to human experience: the stream flees just as time flies, so time must be cherished.

Horace then orders Dellius with an imperative in the fourth stanza. He writes, "Order (someone) to bring here wines and perfumes and short-lived flowers of a rose" (lines 13–14). This tricolon crescens refers to temporal objects that can only be enjoyed in this life. The wines remind one of the Falernian wine of the second stanza and the flowers are short-lived just as life is short-lived. Horace reminds Dellius of his fate by referring in another tricolon crescens to "things and age and the black threads of the three sisters" (lines 15–16).

Horace asks Dellius to cherish life and like his "carpe diem" poem, to make the most of each day, a lesson to be learned by observing the natural world around him.

An excellent response, well-organized and balanced. It accounts for the whole passage. Mastery of the Latin is evident. The student analyzed the text insightfully in response to the question. The authors would award it a 6 by the grading criteria set forth in this workbook.

Second sample

In Horace's time, the natural world served as a contrast to the more ordered world of everyday life. His advice to Dellius, who was deeply enmeshed in politics, is full of nature references to draw him back to Horace's eternal message to enjoy life now, because you can never be sure if there will be a tomorrow.

The first nature reference is in lines 6–8, where Horace recommends spending a festive day in a far-off field with high-quality wine. The image of a field as an isolated but calm location occurs frequently, and mentioning wine is extremely common. Lines 9–11 ("quo pinus . . . ramis?") conjure up the image of two trees, one light and slender, the other dark and large, entwining branches and shadows happily. The image shows trees enjoying the moment as a way to make Dellius enjoy the moment as well. The last two lines in the second stanza, "quid oblique . . . rivo," shows water in a river rushing through a hectic life but with no particular goal mentioned; this symbolizes the way most people rush through life without stopping to enjoy it. The final stanza ushers in the symposium: in lines 13–14, Horace commands someone to bring in wine, perfume, and flowers, which were used to make garlands for the drinkers, and were usually dead by the end of the party. This light and cheerful reference to a common memento mori, coupled with Dellius being addressed as "moriture Delli" in line 4, serves as a reminder that death is imminent, so life should be enjoyed now.

A strong response of a bit less depth of analysis and development than the one above, especially with regard to how Horace's language produces its effects. Although the student evidently understands the Latin, not all Latin references are translated or paraphrased closely enough to show this. The authors would award this essay a 5.

Third sample

In this ode, Horace speaks of living life leisurely and without haste, advice which he believes will make life happier. Opening the poem with paraenesis, Horace is giving advice on how to appease the wearied mind of Dellius, by telling him to envelop himself in nature so that he can relax. Starting off with a physical aspect of Dellius, his "mentem" or mind, Horace then gradually moves on to concrete nature imagery. Horace reminds Dellius to "servare aequam mentem rebus in arduis," or "to keep a level head in difficult circumstances." Dellius like everyone will die someday, and so life must be lived pleasurably. In first describing Dellius' mind as "held back from unaccustomed joy" (lines 3–4) and then reminding him that he will eventually die (moriture Delli), Horace uses juxtaposition well between the first two stanzas.

In stanza two, whether Dellius physically or mentally leads a sad life (line 5), or whether he happily reclines in a remote field (lines 6–7), the "moriture Delli" of line 4 still holds true. Horace advises Dellius to choose the latter of the two hypotheticals, and to enjoy nature. So, with the paraenesis in the first stanza over, Horace brings sympotic imagery and nature imagery as further advice (lines 6–8).

In stanza three Horace addresses why the "drink and relax in nature" image of the previous stanza is ideally suited for life by posing questions concerning the natural flux of action (in nature). Horace uses nature imagery to support his advice: "why live life this way? Why things in nature do what they do?" Horace first asks why two different trees the "pinus ingens" and the "alba populus" (an example of schema horatianum) love to give shade with their branches. Horace then asks why fast waters labor themselves to flow in winding rivers. These two nature images illustrate Horace's idea that life should be lived in leisure/shade and not in haste, but slowed down (no rushing [fugax] in "obliquo rivo").

In stanza 4, Horace continues his sympotic and natural imagery by continuing the paraenesis; telling Dellius (imperatively, "iube") to order someone to bring "wine and perfumes and the too-short flowers" so that he may continue leisurely. The "nimium brevis flores" parallels Horace's idea that life is too short within his nature imagery.

Although this essay demonstrates good understanding of the passage, it is more descriptive than analytical. Some references to the Latin are not translated or are not accompanied by quotation of the Latin or line numbers. The authors would judge this essay to fall toward the top of the 4 range.

Fourth sample

Horace brilliantly uses nature in poem 2.3 to convince Dellius that life would be better if he would simply take his time and enjoy the finer things in life. It is clear through his choice of words and in the structure that Horace has tackled with symposiums before.

In the first stanza, rather than immediately going off into natural references, he begins with his advice. He tells Dellius in lines 1–3 to keep a level mind in both good and bad times and ends the stanza with "moriture Delli" or "(you) Dellius who are about to die." By doing so, Horace ends his first stanza with a hint to the overall moral of the poem: death is inevitable. By placing this short phrase in the end, he emphasizes the words and their meaning.

Moving on to the next stanza, Horace begins to talk about nature, referring to it in very pleasing ways. He states "seu te in remoto gramine per dies festos reclinatum bearis," which means "or whether you will make yourself happy having reclined in remote grass through the holidays." Lines 2 and 3 of this stanza, when juxtaposed with the first thought, which basically says "whether you will have lived sad in all time" (seu maestus omni tempore vixeris) leads the reader to associate happiness (bearis) with nature (reclinatum remoto gramine). By linking the two ideas together, one would think it a very persuasive use of structuring the stanza. Horace also surrounds the "remoto gramine" with pleasing words such as "dies festos" or "holidays" and "bearis" or "you will have made yourself happy." This emphasizes the theory that with nature and all its glory comes happiness.

Furthermore, in the following stanza the poet continues to refer to nature with the best of terms. He begins the stanza with "quo pinus ingens albaque populus umbram hospitalem consociare amant ramis?" or "for what purpose do the huge pine and white poplar love to join together the hospitable shade with (their) branches?" Already, Horace is personifying the trees with the use of "amant" and the feeling he choosing to describe the trees with is love, a very positive angle to go with when you want to convince someone of the greatness of something, like nature in this case. Moreover, Horace describes the shade produced by the trees as hospitable, which makes them seem welcoming in addition to loving.

Last, but not least, Horace concludes the poem with a stanza that also puts into contrast two ideas and clearly vilifies one of the images. He says "huc vina et unguenta et nimium brevis flores amoenae ferre iube rosae," or "order (someone) to bring here wine and perfume and the too-brief flowers of the pleasing rose." Here, once again Horace adorns nature with beautiful, appeasing imagery that would entice anyone. He mentions not only the "pleasing roses," but along with them, wine and perfume, which are essential to enjoyment and lounging and appreciating life. In contrast, Horace blatantly makes the later image less appealing by using words like "atra" or "black" and "aetas" which refer to old age, again alluding to death.

Essentially, once again Horace uses his skill of persuasion consisting of elements of appropriate word choice and tactful structure to create a poem that successfully uses nature to promote life enjoyment.

This essay demonstrates a good understanding of the passage and the question. It omits the image of the brook (lines 11–12) and, although it mentions references to death in the poem, it does not work them into the analysis. Treatment of the last stanza is more descriptive than analytical. The authors would award this essay a 5.

Fifth sample

This ode to Dellius is an example of paraenesis in which Horace gives advice to Dellius. He speaks of the beauty of life and the inevitability of death and encourages Dellius to find balance, or the golden mean, in life and to enjoy an Epicurean symposium. He uses images of nature to convey his message about life.

Horace begins by telling Dellius to maintain the middle ground in life; to keep a level mind in difficult circumstances and a mind held back from unaccustomed joy in good ones (lines 1–4). He contrasts the two extremes of people that Dellius may take after, either one who is always sad (line 5) or one who has made himself happy "in remoto gramine per dies festos reclinatum interiore nota Falerni," having reclined on remote grass through festive days with the inner label of Falernian wine. This is an image of a quiet, peaceful, restful place, conveyed by the adjective remote and the images of grass, where a person can enjoy wine on festive days.

Horace continues with the two rhetorical questions about nature, asking for what purpose a huge pine and white poplar love to unite a hospitable shadow with their branches, and why a fleeing water labors to hurry in a slanting stream (lines 9–12). The first image of the pine and poplar implies through a schema Horatianum dark, huge pine and a slender, white poplar. This image is one of a locus amoenus or pleasing place in which there is a hospitable shadow, or literally, a shadow for a guest to lay and relax. It also conveys a sexual image through the uniting of the branches of the two trees. Thus, life is meant to be enjoyed in a pleasant spot like this. The second image of the fleeing water suggests the brevity of life and the inevitability of death with the river hurrying. This provides more support for why Dellius should follow the Epicurean advice and enjoy a sympotic moment.

The following stanza lists the items necessary for the symposium, including wine, perfume, and roses. Horace refers to the roses as "nimium brevis flores amoenae . . . rosae," the too brief flowers of the pleasing rose, as roses are beautiful but wilt by the end of the symposium. This again brings to light the theme of death and man's inability to avoid it. Thus Dellius should enjoy the pleasing rose for the moment in a symposium before it too dies. Horace concludes the stanza enforcing this point: "dum res et aetas et sororum fila trium patiuntur," while circumstance and age and the black threads of the three sisters allow.

Thus Horace conveys his advice to Dellius in this ode through the use of natural imagery to enjoy the moment because his life is brief, as he is "Dellius moriture," Dellius about to die, and death is swift and inevitable.

The authors would award a 6 to this essay. It develops an insightful analysis of how nature imagery throughout the poem helps Horace convey advice about life, and its mastery and use of Latin support is superior.

APPENDIX C
REVIEW TESTS AND ANSWERS

These practice review tests are provided for you to assess students' mastery as they review the poems listed for each test. Alternatively, feel free to pick and choose questions from different practice tests and combine them in any order. You may xerox these practice test questions for classroom use. To do so, set the copy machine to enlarge by 125%. A scoring key is given in the pages immediately following each practice test.

Each review test is broken into two parts. The first part is a multiple choice section of 15 minutes. The suggested aggregate time for the questions in the second, free-response section is 35 minutes of writing. Allow five minutes as a reading period before the students may begin answering the free-response questions. This practice will accustom them to the 15-minute reading period that precedes the free-response section of the Advanced Placement Exams.

You can establish a rough correspondence between the grading scale of the Advanced Placement Exams and that of one of these practice tests by weighting the multiple choice section 40% of the total score, and the full free-response section 60%. You will come close to the proportionate weights of the several questions on the free-response section of the Advanced Placement Exams if you value the translation and short-answer questions 30% each, and the essay, 40%, of the free-response section.

REVIEW TEST 1
SATIRE 1.9, ODES 1.1, 1.5, 1.9, 1.11, 1.13

I. Multiple Choice *Suggested time: 15 minutes*

The Sibyl offers to sell her books of prophecies to King Tarquinius Superbus of Rome.

> Anus hospita atque incognita ad Tarquinium Superbum regem adiit
> novem libros ferens, quos esse dicebat divina oracula; eos velle
> venundare. Tarquinius pretium percontatus est. Mulier nimium atque
> immensum poposcit; rex, quasi anus aetate desiperet, derisit. Tum
> 5   illa foculum coram cum igni apponit, tres libros ex novem deurit et,
> ecquid reliquos sex eodem pretio emere vellet, regem interrogavit.
> Sed enim Tarquinius id multo risit magis dixitque anum iam procul
> dubio delirare. Mulier ibidem statim tres alios libros exussit atque
> id ipsum denuo placide rogat, ut tres reliquos eodem illo pretio emat.
> 10 Tarquinius ore iam serio atque attentiore animo fit. Libros tres reliquos
> mercatur nihilo minore pretio, quam quod erat petitum pro omnibus.

Aulus Gellius, Noctes Atticae, I.19

anus, -us, f. - *old woman*
hospita, -ae, f. - *foreigner, stranger*
venundo, -are, -dedi, -datus - *to put up for sale*
percontor, -ari, -atus sum - *to inquire*
desipio, -ere - *to act foolishly*
foculum, -i, n. - *stove*
coram - *in (his) presence*
ecquid - *whether*
deliro, -are - *to be crazy*
serius, -a, -um - *serious*

1.   Line 1 states that the old woman was

      a. hospitable   b. in disguise

      c. unknown   d. ignorant

2.   The case of *eos* (line 2) is determined by

      a. *velle*   b. *dicebat*

      c. *quos*   d. *venundare*

3. In line 2, *oracula* is
   - a. accusative plural
   - b. nominative singular
   - c. ablative singular
   - d. nominative plural

4. In line 4, *aetate* is ablative of
   - a. cause
   - b. means
   - c. description
   - d. specification

5. The word *cum* (line 5) is translated
   - a. both
   - b. although
   - c. with
   - d. when

6. In line 5, the woman
   - a. put the stove in the fire
   - b. rewrote three books
   - c. burned three books
   - d. set three books on the ground

7. *vellet* (line 6) is subjunctive in a clause of
   - a. indirect statement
   - b. purpose
   - c. indirect question
   - d. potentiality

8. In line 7, the king laughed because
   - a. he was delirious with old age
   - b. the woman appeared older than she was
   - c. of the woman's large size
   - d. the woman asked for too much money

9. The best translation of *ut* (line 9) is
   - a. as
   - b. in order to
   - c. how
   - d. that

10. *id ipsum*, line 9, refers to
    - a. the book
    - b. the stove
    - c. the offer of sale
    - d. the fire

11. A figure of speech in line 10 is
    - a. hyperbole
    - b. chiasmus
    - c. apostrophe
    - d. ellipsis

12. In line 11, *omnibus* refers to
    - a. the books
    - b. the merchants
    - c. the gods
    - d. the citizens

13. From this passage we learn that
    - a. the sibyl was unwise
    - b. Tarquinius despised prophecy
    - c. the gods punish the proud
    - d. the state paid for oracles

II. Free Response Section
Reading Period *Suggested time: 5 minutes*

Read over the questions and begin planning your answers. You may make notes to yourself on the test sheet, but do not begin writing your answers until told to do so.

IIA. Translation *Suggested time: 5 minutes*

> Quis multa gracilis te puer in rosa
> perfusus liquidis urget odoribus
> grato, Pyrrha, sub antro?
> cui flavam religas comam
>
> simplex munditiis?

Ode 1.5.1–5

Translate the passage as literally as possible.

IIB. Short Analysis Questions *Suggested time: 10 minutes*

> Vides ut alta stet nive candidum
> Soracte, nec iam sustineant onus
> silvae laborantes geluque
> flumina constiterint acuto?
>
> 5 dissolve frigus ligna super foco
> large reponens atque benignius
> deprome quadrimum Sabina,
> o Thaliarche, merum diota.

Ode 1.9.1–8

1. Copy and translate two Latin phrases in lines 2–4 and explain how they set the time of year of the scene depicted in the first stanza.

2. Copy and scan line 5 and name the meter.

3. What action is Thaliarchus told to perform with the command *benignius . . . diota* (lines 6–8)? Support your answer with evidence from the Latin.

4. Name a figure of speech that appears in lines 6–8 and copy the Latin words that contain it.

IIC. Essay *Suggested time: 20 minutes*

> . . . 'Maecenas quomodo tecum?'
> hinc repetit, 'paucorum hominum et mentis bene sanae;
> nemo dexterius fortuna est usus. haberes
> magnum adiutorem, posset qui ferre secundas,
> 5   hunc hominem velles si tradere. dispeream, ni
> summosses omnis.' 'non isto vivimus illic,
> quo tu rere, modo. domus hac nec purior ulla est,
> nec magis his aliena malis. nil mi officit, inquam,
> ditior hic aut est quia doctior: est locus uni
> 10   cuique suus.' 'magnum narras, vix credibile.' 'atqui
> sic habet.' 'accendis, quare cupiam magis illi
> proximus esse.' 'velis tantummodo: quae tua virtus,
> expugnabis, et est, qui vinci possit, eoque
> difficilis aditus primos habet.' 'haud mihi dero:
> 15   muneribus servos corrumpam; non, hodie si
> exclusus fuero, desistam; tempora quaeram,
> occurram in triviis, deducam. nil sine magno
> vita labore dedit mortalibus.'

Satire 1.9.43–60

One of the traditional functions of satire is to present moral values, often by mocking those who fail to display those values. In the passage above, Horace represents himself and the unwanted companion discussing Horace's friend, Maecenas. In a short, well-organized essay, show how this section of dialogue implies beliefs about values that should be present in friendship.

Support your assertions with references to the Latin text **throughout** the passage. All Latin words must be copied or their line numbers provided, AND they must be translated or paraphrased closely enough so that it is clear you understand the Latin. It is your responsibility to convince your reader that you are basing your conclusions on the Latin text and not merely on a general recollection of the passage. Direct your answer to the question; do not merely summarize the passage.

REVIEW TEST 1: ANSWERS

I. Multiple Choice Questions

1—c	2—d	3—a
4—a	5—c	6—c
7—c	8—d	9—d
10—c	11—b	12—a
13—d		

IIA. Translation

8 chunks. One point per chunk.

Quis ... gracilis ... puer	**what slender/thin boy**
multa ... in rosa	**among many a rose/many roses**
perfusus liquidis ... odoribus	**poured over/drenched/doused with liquid odors/perfumes**
te urget ... Pyrrha	**presses upon/pushes you Pyrrha**
grato ... sub antro	**beneath/under/in a pleasing cave/grotto**
cui ... religas	**for whom do you tie back/fasten/untie**
flavam ... comam	**(your) yellow/blond/auburn hair**
simplex munditiis	**simple in/with (your) elegance/neatness**

IIB. Short Answer Questions.

Eight points total.

1. **Four points.**

   One point for each of two Latin phrases copied and translated:
   sustineant ... laborantes **(and) laboring woods (no longer) sustain/hold up their load/burden**
   gelu ... acuto **(and) rivers have stood still with sharp cold/chill**

   One point for each explanation of how the respective phrase sets the time of year as winter: tree branches hold up snow or ice rivers are frozen

2. **Two points.**

   One point for correctly copying and scanning the line:

   – – ∪ – – – ∪ ∪ – ∪ ×
   dissolve frigus ligna super foco

   One point for naming meter as Alcaic.

3. One point for explaining Thaliarchus' task as to bring forth (four-year-old pure) wine in/from a Sabine jar

4. One point for figure of speech with corresponding Latin:
   synchysis: *quadrimum Sabina . . . merum diota*

IIC. Essay

Grade on scale of 0–6.

The student is asked to discuss values that should be present in friendship, as they are implied in the passage. This task involves defining these values and analyzing the text to show how it implies beliefs about them. Because the student is asked to draw references from the whole passage, a competent paper should discuss the speakers' main points. One possible scheme of friendship values implied in the passage: A. friendship is not primarily for furthering one's career, and unwanted companion is wrong to think so; B. friends respect each person for moral qualities, not position or accomplishments; C. unlike the unwanted companion, friends do not disrespect each others' wishes or scruples or make themselves obnoxious. Features of dialogue like word choice, tone, and logic provide material for analysis. Superior essays will demonstrate mastery of the Latin throughout the passage in support of lucid argument about values that the passage implies should exist in friendship. Discerning students may also call into question the values of the two interlocutors. For example, they may point out how the "Horace" character, despite his surface politeness, allows his unwanted companion to convince himself to plan mercenary overtures toward Maecenas; this behavior might conceivably expose Maecenas to annoyance, and it falsely encourages the interlocutor to see Horace as a friend. Essays that earn a grade of 4 may rely more on description, may display inferential thinking but fail to make conclusions explicit (e.g., may characterize the unwanted companion's values but fail to show how they are depicted as faulty), may leave out sections of the passage, and tend to offer less Latin support.

6 – A fully-developed essay, which discusses how the characters' words reveal their values about friendship. The student makes ample reference to specific aspects of the Latin text to support his or her analysis and position. Latin references are properly cited. Even though there may be occasional mistakes, the discussion is coherent and of high quality.

5 – A strong essay. Although the piece has good analysis of values that the passage implies should operate toward friendship, it is not as fully developed nor as supported with references to the text as a paper receiving a 6. Latin references are properly cited. The essay reflects familiarity with the poem. A few parts of the passage may receive thin treatment.

4 – A competent response. There may be uneven development of the two characters' implied values. Although they are limited in quantity, the essay includes accurate and relevant Latin references to support its arguments. The discussion may rely more on recounting what the characters say than on uncovering their value commitments about friendship, or it may point out bad values without drawing from them implied, approved values. Some parts of the passage may be glossed over or omitted.

3 – A limited response. The Latin support is weak and/or inappropriate. Latin references are not properly cited. The answer is descriptive and does not reach the level of analysis. Alternatively, some papers may offer a good, analytical essay without any correct citations of Latin to support the argument.

2 – Some understanding of the poem, but the essay is general and/or vague. The discussion is flawed. The Latin cited demonstrates very limited comprehension.

1 – An incoherent response. While it does contain some relevant information, no substantive argument is presented. The student demonstrates no understanding of the poem.

0 – A response that is off-topic, completely incorrect, or irrelevant. Responses that merely restate the question are also a 0.

REVIEW TEST 2
ODES 1.22, 1.23, 1.24, 1.25, 1.37, 2.3, 2.7

I. Multiple Choice Questions *Suggested time: 15 minutes*

While the Trojans are killing animals for a feast, the Harpies, birds with the heads of women, fly down and seize the food.

    Huc ubi delati portus intravimus, ecce
laeta boum passim campis armenta videmus
caprigenumque pecus nullo custode per herbas.
Inruimus ferro et divos ipsumque vocamus
5   in partem praedamque Iovem; tum litore curvo
exstruimusque toros dapibusque epulamur opimis.
At subitae horrifico lapsu de montibus adsunt
Harpyiae et magnis quatiunt clangoribus alas,
diripiuntque dapes contactuque omnia foedant
10   immundo; tum vox taetrum dira inter odorem.

Vergil, *Aeneid 3.219–228*

armentum, -i, n. - *herd*
caprigenus, -a, -um - *goat(-born)*
daps, -is, f. - *sacrificial feast*
epulor, -ari, -atus sum - *to feast*
opimus, -a, -um - *rich, sumptuous*
quatio, -ere, quassus - *to shake*
foedo, -are, avi, atus - *to defile, pollute*
immundus, -a, -um - *unclean*
taeter, -tra, -trum - *foul*

1. From line 1 we can infer that the Trojans have entered
   - a. the city gates
   - b. a harbor
   - c. wide plains
   - d. after a delay

2. The case of *armenta* (line 2) is determined by
   - a. *laeta*
   - b. *boum*
   - c. *campis*
   - d. *videmus*

3. The case and number of *pecus* (line 3) are
   - a. nominative singular
   - b. accusative plural
   - c. accusative singular
   - d. nominative plural

4. *inruimus ferro* in line 4 is translated
   a. we fall upon the sword
   b. we rush for iron
   c. we hasten to carry
   d. we fall upon them with the sword

5. *Iovem* (line 5) has the same grammatical relationship to *vocamus* (line 4), as does
   a. *divos* (line 4)
   b. *ipsum* (line 4)
   c. *partem* (line 5)
   d. *praedam* (line 5)

6. *partem praedamque* (line 5) is an instance of
   a. prolepsis
   b. pleonasm
   c. zeugma
   d. hendiadys

7. In line 5, *litore* is ablative
   a. of place where
   b. of place from which
   c. absolute
   d. of manner

8. The metrical pattern of the first four feet of line 7 is
   a. dactyl-spondee-spondee-spondee
   b. spondee-spondee-dactyl-spondee
   c. dactyl-dactyl-spondee-spondee
   d. dactyl-dactyl-dactyl-spondee

9. *subitae* (line 7) modifies
   a. *Harpyiae* (line 8)
   b. an implied *nos*
   c. *lapsu* (line 7)
   d. *alas* (line 8)

10. From line 8 we learn that the Harpies
    a. sing with sad voices
    b. have noisy wings
    c. attack many troops
    d. were exiled from the mountains

11. A figure of speech in line 10 is
    a. hyperbole
    b. polysyndeton
    c. metaphor
    d. synchysis

12. The case and number of *dira* (line 10) are
    a. nominative plural
    b. accusative plural
    c. nominative singular
    d. ablative singular

13. The best translation of *tum . . . odorem* (line 10) is
    a. while their frightful voices make a foul sound amidst the odor
    b. then amidst the terrifying odor was a foul sound
    c. when the dire voice sounded among the foul odor
    d. then there was a fearsome voice amidst the foul odor

II. Free Response Section
Reading Period *Suggested time: 5 minutes*

Read over the questions and begin planning your answers. You may make notes to yourself on the test sheet, but do not begin writing your answers until told to do so.

IIA. Translation *Suggested time: 5 minutes*

> namque me silva lupus in Sabina,
> dum meam canto Lalagen et ultra
> terminum curis vagor expeditis,
> fugit inermem
>
> *Ode 1.22.9–12*

Translate the passage as literally as possible.

IIB. Short Analysis Questions *Suggested time: 10 minutes*

> Aequam memento rebus in arduis
> servare mentem, non secus in bonis
> ab insolentia temperatam
> laetitia, moriture Delli,
>
> 5   seu maestus omni tempore vixeris,
> seu te in remoto gramine per dies
> festos reclinatum bearis
> interiore nota Falerni.
>
> *Ode 2.3.1–8*

1. What are two things the poet tells Dellius to do in lines 1–4?

2. What is the significance of the adjective *moriture* (line 4) within the first stanza of this poem (lines 1–4)?

3. Briefly explain the contrast introduced by the words *seu . . . seu* in lines 5–8.

4. Copy and scan line 6 and name the meter.

5. Explain the meaning of *interiore nota Falerni* (line 8).

IIC. Essay *Suggested time: 20 minutes*

accipiter velut
mollis columbas aut leporem citus
 venator in campis nivalis
  Haemoniae, daret ut catenis

5 fatale monstrum, quae generosius
perire quaerens nec muliebriter
 expavit ensem, nec latentis
  classe cita reparavit oras,

ausa et iacentem visere regiam
10 voltu sereno, fortis et asperas
 tractare serpentes, ut atrum
  corpore combiberet venenum.

deliberata morte ferocior:
saevis Liburnis scilicet invidens
15 privata deduci superbo
  non humilis mulier triumpho.

Ode 1.37.17–32

Many readers detect in this passage a remarkably strong tone toward Cleopatra. In a short, well-organized essay, discuss the tone or attitude toward Cleopatra displayed in the passage and show how Horace conveys it.

Support your assertions with references to the Latin text throughout the passage. All Latin words must be copied or their line numbers provided, AND they must be translated or paraphrased closely enough so that it is clear you understand the Latin. It is your responsibility to convince your reader that you are basing your conclusions on the Latin text and not merely on a general recollection of the passage. Direct your answer to the question; do not merely summarize the passage.

REVIEW TEST 2: ANSWERS

I. Multiple Choice Questions

1—b	2—d	3—c
4—d	5—a	6—d
7—a	8—c	9—a
10—b	11—d	12—c
13—d		

IIA. Translation

9 chunks. One point per chunk.

namque	**for in fact/for in truth/for**
me . . . inermem	**(from) me (while I was) unarmed (must be object of fugit)**
silva . . . in Sabina	**in the Sabine woods/forest**
lupus . . . fugit	**a wolf . . . fled (must be perfect tense)**
dum . . . canto	**while I was singing (of)**
meam . . . Lalagen	**my Lalage**
et . . . vagor	**and (I was) wandering/ranging**
ultra terminum	**beyond the/my boundary/property line**
curis . . . expeditis	**with cares cleared away/settled/laid aside**

IIB. Short Analysis Questions

Nine points total.

1. **Two points.**

    One point for each task of Dellius in 1–4:
    to preserve an even mind/calm emotions while in difficulties
    to restrain the mind from insolence while enjoying success

2. **Two points.**

    One point for saying that *moriture* shows that Dellius will/must die.

    One point for a discerning explanation of significance within first stanza: e.g., you could die at any time, so preserve your inner calm and don't be disturbed by changing circumstances.

3.   **Two points.**

   One point for each pole of the contrast:
   a sad life/life of sad circumstances
   a happy life/relaxed life/life of happy circumstances

4.   **One point for correctly copying and scanning the line:**

   $$- \quad - \quad \cup \quad - - \quad - \quad \cup\cup \quad - \quad \cup\times$$
   seu t(e) in remoto gramine per dies

   One point for identifying the meter as Alcaic.

5.   **One point for explaining** *interiore nota Falerni* **as a reference to an older, better wine,**
   whose jar with its mark (*nota***) has been in the back or inner part of the wine cellar.**

IIC. Essay

The question asks the student to discuss the tone or attitude adopted in the passage toward Cleopatra. The student needs to define or characterize the tone and analyze how the passage conveys it. There is no one right characterization of the passage's tone toward Cleopatra; the quality of the essay depends on its success in articulating a position and on showing how the tone, as the student defines it, arises from the language. Likewise, the student need not define the tone in the whole passage with a single word. For example, the student may say that the dove and hare images, contrasted to the image of monster that marks the poem's element of anti-Cleopatra rhetoric, create a tone of sympathy toward her, while word choice and placement in lines 31–32 convey respect. Superior papers will display mastery of the Latin, a clear argumentative structure, and discernment into Horace's poetic technique.

6 – A fully-developed essay which defines the tone or attitude of the passage toward Cleopatra and shows how Horace's language conveys it. The student makes ample reference to specific aspects of the Latin text to support his or her analysis and position. Latin references are properly cited. Even though there may be occasional mistakes, the discussion is coherent and of high quality.

5 – A strong essay. Although the piece has good analysis, it is not as fully developed nor as supported with references to the text as a paper that receives a 6. Latin references are properly cited. The essay reflects familiarity with the poem. A few parts of the passage may receive thin treatment.

4 – A competent response. There may be uneven development of some elements of the passage, and signficant parts may be glossed over or omitted. Although limited in quantity, the essay includes accurate and relevant references in responding to the topic. Although the discussion may rely more on recounting what is said about Cleopatra than on showing how it conveys tone, the student must undertake some analysis and support it with references to the Latin.

3 – A limited response. The Latin support is weak and/or inappropriate. Latin references are not properly cited. The answer is descriptive and does not reach the level of analysis. Alternatively, some papers may offer a good, analytical essay without any correct citations of Latin to support the argument.

2 – Some understanding of the poem, but the essay is general and/or vague. The discussion is flawed. The Latin cited demonstrates very limited comprehension.

1 – An incoherent response. While it does contain some relevant information, no substantive argument is presented. The student demonstrates no understanding of the poem.

0 – A response that is off-topic, completely incorrect, or irrelevant. Responses that merely restate the question are also a 0.

REVIEW TEST 3
ODES 2.10, 2.14, 3.1, 3.9, 3.13, 3.30, 4.7

I. Multiple Choice Questions *Suggested time: 15 minutes*

      Annos undeviginti natus exercitum privato consilio et privata
impensa comparavi, per quem rem publicam a dominatione factionis
oppressam in libertatem vindicavi. Eo nomine senatus decretis
honorificis in ordinem suum me adlegit, C. Pansa et A. Hirtio
5   consulibus, consularem locum sententiae dicendae tribuens, et
imperium mihi dedit. Res publica ne quid detrimenti caperet,
me propraetore simul cum consulibus providere iussit. Populus
autem eodem anno me consulem, cum consul uterque bello cecidisset,
et triumvirum rei publicae constituendae creavit.

                        Caesar Augustus, *Res Gestae Divi Augusti 2*

impensa, -ae, f. - *expense*
vindico, -are, -avi, -atus - *to set free*
adlego, -ere, -legi, -lectus - *to elect*
detrimentum, -i, n. - *damage*
creo, -are, -avi, -atus - *to appoint*

1. From lines 1–2 we learn that the young Augustus
   - a. paid for his own army
   - b. was a private in the army
   - c. served in the army for nineteen years
   - d. trained as a private counselor

2. The antecedent of *quem* (line 2) is
   - a. an understood *me*
   - b. *consilio* (line 1)
   - c. *natus* (line 1)
   - d. *exercitum* (line 1)

3. In lines 2–3 Augustus says that he
   - a. found the republic free
   - b. joined the dominant faction
   - c. liberated the republic
   - d. dominated political affairs

4. *decretis honorificis* (lines 3–4) is ablative
   - a. of manner
   - b. of means
   - c. absolute
   - d. of cause

5. In line 4, *ordinem* refers to
   a. the series of Augustus' actions
   b. enforcement of the laws
   c. the sequence of Roman political offices
   d. the senate

6. *sententiae dicendae* (line 5) is translated
   a. of speaking my opinion
   b. opinions being spoken
   c. of pronouncing sentence
   d. expressing feelings

7. The subject of *dedit* (line 6) is
   a. the consul
   b. consular rank
   c. the empire
   d. the senate

8. In line 6, *ne quid detrimenti caperet* is a clause expressing
   a. purpose
   b. fearing
   c. wish
   d. result

9. The best translation of *cum* (line 8) is
   a. while
   b. since
   c. with
   d. although

10. *uterque* (line 8) refers to
    a. the young Augustus
    b. Hirtius and Pansa
    c. the Roman people
    d. the war

11. The word closest in meaning to *cecidisset* (line 8) is
    a. *interfecisset*
    b. *occisus esset*
    c. *necavisset*
    d. *festinavisset*

12. The job given to the young Augustus in line 9 was to
    a. appoint a triumvirate
    b. appoint a new consul
    c. reestablish the republic
    d. send each consul to war

II. Free Response Section
Reading Period *Suggested time: 5 minutes*

Read over the questions and begin planning your answers. You may make notes to yourself on the test sheet, but do not begin writing your answers until told to do so.

IIA. Translation *Suggested time: 5 minutes*

> dicar, qua violens obstrepit Aufidus
> et qua pauper aquae Daunus agrestium
> regnavit populorum, ex humili potens
> princeps Aeolium carmen ad Italos
> 5   deduxisse modos.
>
> *Ode 3.30.10–14*

Translate the passage as literally as possible.

IIB. Short Analysis Questions *Suggested time: 10 minutes*

> linquenda tellus et domus et placens
> uxor, neque harum, quas colis, arborum
>   te praeter invisas cupressos
>   ulla brevem dominum sequetur,
>
> 5   absumet heres Caecuba dignior
> servata centum clavibus et mero
>   tinguet pavimentum superbo,
>   pontificum potiore cenis.
>
> *Ode 2.14.21–28*

1. According to lines 1–2, what are three things that must be done?

2. Explain the signficance of the phrases *invisas cupressos* and *brevem dominum* in their context (lines 3–4).

3. What is accomplished by the poet's description of the *heres* as *dignior* (line 5)?

4. Name a figure of speech that appears in lines 6–8 and write out the Latin words that contain it.

5. Write out and scan line 2.

IIC. Essay *Suggested time: 20 minutes*

> regum timendorum in proprios greges,
> reges in ipsos imperium est Iovis,
>   clari Giganteo triumpho,
>   cuncta supercilio moventis.
>
> 5   est, ut viro vir latius ordinet
>   arbusta sulcis, hic generosior
>   descendat in campum petitor,
>   moribus hic meliorque fama
>
>   contendat, illi turba clientium
> 10   sit maior: aequa lege Necessitas
>   sortitur insignis et imos,
>   omne capax movet urna nomen.

Ode 3.1.5–16

In this passage, Horace reflects on difference in status among people and on the human condition that puts all people on the same level. In a short, well-organized essay, discuss how he develops a connection between these two themes.

Support your assertions with references to the Latin text throughout the passage. All Latin words must be copied or their line numbers provided, AND they must be translated or paraphrased closely enough so that it is clear you understand the Latin. It is your responsibility to convince your reader that you are basing your conclusions on the Latin text and not merely on a general recollection of the passage. Direct your answer to the question; do not merely summarize the passage.

REVIEW TEST 3: ANSWERS

I. Multiple Choice Questions

1—a	2—d	3—c
4—b	5—d	6—a
7—d	8—a	9—b
10—b	11—b	12—c

IIA. Translation

9 chunks. One point per chunk.

dicar, qua	I shall/will be said/spoken of where
violens obstrepit Aufidus	(the) violent/vehement Aufidus roars/makes a loud noise
et qua . . . Daunus	and where Daunus
pauper aquae	poor in/of water
agrestium regnavit populorum	(has) ruled (over) the rustic/rural/country peoples
ex humili potens	powerful/potent/able from a low/humble position
princeps . . . deduxisse	first to have adapted/composed/led down/escorted
Aeolium carmen	(the) Aeolic/Aeolian song/(lyric) poetry/poem
ad Italos . . . modos	to Italian patterns/poetry/ways

IIB. Short Analysis Questions

Nine points total.

1. **Two points.**

    One point for identifying the action as leaving/abandoning, *linquenda*.

    One point for identifying all three things: earth, house, wife.

2. **Three points.**

    One point for explaining *invisas cupressos* as a reference to funerals.

    One additional point for making explicit the inference from this image that death awaits the owner/Postumus/the addressee.

    One point for explaining *brevem dominum* as reference to the fact that the owner/Postumus is short-lived/shorter-lived than the trees.

3. **Two points.**

   One point for incorporating correct translation or paraphrase of *heres* and *dignior.*

   One point for an explanation that is consistent with the passage: e.g., the heir is more worthy because he uses the wine/property, unlike the owner

   OR

   the heir is more worthy because he is still alive, unlike the dead owner.

4. One point for a figure with supporting Latin:
   hyperbole: *centum clavibus*
   transferred epithet or personification: *mero . . . superbo*
   alliteration: *pavimentum . . . pontificum potiore*

5. One point for correctly copying and scanning the line:

   $$– \; – \quad \cup \qquad – \; – \qquad – \; \cup\cup \; – \; \cup \times$$
   uxor, nequ(e) harum, quas colis, arborum

IIC. Essay

The student is asked to show how Horace develops a connection between the themes of people's dif-ference in status and their sameness as subjects of the human condition. A student who successfully discusses the whole passage may select these references to status difference: kings rule humans by authority, Jupiter rules kings; men differ in wealth, political influence, and fame; all people are put on a level as subjects of kings and gods, as ruled by Necessity, as subject to death. Discerning students may notice that the two themes are bridged by the images of Necessity, who allots differences in status to people by a fair law, and of the urn, which holds names of different social lustre but selects the next one for death indiscriminately. Superior essays will conclude their argument with an attempt to show how the themes intersect: e.g., we should not entrust our happiness to advantages of circumstance, which are controlled by powers beyond us.

6 – A fully-developed essay, which shows by analysis how the passage develops and connects the two themes. The student makes ample reference, correctly cited and rendered, to specific aspects of the Latin text to support his or her analysis and position. Even though there may be occasional mistakes, the discussion is coherent and of high quality.

5 – A strong essay. Although the piece has good analysis, it is not as fully developed nor as supported with references to the text as a paper that receives a 6. Latin references are properly cited. The essay reflects familiarity with the poem. A few parts of the passage may receive thin treatment.

4 – A competent response. There may be uneven development of some elements of the passage, and signficant parts may be glossed over or omitted. Although limited in quantity, the essay includes ac-curate and relevant references in responding to the topic. The discussion may rely more on describing the people and divinities in the passage than analyzing how it develops the two themes. Nevertheless, the student undertakes some analysis and supports it with references to the Latin.

3 – A limited response. The Latin support is weak and/or inappropriate. Latin references are not properly cited. The answer is descriptive and does not reach the level of analysis. Alternatively, some papers may offer a good, analytical essay without any correct citations of Latin to support the argument.

2 – Some understanding of the poem, but the essay is general and/or vague. The discussion is flawed. The Latin cited demonstrates very limited comprehension.

1 – An incoherent response. While it does contain some relevant information, no substantive argument is presented. The student demonstrates no understanding of the poem.

0 – A response that is off-topic, completely incorrect, or irrelevant. Responses that merely restate the question are also a 0.

A COMPLETE VOCABULARY

In general, only long vowels in metrically indeterminate positions are marked. For example, the length of the "a" in "accipiter" need not be marked as long or short because the syllable in which it is contained must be long, regardless of the length of the vowel, because the vowel is followed by two consonants, "cc," (not a combination like "tr" which can create indeterminacy), while the "a" in "beātus" must be marked long because it occurs in a position where metrical rules cannot determine the length of the syllable in which it occurs.

A

ā/ab, prep. with abl., *from, by*

abeō, abīre, abiī, abitum, *go away, depart*

abrumpō, abrumpere, abrūpī, abruptum, *break, break apart*

absum, abesse, āfuī, āfutūrus, *be away, be absent*

absūmō, absūmere, absumpsī, absumptum, *spend, consume*

ac, conj., *and*

accendō, accendere, accendī, accensum, *kindle, arouse, ignite*

accipiter, accipitris, m., *hawk*

accurrō, accurrere, accurrī/accucurrī, accursum, *run or hurry up to*

Achaemenius, -a, -um, adj., *Persian, Parthian*

acūtus, -a, -um, adj., *sharp, severe*

ad, prep. with acc., *to, towards, near*

adferō, adferre, attulī, allātum, *bring, add*

adiciō, adicere, adiēcī, adiectum, *throw to, add*

adimō, adimere, adēmī, ademptum, *take away*

aditus, -ūs, m., *approach, access*

adiūtor, adiūtōris, m., *helper*

adlabōrō, adlabōrāre, *add to by taking trouble*

adolescō, adolescere, adolēvī, adultum, *grow up,* (of a season or time) *reach its peak*

adpōnō, adpōnere, adposuī, adpositum, *add; treat as, count as* (with lucrum)

adrogans, adrogantis, adj., *arrogant, insolent*

adsector, adsectārī, adsectātus sum, *follow closely, attend, escort*

adsum, adesse, adfuī, *be present;* in technical sense, *be present in court as a friend or adviser*

adurgeō, adurgēre, *press hard upon, pursue closely*

adventus, -ūs, m., *arrival, approach*

adversārius, adversāriī, m., *adversary, opponent*

Aenēās, Aenēae, m., *Aeneas,* son of Venus and Anchises, Trojan leader who brought his followers to Italy after the Trojan War and founded what would become the Roman state; hero of Vergil's *Aeneid*

aēneus, -a, -um, adj., *of bronze*

Aeolidēs, Aeolidae, m., *a son or more remote descendant of Aeolus*

Aeolius, -a, -um, adj., *Aeolian, Aeolic;* referring to Aeolia, the Greek area of Asia Minor, including the island of Lesbos where the Greek poets Sappho and Alcaeus lived, as well as to the dialect of Greek in which they wrote

aequor, aequoris, n., *a flat level surface, the flat surface of the sea,* (often used in pl.)

aequus, -a, -um, adj., *equal, even, impartial, fair*

āēr, āeris, m., *air, weather, mist*

aerātus, -a, -um, adj., *made of or fitted with bronze or brass*

aes, aeris, n., *copper, bronze, money*

aesculētum, -ī, n., *oak forest*

aestās, aestātis, f., *summer*

aestīvus, -a, -um, adj., *summer*

aestuōsus, -a, -um, adj., *very hot, agitated*

aetās, aetātis, f., *time, age*

aeternus, -a, -um, adj., *eternal, everlasting*

Āfricus, -a, -um, adj., *African*

ager, agrī, m., *field, territory*

agitō, agitāre, agitāvī, agitātum, *stir, drive, agitate, excite*

agō, agere, ēgī, actum, *do, drive*

agrestis, -e, adj., *of the country, rustic, rural*

āiō, defective verb, *say yes, say*

albus, -a, -um, adj., *white, bright*

aliās, adv., *at another time*

aliēnus, -a, -um, adj., *of another, alien, strange* (with abl. or dat.)

alius, alia, aliud, adj., *other, another*

almus, -a, -um, adj., *providing nurture, kindly, gracious*

alō, alere, aluī, altum, *nourish*

alter, altera, alterum, adj., *another, one of two, the one, the other*

altum, -ī, n., *high place or position, heaven, sea, the deep*

altus, -a, -um, adj., *high, deep, tall*

amābilis, -e, adj., *lovable, delightful*

amīcus, -ī, m., *friend*

amō, amāre, amāvī, amātum, *love*

amoenus, -a, -um, adj., *charming, pleasing*

amor, amōris, m., *love*

amplius, adv., *more*

amplus, -a, -um, adj., *large, spacious*

an, conj., *whether, or*

Ancus, -ī, m., *Ancus Martius,* fourth king of Rome

angiportus, -ūs, m., *alley*

angulus, -ī, m., *angle, corner*

angustus, -a, -um, adj., *narrow, limited, difficult* (of circumstances)

anima, -ae, f., *breath, life, darling*

animōsus, -a, -um, adj., *spirited, bold*

animus, -ī, m., *mind; mind, as standing for the whole person*

annus, -ī, m., *year*

antehāc, adv., *previously*

antestor, antestārī, antestātus sum, *call as a witness*

antrum, -ī, n., *cave, hollow space*

anus, -ūs, f., *old woman*

aper, aprī, m., *wild boar*

apium, apiī, n., *parsley, celery*

Apollō, Apollinis, m., *Apollo,* son of Jupiter and Latona, brother of Diana, god of archery, music, poetry, etc.

apparātus, -ūs, m., *preparation, show, sumptuousness, paraphernalia*

appāreō, appārēre, appāruī, appāritum, *appear*

aqua, -ae, f., *water, body of water*

Aquilō, Aquilōnis, m., *the north wind*

arbiter, arbitrī, m., *judge, overseer*

arbitrium, arbitriī, n., *decision, judgement*

arbor, arboris, f., *tree*

arbustum, -ī, n., *wood, plantation,* (pl.) *trees*

arbutus, -ī, f., *the wild strawberry or arbutus tree*

arceō, arcēre, arcuī, *contain, keep away, spurn*

Arctūrus, -ī, m., *Arcturus,* the brightest star of the constellation Boōtes

arcus, -ūs, m., *bow*

ardeō, ardēre, arsī, *be on fire, burn, be in love* (with abl.)

arduus, -a, -um, adj., *steep, towering, lofty, high, difficult*

ārea, -ae, f., *open space, threshing floor*

arguō, arguere, arguī, argūtum, *prove, show*

āridus, -a, -um, adj., *dry*

Aristius, Aristiī, m., *Aristius Fuscus,* Horace's literary friend; cf. *Satire 1.9* and *Ode 1.22*

arripiō, arripere, arripuī, arreptum, *seize, take hold of, arrest, bring before a court*

artus, -a, -um, adj., *close, thrifty, dense, economical*

asellus, -ī, m., *young ass, young donkey*

asper, aspera, asperum, adj., *fierce, rough*

at, conj., *but*

atavus, -ī, m., *a great-great-great grandfather, or remote ancestor*

āter, ātra, ātrum, adj., *black, dark, gloomy*

atque, conj., *and;* after comparatives, *than;* also, cf. **simul**

atquī, conj., *but, nevertheless*

ātrium, ātriī, n., *hall, first main room in a Roman-style house*

atrox, atrōcis, adj., *dreadful, fierce, cruel*

Attalicus, -a, -um, adj., *of King Attalus or his dynasty, rich, splendid*

audeō, audēre, ausus sum, *dare, wish*

audiō, audīre, audīvī, audītum, *hear, heed*

auferō, auferre, abstulī, ablātum, *take away, carry off, kill*

Aufidus, -ī, m., *Aufidus,* river in Apulia

aula, aulae, f., *noble residence, palace, hall*

aura, -ae, f., *breeze*

aureus, -a, -um, adj., *golden, splendid*

auricula, -ae, f., *ear*

auris, auris, f., *ear*

Auster, Austrī, m., *south wind*

aut, conj., *or;* **aut . . . aut,** *either . . . or*

autumnus, -ī, m., *autumn*

avidus, -a, -um, adj., *greedy, avaricious, eager*

avis, avis, f., *bird*

avītus, -a, -um, adj., *of a grandfather, ancestral*

āvius, -a, -um, adj., *pathless, remote*

B

Babylōnius, -a, -um, adj., *Babylonian*

bacchor, bacchārī, bacchātus sum, *celebrate the festival of Bacchus, rave, rage*

Bandusia, -ae, f., *Bandusia,* name of a spring, perhaps at Horace's Sabine farm or near Apulia, the area on which his hometown bordered.

barbarē, adv., *roughly, cruelly*

barbitos, barbitī, m., *lyre*

beātus, -a, -um, adj., *happy, fortunate*

bellum, -ī, n., *war*

bene, adv., *well;* with adj. or adv., *quite*

benignē, adv., *lavishly, liberally*

beō, beāre, beāvī, beātum, *bless, make happy*

bibō, bibere, bibī, *drink*

bīlis, bīlis, f., *gall, bile, anger*

bis, adv., *twice*

blandus, -a, -um, adj., *charming, persuasive, seductive*

Bōlānus, -ī, m., *Bolanus,* Roman cognomen

bonus, -a, -um, adj., *good*

brāchium, brāchiī, n., *arm*

brevis, -e, adj., *short, brief*

brūma, -ae, f., *the shortest day, winter, wintry weather*

Brūtus, -ī, m., *Marcus Iunius Brutus,* one of the leaders, along with Cassius, of the conspiracy to kill Julius Caesar.

C

cadō, cadere, cecidī, cāsum, *fall, die, set* (of heavenly bodies)

cadus, -ī, m., *jar, flask* (especially for wine)

Caecubum, -ī, n., *choice wine from Caecubum,* a district in south Latium

caelestis, -e, adj., *of the sky, celestial, divine*

caelum, -ī, n., *sky, heavens, weather, world*

caementum, -ī, n., *small stones, rubble*

Caesar, Caesaris, m., *Caesar;* Octavian (later Augustus), in *Ode 1.37;* in *Satire 1.9,* Julius Caesar, (100–44 BCE), Roman general who defeated Pompey at the battle of Pharsalus in 48 BCE and was made dictator for life in 44 BCE, shortly before his assassination in the conspiracy led by Brutus and Cassius.

Calais, Calais, m., *Calais,* man's name

campus, -ī, m., *plain, level surface; plain, field;* often refers specifically to the Campus Martius in Rome

candidus, -a, -um, adj., *bright, radiant, white*

canīcula, -ae, f., *the Dog Star, Sirius,* in the constellation Canis Major, brightest star in the sky, thought to bring hot weather

cānitiēs, cānitiēī, f., *white or grey coloring, grey or white hair*

canō, canere, cecinī, cantum, *sing, sing about, recite, prophesy, foretell*

cantō, cantāre, cantāvī, cantātum, *sing, sing about, recite*

cantus, -ūs, m., *singing, song, poetry*

capax, capācis, adj., *spacious, capable*

Capitōlium, Capitōliī, n., *Capitolium,* the Capitoline hill in Rome on which the Capitoline gods, Jupiter, Juno, and Minerva, were worshipped

caput, capitis, n., *head, top, source, person, person's life*

cardō, cardinis, m., *hinge*

careō, carēre, caruī, caritum, *lack, be without* (with abl.)

carmen, carminis, n., *solemn or ritual utterance, song, poem, lyric poetry*

carpō, carpere, carpsī, carptum, *pluck, seize*

cārus, -a, -um, adj., *dear, beloved*

castra, castrōrum, n. pl., *military camp*

cāsus, -ūs, m., *fall, event, misfortune, chance*

catēna, -ae, f., *chain*

catulus, -ī, m., *a young animal,* especially *a young dog*

Caucasus, -ī, m., *Caucasus mountains*

cautus, -a, -um, adj., *on one's guard, wary, cautious, prudent*

cavus, -a, -um, adj., *hollow, concave*

cēdō, cēdere, cessī, cessum, *go, yield, withdraw*

celer, celeris, celere, adj., *swift, quick*

cella, -ae, f., *storeroom, wine cellar*

celsus, -a, -um, adj., *high, lofty, proud*

cēna, -ae, f., *dinner*

centum, indecl. adj., *a hundred*

cerebrum, -ī, n., *brain, seat of intelligence, seat of anger, anger*

cēreus, -a, -um, adj., *waxen, supple*

certō, certāre, certāvī, certātum, *contend, strive*

certus, -a, -um, adj., *certain, definite*

cerva, -ae, f., *deer, female deer*

cervix, cervīcis, f., *neck*

cēterus, -a, -um, adj., *the rest,* usually found in plural

Chloē, Chloēs, f., *Chloe,* Greek woman's name

chorēa, -ae, f., *dance*

chorus, -ī, m., *choral dance, people singing and dancing, crowd, troop*

cibōrium, cibōriī, n., *a kind of drinking cup*

cingō, cingere, cinxī, cinctum, *surround, encircle*

circā, prep. with acc., *around*

circumagō, circumagere, circumēgī, circumactum, *drive or lead around, lead around in circles*

cithara, -ae, f., *lyre*

citius, adv., *quicker, sooner*

citus, -a, -um, adj., *swift, quick*

cīvīlis, -e, adj., *civil*

clāmor, clāmōris, m., *shout, shouting, clamor*

clārus, -a, -um, adj., *clear, bright, famous*

classis, classis, f., *fleet, political class*

clāvis, clāvis, f., *key*

cliens, clientis, m., *client;* one who attaches himself to a person of greater influence or political power (**patrōnus**) for protection

Cōcȳtos, Cōcȳtī, m., *Cocytus,* one of the rivers of the underworld

coemō, coemere, coēmī, coemptum, *buy up*

coepī, coepisse, coeptum (typically appears in perfect system), *begin*

cognātus, -a, -um, adj., *related*

cōgō, cōgere, coēgī, coactum, *drive together, force*

cohibeō, cohibēre, cohibuī, cohibitum, *hold together, hold back, confine*

colligō, colligere, collēgī, collectum, *to gather or bring together, collect*

colō, colere, coluī, cultum, *cultivate, cherish*

colōnus, -ī, m., *farmer, settler*

color, colōris, m., *color*

columba, -ae, f., *dove, pigeon*

coma, -ae, f., *hair*

combibō, combibere, combibī, *drink up, drink completely*

compellō, compellere, compulī, compulsum, *bring together, drive together, round up*

compescō, compescere, compescuī, *confine, restrain, check*

compōnō, compōnere, composuī, compositum, *put together, arrange, compose, calm, bury*

concha, -ae, f., *shell fish, sea shell, perfume dish*

concursus, -ūs, m., *running to and fro*

condiciō, condiciōnis, f., *condition, term, agreement*

condō, condere, condidī, conditum, *found, establish, store up*

conficiō, conficere, confēcī, confectum, *complete, destroy, finish off, kill*

coniunx, coniugis, c., *spouse, wife, husband*

consistō, consistere, constitī, *stop, pause, stand still, take a position*

consociō, consociāre, consociāvī, consociātum, *unite, connect, share*

constō, constāre, constitī, *stand together, stand still*

consūmō, consūmere, consumpsī, consumptum, *consume, destroy, kill*

contāminātus, -a, -um, adj., *morally foul, impure*

contendō, contendere, contendī, contentum, *stretch, hasten, compete, contend*

contrahō, contrahere, contraxī, contractum, *draw together, narrow*

cōpula, -ae, f., *bond, link*

cor, cordis, n., *heart*

cornū, -ūs, n., *horn, anything horn-shaped*

corōna, -ae, f., *crown, garland*

corōnō, corōnāre, corōnāvī, corōnātum, *put a garland on, crown*

corpus, corporis, n., *body*

corrigō, corrigere, correxī, correctum, *make straight, correct, remedy*

corrumpō, corrumpere, corrūpī, corruptum, *damage, spoil, bribe, seduce*

cortex, corticis, m., *bark, rind, cork*

costum, -ī, n., *an aromatic plant*

crās, adv., *tomorrow*

crastinus, -a, -um, adj., *of tomorrow*

crēber, crēbra, crēbrum, adj., *crowded together, frequent*

crēdibilis, -e, adj., *believable*

crēdō, crēdere, crēdidī, crēditum, *trust, believe,
entrust*

crēdulus, -a, -um, adj., *credulous, trustful*

crescō, crescere, crēvī, crētum, *arise, multiply, expand,
increase*

cruentus, -a, -um, adj., *bloody, gory, cruel*

cubō, cubāre, cubuī, cubitum, *lie down or be lying
down, recline, be in bed or on one's couch, be confined
to bed by illness, recline at table*

culpō, culpāre, culpāvī, culpātum, *blame*

culter, cultrī, m., *knife*

cum, prep. with abl., *with;* conj., *when, since, although*

cumba, -ae, f., *small boat,* especially that in which
Charon ferries the dead across the river Styx

cunctus, -a, -um, adj., *the whole of, all*

cupiō, cupere, cupīvī, cupītum, *wish, desire, long for*

cupressus, -ī, f., *cypress*

cūr, adv., *why*

cūra, -ae, f., *care, concern, worry, a person or thing
constituting an object of care*

cūrō, cūrāre, cūrāvī, cūrātum, *care about, take care of,
attend to*

curriculum, -ī, n., *a running, course, race, racing chariot*

currus, -ūs, m., *chariot*

curtus, -a, -um, adj., *having a part missing, mutilated,
circumcized*

Cyprius, -a, -um, adj., *Cyprian, of the island of Cyprus*

D

damnō, damnāre, damnāvī, damnātum, *condemn,
sentence*

damnum, -ī, n., *loss*

Danaus, -ī, m., *Danaus;* all but one of his fifty
daughters, the Danaids, on instructions from their
father, killed their husbands on their wedding
night; they are punished in the underworld by
having continuously to fill up leaky jars

daps, dapis, f., *feast, banquet*

Daunias, Dauniadis, f., *Apulia,* region of
southeastern Italy

Daunus, -ī, m., *Daunus,* legendary king of Apulia

dē, prep. with abl., *about, concerning, down from, from*

dēbeō, dēbēre, dēbuī, dēbitum, *owe, ought, should,
must*

dēbilitō, dēbilitāre, dēbilitāvī, dēbilitātum, *weaken*

dēcēdō, dēcēdere, dēcessī, dēcessum, *go away, depart,
withdraw* (with abl.)

dēcidō, dēcidere, dēcidī, *fall down, die*

dēcrescō, dēcrescere, dēcrēvī, dēcrētum, *decrease,
grow smaller, shrink*

decus, decoris, n., *that which adorns or beautifies, honor,
glory*

dēdecet, dēdecēre, dēdecuit, used in third person, *be
unsuitable for, be unbecoming to*

dēdicō, dēdicāre, dēdicāvī, dēdicātum, *dedicate*

dēdūcō, dēdūcere, dēduxi, dēductum, *lead away,
lead down, escort, bring a person or army back with
one to Rome, bring home in procession as a bride, spin,
compose, adapt*

dēlēniō, dēlēnīre, dēlēnīvī, dēlēnītum, *soothe*

dēlīberō, dēlīberāre, dēlīberāvī, dēlīberātum,
consider carefully, deliberate, decide

Dellius, Delliī, m., *Quintus Dellius,* who first joined
Dolabella, then Cassius, then Antony, and finally
Octavian, right before Actium

Delphicus, -a, -um, adj., *Delphic, of Delphi* (the site of
the oracle of Apollo, god of poetry and the arts,
among other things)

dēmens, dēmentis, adj., *out of one's senses, mad, insane*

dēmittō, dēmittere, dēmīsī, dēmissum, *let down, let
fall, lower, sink*

dēmō, dēmere, dempsī, demptum, *take away, subtract*

dēmoveō, dēmovēre, dēmōvī, dēmōtum, *remove,
drive out*

dens, dentis, m., *tooth*

densus, -a, -um, adj., *thick, dense*

dēpōnō, dēpōnere, dēposuī, dēpositum, *lay down*

dēproelior, dēproeliārī, *fight fiercely, struggle violently*

dēprōmō, dēprōmere, dēprompsī, dēpromptum,
bring out, produce

dēproperō, dēproperāre, *hurry to complete*

dēripiō, dēripere, dēripuī, dēreptum, *tear down,
snatch away*

descendō, descendere, descendī, descensum, *come or
go down, descend*

dēsīderium, desideriī, n., *desire, longing* (for
something or someone lost or absent)

dēsīderō, dēsīderāre, dēsīderāvī, dēsīderātum,
desire, want, long for

dēsiliō, dēsilīre, dēsiluī, *leap or jump down*

dēsinō, dēsinere, dēsiī, dēsitum, *stop, cease*

dēsistō, dēsistere, destitī, *cease, desist*

destinō, destināre, destināvī, destinātum, *fix, determine, intend, destine, earmark*

destringō, destringere, destrinxī, destrictum, *strip off, scrape lightly, draw or unsheathe* (a weapon)

dēsum, dēesse, dēfuī, *be missing, fail* (with dat. of person)

dētestor, dētestārī, dētestātus sum, *pray against, curse*

deus, -ī, m., *god;* **dī,** alternate form of **deī,** nom. pl., **dīs,** alternate form of **deīs,** dat. and abl. pl.

dexter, dextra, dextrum, adj., *right, skillful*

Diāna, -ae, f., *the goddess Diana,* daughter of Jupiter and Latona

dīcō, dīcere, dixī, dictum, *say, tell, call*

dīdūcō, dīdūcere, dīduxī, dīductum, *separate, split*

diēs, diēī, m., (f.) *day*

difficilis, -e, adj., *difficult, troublesome, hard to manage*

diffugiō, diffugere, diffūgī, *flee in several directions, disperse, scatter*

digitus, -ī, m., *finger*

dignus, -a, -um, adj., *worthy, worthy of, deserving* (with abl.)

dīligō, dīligere, dīlexī, dīlectum, *love, esteem, hold dear, have special regard for*

dīmoveō, dīmovēre, dīmōvī, dīmōtum, *move apart, separate*

diōta, -ae, f., *two-handled wine jar*

dīruō, dīruere, dīruī, dīrutum, *cause to fall in ruin, demolish*

dīrus, -a, -um, adj., *terrible, awful, dire*

dīs, dītis, adj., *rich, wealthy*

discēdō, discēdere, discessi, discessum, *go away, depart*

dispereō, disperīre, disperiī, *perish, be destroyed* (frequently hyperbolic)

displiceō, displicēre, displicuī, displicitum, *displease*

dissimulō, dissimulāre, dissimulāvī, dissimulātum, *pretend that something is not what it is, pretend not to notice, ignore*

dissolvō, dissolvere, dissolvī, dissolūtum, *dissolve, free*

distorqueō, distorquēre, distorsī, distortum, *twist this way and that, distort, torment*

dīvellō, dīvellere, dīvellī, dīvolsum, *tear apart*

dīves, dīvitis, adj., *rich, wealthy*

dīvīnus, -a, -um, adj., *divine*

dīvitiae, dīvitiārum, f. pl., *wealth, riches*

dīvum, -ī, n., *sky*

dīvus, -a, -um, adj., *divine*

dīvus, -ī, m., *god*

dō, dare, dedī, datum, *give*

doctus, -a, -um, *learned, taught*

doleō, dolēre, doluī, dolitum, *suffer mental or physical pain, be in pain, grieve*

dolor, dolōris, m., *pain, anguish, grief*

dominus, -ī, m., *master, lord, ruler*

domus, -ūs/-ī, f., *house, home*

dōnec, conj., *as long as, while*

dōnō, dōnāre, dōnāvī, dōnātum, *present, endow, reward* (with), with abl. of thing given

dormiō, dormīre, dormīvī, dormītum, *sleep*

dorsum, -ī, n., *back*

dubius, -a, -um, adj., *uncertain, indecisive*

dūcō, dūcere, duxī, ductum, *lead, take, consider*

dudum, adv., *some time ago, previously, just now; for a long time* (with **iam**)

dulce, adv., *sweetly*

dulcis, -e, adj., *sweet,* (of persons) *dear, beloved*

dum, conj., *while, as long as, provided that, if only, until*

dūrus, -a, -um, adj., *hard, harsh*

dux, ducis, m., *leader, general, commander*

E

ē/ex, prep. with abl., *out of, from*

ēbrius, -a, -um, adj., *drunk*

ecce, interj., *look, behold*

edax, edācis, adj., *greedy, devouring, destructive*

ēditus, -a, -um, adj. (from **ēdō**), *descended from*

ēdō, ēdere, ēdidī, ēditum, *put forth, give out, give birth to*

Ēdōnus, -a, -um, adj., *Thracian;* the **Ēdōnī** were a tribe celebrated for their orgiastic worship of Bacchus

effundō, effundere, effūdī, effūsum, *pour out, pour forth*

egeō, egēre, eguī, *need, want* (with abl.)

ego, meī, mihi/mī, mē, mē, pron., *I, me*

ēheu, interj. (expressing grief or pain), *alas*

ēlabōrō, ēlabōrāre, ēlabōrāvī, ēlabōrātum, *strive, work out, develop, perfect* ēmīror, ēmīrārī, *wonder at exceedingly, be astonished at*

ēnāvigō, ēnāvigāre, ēnāvigāvī, ēnāvigātum, *sail across, sail forth*

enim, conj., *for, truly*

ensis, ensis, m., *sword*

eō, adv., abl. of is, *therefore*

eō, īre, īvī/iī, itum, *go*

eōdem, adv., *to the same place*

eques, equitis, m., *horseman, rider, member of the cavalry, member of the equestrian order*

equus, -ī, m., *horse*

ergō, particle, *then, consequently, therefore*

ēripiō, ēripere, ēripuī, ēreptum, *snatch away, rescue*

errō, errāre, errāvī, errātum, *wander, make a mistake*

et, conj., *and, even;* et . . . et, *both . . . and*

Euterpē, Euterpēs, f., *Euterpe, one of the Muses.*

ēvehō, ēvehere, ēvexī, ēvectum, *carry out, lift up, raise*

ēvītō, ēvītāre, ēvītāvī, ēvītātum, *avoid*

exclūdō, exclūdere, exclūsī, exclūsum, *shut out, exclude*

excutiō, excutere, excussī, excussum, *shake out, drive out, banish*

exeō, exīre, exiī, exitum, *go out, come out, emerge*

exigō, exigere, exēgī, exactum, *drive out, complete, execute*

exilium, exiliī, n., *exile*

expavescō, expavescere, expāvī, *become frightened of, dread*

expediō, expedīre, expedīvī, expedītum, *free, extricate, release*

expleō, explēre, explēvī, explētum, *fill up*

expugnō, expugnāre, expugnāvī, expugnātum, *storm, conquer, overcome*

exstruō, exstruere, exstruxī, exstructum, *heap up, pile up, construct*

F

fābulōsus, -a, -um, adj., *legendary, storied*

facilis, -e, adj., *easy, quick*

faciō, facere, fēcī, factum, *make, do, regard*

fācundia, -ae, f., *eloquence*

Falernum, -ī, n., *Falernian wine,* wine from a district in northern Campania famous for its wine

Falernus, -a, -um, adj., *Falernian,* of a district in northern Campania famous for its wine

fallax, fallācis, adj., *deceitful, deceptive*

fāma, -ae, f., *fame, reputation*

famulus, -ī, m., *servant, attendant, slave*

fastīdiō, fastīdīre, fastīdīvī, fastīdītum, *show aversion to, scorn*

fastīdiōsus, -a, -um, adj., *critical, exacting, disdainful*

fātālis, -e, adj., *deadly, fatal*

fātum, -ī, n., *fate,* pl., *the Fates*

faveō, favēre, fāvī, fautum, *favor;* with linguīs (abl.), *avoid words of ill omen, be silent*

fax, facis, f., *torch, torch used at funerals and marriages, marriage, death*

fēlix, fēlīcis, adj., *happy, fortunate*

fenestra, -ae, f., *window*

feriō, ferīre, *strike, hit*

ferō, ferre, tulī, lātum, *bear, bring, carry, play* (a part, role)

ferox, ferōcis, adj., *bold*

fervens, ferventis, adj., *boiling, seething*

fervidus, -a, -um, adj., *boiling, burning, hot, impetuous*

fessus, -a, -um, adj., *tired, weary*

festus, -a, -um, adj., *festal, on holiday, festive*

fidēlis, -e, adj., *faithful*

fidēs, fideī, f., *trust, belief, faith, honesty, honor*

fidēs, fidis, f., *lyre*

fīlius, fīliī, m., *son*

fīlum, -ī, n., *thread*

findō, findere, fidī, fissum, *split, separate, divide*

fīnis, fīnis, m., *boundary, limit, end*

fīō, fīerī, factus sum, *be made, become*

flagrans, flagrantis, adj., *hot, blazing, passionate*

flāvus, -a, -um, adj., *yellow, golden, blonde, auburn*

flēbilis, -e, adj., *worthy of tears, lamentable*

fleō, flēre, flēvī, flētum, *weep for, lament*

flōs, flōris, m., *flower*

fluctus, -ūs, m., *a flowing, wave, disturbance*

flūmen, flūminis, n., *river, waters of a river*

focus, -ī, m., *hearth, fireplace*

folium, foliī, n., *leaf*

fons, fontis, m., *spring, source*

fors, fortis, f., *chance, luck*

forte, adv., *by chance, as luck would have it, as it so happened*

fortis, -e, adj., *brave*

fortūna, -ae, f., *fortune, chance, luck*

frangō, frangere, frēgī, fractum, *break, crush*

frequens, frequentis, adj., *crowded, assiduous, constant, regular*

fretum, -ī, n., *strait, sea, violence*

frīgidus, -a, -um, *cold*

frīgus, frigoris, n., *cold*

frons, frondis, f., *leaf*

frons, frontis, f., *forehead, brow, front*

fruor, fruī, fructus sum, *enjoy* (with abl.)

frustrā, adv., *in vain, to no purpose*

frux, frūgis, f., usually in pl., *fruit, crops*

fuga, -ae, f., *flight, rout*

fugax, fugācis, adj., *swift, fugitive, elusive*

fugiō, fugere, fūgī, fugitum, *flee, flee from, avoid*

fulgur, fulguris, n., *a flash of lightning, flash of light*

fundō, fundere, fūdī, fūsum, *pour, spread, scatter, defeat*

fundus, -ī, m., *bottom, farm, estate*

fūnus, fūneris, n., *funeral, death, destruction*

furens, furentis, adj., *mad, wild*

furiō, furiāre, furiāvī, furiātum, *madden*

furō, furere, *behave wildly, be crazy*

furor, furōris, m., *madness, frenzy, fury*

furtim, adv., *secretly*

Fuscus, -ī, m., *Aristius Fuscus,* Horace's literary friend; cf. *Satire* 1.9 and *Ode* 1.22

G

Gaetūlus, -a, -um, adj., *Gaetulian, of Gaetulia,* region of northwest Africa known for its lions

garriō, garrīre, garrīvī, *talk rapidly, chatter,* (do this in writing)

garrulus, -a, -um, adj., *talkative, loquacious*

gaudeō, gaudēre, gāvīsus sum, *rejoice, delight in* (with abl.)

gelidus, -a, -um, adj., *cold, icy*

gelū, -ūs, n., *frost, cold, chill*

geminus, -a, -um, adj., *twin, double*

gena, -ae, f., *cheek*

generō, generāre, generāvī, generātum, *produce, create*

generōsē, adv., *nobly, with dignity*

generōsus, -a, -um, adj., *of noble birth, noble*

gens, gentis, f., *clan, tribe, family*

genū, -ūs, n., *knee*

genus, generis, n., *birth, race, kind, offspring*

Gēryōn, Gēryonis, m., *Geryon;* triple-headed or triple-bodied king whom Hercules killed when carrying off his cattle

Gigantēus, -a, -um, adj., *of the Giants,* a mythical race, who fought and were defeated by the Olympian gods

gracilis, -e, adj., *slender, thin*

grāmen, grāminis, n., *grass*

grandō, grandinis, f., *hail*

grātia, -ae, f., *goodwill, kindness, charm, attraction,* pl. personified, *the Graces,* goddesses (usually three in number) embodying charm and beauty

grātus, -a, -um, adj., *pleasing*

gravidus, -a, -um, adj., *laden, weighed down*

gravis, -e, adj., *heavy, weighty, serious*

grex, gregis, m., *flock, herd, company, crowd*

H

habeō, habēre, habuī, habitum, *have, hold, consider, keep*

Hadria, -ae, m., *Adriatic Sea*

haedus, -ī, m., *young goat, kid;* two stars in the constellation Auriga

Haemonia, -ae, f., *Thessaly*

haud, adv., *not*

Hebrus, -ī, m., *Hebrus,* river in Thrace

hedera, -ae, f., *ivy*

hērēs, hērēdis, c., *heir*

Hermogenēs, Hermogenis, m., *Hermogenes;* in *Satire 1.10.80* Horace places a Hermogenes Tegellius in a group of people whose opinions do not matter to him as opposed to those of his literary friends.

heu, interj., expressing grief or pain, *oh, alas*

hīc, adv., *here, at this point*

hic, haec, hoc, demonstr. pron. and adj., *this, the latter*

hiems, hiemis, f., *winter, storm*

hinc, adv., *from here, here*

Hippolytus, -ī, m., *Hippolytus,* son of Theseus, whose rejection of the sexual advances of his stepmother, Phaedra, resulted in his death.

hodiē, adv., *today*

hodiernus, -a, -um, adj., *of today*

homō, hominis, m., *person, human being*

honor (honōs), honōris, m., *honor, office*

hōra, -ae, f., *hour, time, season*

horrescō, horrescere, horruī, *shudder at, tremble at*

horreum, -ī, n., *storehouse, granary*

horridus, -a, -um, adj., *rough, harsh, dreadful*

hortus, -ī, m., *garden;* usually in pl., *pleasure grounds or gardens*

hospitālis, -e, adj., *hospitable, belonging to a host or guest*

hosticus, -a, -um, adj., *belonging to an enemy*

hostis, hostis, c., *enemy*

hūc, adv., *to here, here*

humilis, -e, adj., *humble, low;* neuter as noun, *low position*

Hydaspēs, Hydaspis, m., *Hydaspes,* tributary of river Indus, the Jhelum

I

iaceō, iacēre, iacuī, *lie, be in ruins*

iaciō, iacere, iēcī, iactum, *throw, lay foundations*

iactus, -ūs, m., *throwing, hurling*

iaculum, -ī, n., *javelin*

iam, adv., *already, now*

iānua, -ae, f., *door*

Īcarius, -a, -um, adj., *of Icarus, Icarian*

īdem, eadem, idem, pron. and adj., *the same, too, likewise*

iecur, iecoris, n., *liver, the seat of the feelings*

ignis, ignis, m., *fire*

ignoscō, ignoscere, ignōvī, ignōtum, *forgive, pardon*

īlex, īlicis, f., *holm oak, ilex*

Īlia, -ae, f., *Ilia or Rhea Silvia,* mother of Romulus and Remus

ille, illa, illud, demonstr. pron. and adj., *that, the former*

illīc, adv., *there*

imāgō, imāginis, f., *image, likeness, shape*

imber, imbris, m., *rain, rain shower, water*

imbuō, imbuere, imbuī, imbūtum, *wet, fill, inspire*

imperium, imperiī, n., *power, command, government*

impetus, -ūs, m., *attack, onset, rapid motion*

impius, -a, -um, adj., *impious, undutiful, disloyal*

īmus, -a, -um, adj., *lowest, bottom of*

in, prep. with abl., *in, on;* prep. with acc., *into, onto, against, over*

Īnachus, -ī, m., *Inachus,* first king of Argos

incipiō, incipere, incēpī, inceptum, *begin*

inclāmō, inclāmāre, inclāmāvī, inclāmātum, *call out, cry out*

incorruptus, -a, -um, adj., *uncorrupted, upright*

indicō, indicāre, indicāvī, indicātum, *point out, show, declare*

indocilis, -e, adj., *untrained, hard to instruct*

indomitus, -a, -um, adj., *unconquered, unconquerable*

inermis, -e, adj., *unarmed*

iners, inertis, adj., *lacking skill, inactive, lazy, impotent*

infāmis, -e, adj., *infamous, disreputable*

infernus, -a, -um, adj., *lower, of the lower world, infernal*

infestus, -a, -um, adj., *dangerous, hostile, insecure*

inficiō, inficere, infēcī, infectum, *dye, imbue, taint, stain*

infimus, -a, -um, adj., *lowest, most humble*

infirmus, -a, -um, adj., *weak, lacking strength of purpose, not resolute*

informis, -e, adj., *shapeless, deformed, ugly*

ingens, ingentis, adj., *huge*

inhorrescō, inhorrescere, inhorruī, *begin to tremble, bristle, become stiffly erect*

inhospitālis, -e, adj., *inhospitable*

inīquus, -a, -um, adj., *uneven, unfavorable, treacherous, discontented*

inlacrimābilis, -e, adj., *pitiless*

inmemor, inmemoris, adj., *forgetful, unmindful*

inmodicus, -a, -um, adj., *immoderate*

inmortālis, -e, adj., *immortal*

īn(n)uleus, -ī, m., *fawn*

innumerābilis, -e, adj., *countless, numberless*

inops, inopis, adj., *lacking wealth, poor*

inpōnō, inpōnere, inposuī, inpositum, *place on or over, build on*

inpotens, inpotentis, adj., *powerless, weak, wild, violent*

inprimō, inprimere, inpressī, inpressum, *press upon*

inprobus, -a, -um, adj., *unprincipled, immoderate, unruly, relentless, shameless*

inquam, inquit, defective verb, only a few forms occur, most often used parenthetically or before or after a quotation, *say*

inruptus, -a, -um, *broken into, interrupted; unbroken*

inserō, inserere, inseruī, insertum, *introduce, insert, put in or among*

insignis, -e, adj., *distinguished*

insolens, insolentis, adj., *unaccustomed, excessive*

instans, instantis, adj., *pressing, urgent*

instō, instāre, institī, *be pressing, loom, threaten*

integer, integra, integrum, adj., *whole, untouched, upright*

intemptātus, -a, -um, adj., *untried, unattempted*

interdum, adv., *at times*

intereō, interīre, interiī, interitum, *perish, die*

interior, interius, adj., *inner, interior, private*

interlūnium, interlūniī, n., *the period between the old moon and the new*

interpellō, interpellāre, interpellāvī, interpellātum, *interrupt, break in on, impede*

intersum, interesse, interfuī, when used impersonally, *it makes a difference, it matters, it is of importance*

intumus, -a, -um, adj., *innermost, most secret*

inveniō, invenīre, invēnī, inventum, *find*

invicem, adv., *in turn*

invideō, invidēre, invīdī, invīsum, *envy, begrudge, refuse*

invidus, -a, -um, adj., *envious, jealous*

invīsus, -a, -um, adj., *hateful, odious*

ipse, ipsa, ipsum, pron., adj., *himself, herself, itself, oneself* etc.

īrācundus, -a, -um, adj., *angry, hot-tempered, prone to anger*

is, ea, id, pron. and adj., *he, she, it, this, that*

iste, ista, istud, pron. and adj., *that of yours, this, that* (often with derogatory sense)

ita, adv., *thus, so*

Italia, -ae, f., *Italy*

Italus, -a, -um, adj., *Italian*

iter, itineris, n., *journey*

Iuba, -ae, m., *Juba; Juba I, Numidian king who supported Pompey in the civil war; Juba II, son of Juba I, fought for Octavian (Augustus) at the battle of Actium, made king of Mauretania by Augustus, known for his learning*

iubeō, iubēre, iussī, iussum, *order, command, bid*

Iūdaeus, -ī, m., *Jew*

iugum, -ī, n., *yoke, bond*

iungō, iungere, iunxī, iunctum, *join, yoke, mate*

Iuppiter, Iovis, m., *Jupiter, supreme god of the Romans, god of sky and weather*

iūs, iūris, n., *law, right, court*

iustitia, -ae, f., *justice*

iuvenis, iuvenis, m., (f.), *young man, young woman*

iuvō, iuvāre, iūvī, iūtum, *please, delight, help*

L

lābor, lābī, lapsus sum, *glide, slip, pass*

labor, labōris, m., *work, effort, task*

labōrō, labōrāre, labōrāvī, labōrātum, *work, suffer, labor*

labrum, -ī, n., *lip*

lacerta, -ae, f., *lizard*

lacertus, -ī, m., *upper arm*

laedō, laedere, laesī, laesum, *harm, strike*

laetitia, -ae, f., *happiness, joy*

laetus, -a, -um, adj., *happy, glad, fertile*

Lalagē, Lalagēs, f., *Lalage, woman's name; Greek for "chatterer"*

lambō, lambere, lambī, *lick, wash*

languidus, -a, -um, adj., *languid, sluggish, slow*

lapis, lapidis, m., *stone*

largē, adv., *generously, plentifully*

lascīvus, -a, -um, adj., *playful, frisky, wanton*

lateō, latēre, latuī, *lie hidden*

lātus, -a, -um, adj., *wide*

latus, lateris, n., *side, extreme part or region, flank, lungs, body*

laudō, laudāre, laudāvī, laudātum, *praise*

laurus, -ī/-ūs, f., *laurel tree*

laus, laudis, f., *praise*

lavō, lavāre/lavere, lāvī, lavātum/lautum/lōtum, *wash*

lēnis, -e, adj., *smooth, gentle, mild, soft*

lentus, -a, -um, adj., *slow, lingering, unresponsive*

leō, leōnis, m., *lion*

lepus, leporis, m., *hare, rabbit*

Lesbōus, -a, -um, adj., *Lesbian, of the Greek island of Lesbos*

Lēthaeus, -a, -um, adj., *relating to Lethe or the underworld; Lethe is a place or river in the underworld whose waters, if drunk, were supposed to induce sleepiness or forgetfulness.*

Leuconoē, Leuconoēs, f., *Leuconoe, woman's name*

levis, -e, adj., *light, swift, gentle, unimportant, fickle* lēvis, -e, adj., *smooth, smooth* (from polishing)

lex, lēgis, f., *law, rule, particular condition or term*

libens, libentis, adj., *willing*

līber, lībera, līberum, adj., *free*

līberō, līberāre, līberāvī, līberātum, *free*

libīdō, libīdinis, f., *desire, lust*

Libitīna, -ae, f., *Libitina,* the goddess of funerals, *funeral couch*

Liburna, -ae, f., *light, fast sailing warship, galley;* name taken from the Liburnians, a people of Illyricum

Libycus, -a, -um, adj., *Libyan,* sometimes *African,* in general

licet, licēre, licuit/licitum est, impersonal verb, *it is permitted*

Licinius, Liciniī, m., *Licinius;* maybe Lucius Licinius Murena, brother-in- law of Maecenas, who was executed when trying to escape after his alleged participation in a conspiracy against Augustus

lignum, -ī, n., *wood* (often in pl.)

līmen, līminis, n., *threshold*

lingua, -ae, f., *tongue, language*

linquō, linquere, līquī, *go away from, abandon, leave behind*

liquidus, -a, -um, adj., *flowing, clear, melodious, liquid*

liquō, liquāre, liquāvī, liquātum, *melt, strain*

līs, lītis, f., *quarrel, lawsuit*

lītus, lītoris, n., *shore, coast, beach*

lituus, lituī, m., *curved cavalry trumpet*

locus, -ī, m., *place, occasion;* m. pl., -ī; n. pl., -a

longē, adv., *far, far off, far away in time*

longus, -a, -um, adj., *long*

loquax, loquācis, adj., *talkative, loquacious, talking*

loquor, loquī, locūtus sum, *speak*

lucrum, -ī, n., *profit, gain*

luctor, luctārī, luctātus sum, *wrestle, struggle, contend*

lūgubris, -e, adj., *mournful*

lūna, -ae, f., *moon*

lupus, -ī, m., *wolf*

Lȳdia, -ae, f., *Lydia,* woman's name

lympha, -ae, f., *water*

lymphātus, -a, -um, adj., *frenzied, distracted, frantic*

lyricus, -a, -um, adj., *of the lyre, lyric*

M

mācerō, mācerāre, mācerāvī, mācerātum, *soften, make weak, torment*

Maecēnās, Maecēnātis, m., *Gaius Cilnius Maecenas,* friend and supporter of Horace and of other contemporary poets, including Vergil

maestus, -a, -um, adj., *sad, sorrowful, dejected, gloomy*

magis, adv., *more*

magnus, -a, -um, adj., *large, big, great*

maior, maius, adj., *greater, larger*

male, adv., *badly, insufficiently, wickedly, scarcely*

mālobathrum, -ī, n., *the tree Cinnamomum tamala or its oil*

malus, -a, -um, adj., *bad, nasty, hostile, unfavorable*

maneō, manēre, mansī, mansum, *remain, stay, endure*

mānō, mānāre, mānāvī, mānātum, *flow, spread*

manus, -ūs, f., *hand, band*

mare, maris, n., *sea*

Mareōticum, -ī, n., *wine from Mareotis,* area around Alexandria in Egypt

Mars, Martis, m., *Mars,* god of war

Marsus, -a, -um, adj., *Marsian, of the* Marsī, a people of central Italy

Massicum, -ī, n., *Massic wine, wine from the area of* Massicus, a mountain in Campania

Massicus, -a, -um, adj., *Massic*

māter, mātris, f., *mother*

Maurus, -a, -um, adj., *Moorish, African*

mēcum = cum mē

mediocritās, mediocritātis, f., *mean, moderation, keeping of a middle course*

meditor, meditārī, meditātus sum, *think over, contemplate, practice*

melior, melius, adj., *better*

Melpomenē, Melpomenēs, f., *Melpomene,* one of the Muses

membrum, -ī, n., *limb or member of the body, limb, member, part of anything*

meminī, meminisse (perf. with pres. meaning), *remember, recollect*

memor, memoris, adj., *mindful, remembering*

mendax, mendācis, adj., *lying, false*

mens, mentis, f., *mind*

mentum, -ī, n., *chin*

mercātor, mercātōris, m., *merchant*

Mercurius, Mercuriī, m., *Mercury,* son of Jupiter and Maia

meritum, -ī, n., *that which one deserves, due reward, service, meritorious action*

merus, -a, -um, adj., *pure, unmixed;* with **vīnum** or with **vīnum** understood, *wine not mixed with water*

mēta, -ae, f., *turning point, end*

metuō, metuere, metuī, metūtum, *fear, be afraid of, be afraid*

metus, -ūs, m., *fear*

meus, -a, -um, adj., *my*

mī = mihi

mīlitāris, -e, adj., *military*

mīlitia, -ae, f., *military service, war, army*

minae, -ārum, f. pl., *threats, warning signs*

minax, minācis, adj., *threatening, projecting*

minimus, -a, -um, adj., *smallest, least*

minister, ministrī, m., *servant, assistant*

Mīnōs, Mīnōis/Minōnis, m., *Minos,* king of Crete, and later a judge in the underworld

minuō, minuere, minuī, minūtum, *make smaller, reduce, weaken*

minus, adv., *less*

misceō, miscēre, miscuī, mixtum, *mix, mingle*

miser, misera, miserum, adj., *unhappy, pitiful*

miserē, adv., *pitifully, desperately*

miseror, miserārī, miserātus sum, *pity, lament*

mītescō, mītescere, *become mild, soft, or ripe*

mittō, mittere, mīsī, missum, *release, let go, abandon, send*

mōbilis, -e, adj., *moveable, changeable, inconstant, pliant*

moderor, moderārī, moderātus sum, *handle, control, play*

modo, adv., *only, just now*

modus, -ī, m., *limit, way, rhythmic pattern;* in pl., *poetry*

moechus, -ī, m., *adulterer*

mōlēs, mōlis, f., *mass, bulk, massive structure*

mōlior, mōlīrī, mōlītus sum, *labor at, build*

mollis, -e, adj., *soft, gentle, flexible, voluptuous*

moneō, monēre, monuī, monitum, *bring to the notice of, remind, tell* (of), *warn*

mons, montis, m., *mountain*

monstrum, -ī, n., *portent, marvel, monster*

monumentum, -ī, n., *monument, memorial*

mora, -ae, f., *delay, hindrance*

morbus, -ī, m., *sickness, disease*

morior, morī, mortuus sum, *die*

moror, morārī, morātus sum, *delay, linger, be late in appearing*

mōrōsus, -a, -um, adj., *difficult*

mors, mortis, f., *death*

mortālis, -e, adj., *mortal*

mōs, mōris, m., *custom, tradition;* (pl.) *character, habits*

moveō, movēre, mōvī, mōtum, *move*

mox, adv., *soon*

muliebriter, adv., *like a woman*

mulier, mulieris, f., *woman, wife*

multum, adv., *much*

multus, -a, -um, *much, many, large* (with sing. noun)

munditia, -ae, f., *neatness, elegance*

mundus, -ī, m., *world*

mūnus, mūneris, n., *service, duty, gift, entertainment*

Mūsa, -ae, f., *muse;* one of the nine Muses, goddesses who were daughters of Zeus and Mnemosyne and presided over the arts

mūtō, mūtāre, mūtāvī, mūtātum, *change*

mūtuus, -a, -um, adj., *mutual, reciprocal*

Myrtōus, -a, -um, adj., *Myrtoan*

myrtus, -ī, f., *myrtle*

N

nam, conj., *for, because*

namque, conj., *for, because*

narrō, narrāre, narrāvī, narrātum, *tell*

nascor, nascī, nātus sum, *be born*

nauta, -ae, m., *sailor*

nāvis, nāvis, f., *ship*

nē, negative adv. and conj., *not, that not, so that not, lest;* used in negative purpose clauses and prohibitions, among other constructions

-ne, interr. particle, in direct questions; in indirect questions with alternatives, often used with **an,** *whether . . . or;* affirmative particle often used with infinitive in exclamations, *indeed*

nebula, -ae, f., *mist, fog*

nec, conj., *and not;* **nec . . . nec,** *neither . . . nor*

nectar, nectaris, n., *nectar,* drink of the gods

nectō, nectere, nexī, nexum, *tie, weave, bind, compose*

nefās, n., indecl., *crime, offense against divine law, sacrilege* negō, negāre, negāvī, negātum, *say no, deny, refuse*

nēmō, nēminis, m., pron., *no one, nobody*

nemus, nemoris, n., *grove, forest*

neque, conj., *and not;* neque . . . neque, *neither . . . nor*

nesciō, nescīre, nescīvī, nescītum, *not know, be ignorant of, not to know how to, not to be able to*

nescius, -a, -um, adj., *ignorant, unaware*

niger, nigra, nigrum, adj., *black, dark, gloomy, black as a color of ill omen, evil*

nihil, n., indecl., *nothing*

nīl = nihil

nimium, adv., *too, too much, very*

nisi, conj., *if not, unless*

niteō, nitēre, nituī, *shine, be radiant with beauty*

nivālis, -e, adj., *snowy*

nix, nivis, f., *snow*

nōbilis, -e, adj., *noble*

noceō, nocēre, nocuī, nocitum, *harm* (with dat.)

nōmen, nōminis, n., *name*

nōn, adv., *not*

nōs, nostrī/nostrum, nōbīs, nōs, nōbīs, pron., *we, us*

noscō, noscere, nōvī, nōtum, *get to know learn; know* (in perfect tense)

nota, -ae, f., *mark, sign, wine of a specified quality or vintage*

nōtus, -a, -um, adj., *known, familiar*

novus, -a, -um, adj., *new, strange*

nox, noctis, f., *night*

nūdus, -a, -um, adj., *naked, bare, plain*

nūgae, -ārum, f. pl., *trifles, nonsense, things of no importance*

nullus, -a, -um, adj., *no, not any*

num, interr. particle, *certainly not*

numerus, -ī, m., *number*

numquam, adv., *never*

numquid, interr. particle, introduces question where a negative answer is expected, *surely . . . not; you don't, do you?*

nunc, adv., *now*

nūtō, nūtāre, nūtāvī, nūtātum, *nod with the head, nod, hesitate*

nūtrix, nūtrīcis, f., *nurse,* especially a *wet-nurse*

nympha, -ae, f., *nymph,* semi-divine female spirit of nature

O

ō, interj., *O* (with voc.)

obeō, obīre, obiī, obitum, *go to, meet, die*

obligō, obligāre, obligāvī, obligātum, *tie up, pledge, dedicate*

oblīquus, -a, -um, adj., *slanting, zigzag*

oblīviōsus, -a, -um, adj., *producing forgetfulness, forgetful*

obsolētus, -a, -um, adj., *worn out, shabby, ordinary*

obstrepō, obstrepere, obstrepuī, obstrepitum, *make a loud noise, roar, drown by louder noise*

obvius, -a, -um, adj. (with dat.), *in the way, placed so as to meet, situated so as to confront*

occidō, occidere, occidī, occāsum, *fall, die*

occupō, occupāre, occupāvī, occupātum, *seize, forestall, take the lead over*

occurrō, occurrere, occurrī/occucurrī, occursum, *meet, hurry to meet, arrive, turn up*

ōcius, adv., *sooner, quicker*

oculus, -ī, m., *eye*

ōdī, ōdisse, ōsum (perfect with present sense), *have an aversion to, hate*

odor, odōris, m., *smell, odor, perfume*

officiō, officere, offēcī, offectum, *impede, interfere with* (with dat.)

ōlim, adv., *formerly, once, on an occasion, at some future date*

Olympicus, -a, -um, adj., *Olympic, Olympian*

omnis, -e, adj., *all, every*

onus, oneris, n., *burden*

operōsus, -a, -um, adj., *toilsome, laborious, painstaking, industrious*

oppēdō, oppēdere, *fart in the face of* (with dat.)

oppidum, -ī, n., *town*

oppōnō, oppōnere, opposuī, oppositum, *place against, place in front,* especially *put before someone for acceptance, proffer*

oppositus, -a, -um, *placed against, hostile*

opus, operis, n., *work, business, task, genre;* with esse, *be necessary, be needed* (with abl. of thing needed and dat. of person with the need)

ōra, -ae, f., *shore*

Orcus, Orcī, m., *Orcus,* the god of the lower world, the lower world, death

ordinō, ordināre, ordināvī, ordinātum, *set in order, arrange* orior, orīrī, ortus sum, *rise, be born*

ornō, ornāre, ornāvī, ornātum, *prepare, decorate, adorn, honor* (with abl.)

ornus, -ī, f., *flowering ash tree*

Ornytus, -ī, m., *Ornytus,* man's name

Orpheus, -ī, m., *Orpheus;* he was able to charm animals and nature with his music.

osculum, -ī, n., *kiss, mouth, lips* (as used in kissing)

ōtium, ōtiī, n., *free time, leisure, peace*

P

palma, -ae, f., *palm tree, palm branch, palm wreath, token of victory*

pār, paris, adj., *equal*

parcē, adv., *sparingly*

parcō, parcere, pepercī, parsum, *spare* (with dat.)

pariēs, parietis, m., *wall*

parmula, -ae, f., *little shield*

parō, parāre, parāvī, parātum, *prepare*

pars, partis, f., *part, party; stage role* (usually in pl.)

pateō, patēre, patuī, *be open*

pater, patris, m., *father*

patientia, -ae, f., *patience*

patior, patī, passus sum, *suffer, undergo, experience, endure, allow*

patrius, -a, -um, adj., *of a father, ancestral, native, inherited, belonging to one's country*

paucus, -a, -um, adj., in pl., *few*

paulum, adv., *for a short while*

paulum, -ī, n., *a little*

pauper, pauperis, adj., *poor* (with gen.)

pauperiēs, pauperiēī, f., *poverty*

paveō, pavēre, *be frightened, be terrified*

pavidus, -a, -um, adj., *frightened, terrified, trembling, fearful*

pavīmentum, -ī, n., *pavement, floor*

pectus, pectoris, n., *breast, chest*

pecus, pecoris, n., *farm animal;* sing. as collective, *farm animals, livestock,* especially *sheep and cattle*

pendeō, pendēre, pependī, *hang, hover, hang down, be suspended*

penitus, adv., *deeply*

per, prep. with acc., *through*

perdō, perdere, perdidī, perditum, *destroy, lose*

perennis, -e, adj., *lasting throughout the year, lasting for many years, enduring*

pereō, perīre, periī, peritum, *perish, die*

perfundō, perfundere, perfūdī, perfūsum, *pour over, fill with*

permisceō, permiscēre, permiscuī, permixtum, *mix together, confuse*

permittō, permittere, permīsī, permissum, *let go, allow, entrust*

permūtō, permūtāre, permūtāvī, permūtātum, *exchange, receive in exchange for* (with acc. of thing received and abl. of thing given up)

perpetuus, -a, -um, adj., *continuing, permanent, connected*

Persae, Persārum, m. pl., *Persians*

persequor, persequī, persecūtus sum, *pursue, chase*

Persicus, -a, -um, adj., *Persian*

pertinax, pertinācis, adj., *very tenacious, holding fast, persisting*

pēs, pedis, m., *foot, metrical foot*

petītor, petītōris, m., *seeker, candidate*

pharetra, -ae, f., *quiver*

Philippī, -ōrum, m. pl., *Philippi,* town in eastern Macedonia where Brutus and Cassius were defeated

philyra, -ae, f., *fibrous membrane under the bark of the linden or lime tree, bast;* used to bind together elaborate garlands of flowers

Phrygius, -a, -um, adj., *Phrygian*

pietās, pietātis, f., *duty, devotion*

piger, pigra, pigrum, adj., *inactive, lazy*

pignus, pigneris/pignoris, n., *pledge, token, symbol*

pīnus, -ūs, f., *pine*

Pīrithous, -ī, m., *Pirithous,* a king of the Lapiths who fights with the Centaurs; son by Dia of Zeus or Ixion

piscis, piscis, m., *fish*

pius, -a, -um, adj., *dutiful, devoted*

placeō, placēre, placuī, placitum, *please*

plācō, plācāre, plācāvī, plācātum, *appease, calm*

plaga, -ae, f., *hunting net, trap*

plūs, plūris, n., *more;* plūrēs, plūra, pl. adj., *more*

Plūtō, Plūtōnis, m., *Pluto,* king of the underworld

pōculum, -ī, n., *cup, drink*

podagra, -ae, f., *gout*

Polyhymnia, -ae, f., *Polyhymnia,* one of the Muses

pōmifer, pōmifera, pōmiferum, adj., *fruit-bearing, fruitful*

Pompēius, Pompēiī, m., *Pompeius;* identity unknown

pōnō, pōnere, posuī, positum, *put, place*

pontifex, pontificis, m., *high priest, pontiff*

pōpulus, -ī, f., *poplar tree*

populus, -ī, m., *people, public, multitude*

portentum, -ī, n., *portent, abnormal phenomenon*

poscō, poscere, poposcī, *demand*

possum, posse, potuī, *be able, can*

post, prep. with acc., *behind, after*

posterus, -a, -um, adj., *next, following, future, later*

postis, postis, m., *door-post, door*

Postumus, -ī, m., *Postumus;* this name was often given to boys who were born after the death of their fathers

potens, potentis, adj., *able, powerful, potent*

potior, potīrī, potītus sum, *get possession of, obtain, possess*

potior, potius, adj., *more able, more powerful, preferable*

praebeō, praebēre, praebuī, praebitum, *give, supply, provide*

praecēdō, praecēdere, praecessī, praecessum, *go in front, go on ahead*

praecipiō, praecipere, praecēpī, praeceptum, *take beforehand, teach*

praemium, praemiī, n., *prize, reward*

praeparō, praeparāre, praeparāvī, praeparātum, *prepare*

praesidium, praesidiī, n., *protection, defense*

praeter, prep. with acc., *except, beyond*

praetereō, praeterīre, praeteriī, praeteritum, *go by, go past, pass by, go beyond, omit*

premō, premere, pressī, pressum, *press, follow closely*

pressō, pressāre, pressāvī, pressātum, *press*

prex, precis, f., *prayer*

prīmus, -a, -um, adj., *first*

princeps, principis, adj., *first in time, leading, first*

priscus, -a, -um, adj., *ancient, former*

prius, adv., *previously, before*

prīvātus, -a, -um, adj., *private, not in public life*

prō, prep. with abl., *for, on behalf of, in front of*

procella, -ae, f., *storm, trouble*

prōditor, prōditōris, m., *betrayer, traitor*

proelium, proeliī, n., *battle*

profānus, -a, -um, adj., *profane, secular, impious, uninitiated*

prope, prep. with acc., *near*

properō, properāre, properāvī, properātum, *hurry, hasten*

propinquus, -a, -um, adj., *near, neighboring*

proprius, -a, -um, adj., *one's own, personal*

prōterō, prōterere, prōtrīvī, prōtrītum, *trample down, crush*

protervus, -am, -um, adj., *bold, violent*

proxumus, -a, -um, adj., *nearest, next*

pūbēs, pūbis, f., *adult population, age of puberty, the pubic region*

pudīcus, -a, -um, adj., *having a sense of modesty or shame, modest, honorable, chaste*

pudor, pudōris, m., *restraint, feeling of shame*

puella, -ae, f., *girl, young woman, girlfriend*

puer, puerī, m., *boy, non-adult male, male beloved, (young) male slave*

pulcher, pulchra, pulchrum, adj., *beautiful*

pullus, -a, -um, adj., *gray, somber*

pulsō, pulsāre, pulsāvī, pulsātum, *beat, strike repeatedly*

pulvīnar, pulvīnāris, n., *sacred couch on which the image of a god was placed*

pulvis, pulveris, m., *dust*

pūmex, pūmicis, m., *pumice-stone*

purpura, -ae, f., *shellfish yielding a purple dye, the purple dye from the shellfish, purple-dyed cloth, purple*

pūrus, -a, -um, adj., *pure, innocent*

pȳramis, pȳramidis, f., *pyramid*

Pyrrha, -ae, f., *Pyrrha,* woman's name

Q

quā, adv., *where*

quadrīmus, -a, -um, adj., *four-year-old*

quaerō, quaerere, quaesīvī, quaesītum, *look for, seek, ask, acquire, earn*

quālis, -e, rel. adj., *of which sort*

quam, interr. and rel. adv., *how;* with the superlative, *as . . . as possible;* after a comparative, *than*

quamquam, conj., *although*

quandō, interr. adv., *when*

quandōcumque, adv., *at some time or other*

quārē, interr. and rel. adv., *in what way, how, why, because, therefore* quartus, -a, -um, adj., *fourth*

quatiō, quatere, quassum, *shake, beat upon*

-que, enclitic conj., *and*

querimōnia, -ae, f., *complaint*

questus, -ūs, m., *complaint, lament*

quī, quae, quod, rel. pron., *who, which, that;* interr. adj., *what, which*

quia, conj., *because*

quīcumque, quaecumque, quodcumque, indef. pron., *whoever, whichever, whatever*

quid, adv., *why*

quīdam, quaedam, quiddam, pron., *a certain person, a certain thing*

quīlibet, quaelibet, quidlibet, pron., *anyone or anything whatever, whoever or whatever you please*

Quintilius, Quintiliī, m., *Quintilius Varus,* friend of Horace and Vergil

quintus, -a, -um, adj., *fifth*

Quirīs, Quirītis, m., *Roman citizen*

quis, quid, interr. pron., *who, what;* indef. pron., *anyone, anything*

quisquam, quicquam, pron., *anyone, anything*

quisque, quaeque, quidque, pron., *each one*

quisquis, quidquid (or quicquid), pron. and adj., *whoever, whatever*

quō, adv., *where, for what purpose*

quod, conj., *because*

quodsī, conj., *but if*

quōmodo, interr., rel. adv., *how, in the manner in which*

quondam, adv., *once, formerly, sometimes, in the future*

quoque, adv., *also, too*

quotiens, adv., *how often*

quotquot, indecl. adj., *however many*

R

rāmus, -ī, m., *branch*

rapiō, rapere, rapuī, raptum, *seize, snatch away*

ratis, ratis, f., *raft, boat, ship*

raucus, -a, -um, adj., *hoarse, noisy, raucous*

recens, recentis, adj., *fresh, recent, modern*

recipiō, recipere, recēpī, receptum, *take back, accept, regain*

reclīnō, reclīnāre, reclīnāvī, reclīnātum, *cause to lean back*

reclūdō, reclūdere, reclūsī, reclūsum, *open up, undo*

recreō, recreāre, recreāvī, recreātum, *recreate, restore, revive*

rectus, -a, -um, adj., *straight, right, correct, proper*

recurrō, recurrere, recurrī, recursum, *run back, return*

reddō, reddere, reddidī, redditum, *give back, deliver*

redemptor, redemptōris, m., *contractor*

redeō, redīre, rediī, reditum, *go back, come back, return*

redigō, redigere, redēgī, redactum, *drive back, reduce*

redōnō, redōnāre, redōnāvī, redōnātum, *give back*

redūcō, redūcere, reduxī, reductum, *bring back*

reficiō, reficere, refēcī, refectum, *make again, repair*

refugiō, refugere, refūgī, *run away, avoid*

rēgālis, -e, adj., *royal, regal*

rēgia, -ae, f., *palace*

rēgīna, -ae, f., *queen*

regnō, regnāre, regnāvī, regnātum, *rule, rule over*

regō, regere, rexī, rectum, *guide, direct, rule*

rēiciō, rēicere, rēiēcī, rēiectum, *throw back, drive back, reject*

religiō, religiōnis, f., *religious awe or conscience, religious practice, particular set of religious observances, cult, religious feeling, superstition*

religō, religāre, religāvī, religātum, *tie, fasten behind; untie* (occasionally)

relinquō, relinquere, relīquī, relictum, *leave, leave behind, abandon*

removeō, removēre, remōvī, remōtum, *move back*

rēmus, -ī, m., *oar*

reor, rērī, ratus sum, *think*

reparō, reparāre, reparāvī, reparātum, *obtain in exchange for, recover*

repetō, repetere, repetīvī, repetītum, *seek again, recall, resume*

repōnō, repōnere, reposuī, repositum, *put down, place*

rēs, reī, f., *wealth, thing, circumstance, affair, legal matter*

resecō, resecāre, resecuī, resectum, *cut back, prune, restrain*

resorbeō, resorbēre, *suck back, swallow again*

respondeō, respondēre, respondī, responsum, *answer, reply;* technical sense, *appear in court*

restituō, restituere, restituī, restitūtum, *restore, revive*

restō, restāre, restitī, *remain, remain to be dealt with*
rex, rēgis, m., *king*
rīdeō, rīdēre, rīsī, rīsum, *laugh*
rīpa, -ae, f., *bank of a river, shore*
rīsus, -ūs, m., *laughter*
rītus, -ūs, m., *ritual, custom, manner, style*
rīvus, -ī, m., *stream*
rixa, -ae, f., *fight*
rogō, rogāre, rogāvī, rogātum, *ask, ask for*
Rōmānus, -a, -um, adj., *Roman*
rosa, -ae, f., *rose*
roseus, -a, -um, adj., *rosy*
rota, -ae, f., *wheel*
ruber, rubra, rubrum, adj., *red*
rubus, -ī, m., *bramble, prickly bush*
rūga, -ae, f., *wrinkle*
ruīna, -ae, f., *collapse, ruin*
rumpō, rumpere, rūpī, ruptum, *break, shatter, destroy*
rursus, adv., *back, again*
rūs, rūris, n., *the country* (as opposed to the town), *farm, estate*

S

sabbata, sabbatōrum, n. pl., *the Jewish sabbath*
Sabellus, -a, -um, adj., *Sabine;* the Sabines were a people of central Italy.
Sabīnus, -a, -um, adj., *Sabine;* the Sabines were a people of central Italy.
sacer, sacra, sacrum, adj., *sacred, holy*
sacerdōs, sacerdōtis, c., *priest or priestess*
saepe, adv., *often*
saeviō, saevīre, saeviī, saevītum, *rage, rave*
saevus, -a, -um, adj., *cruel, savage*
sagitta, -ae, f., *arrow*
Saliāris, -e, adj., *of the Salii,* who were a group of priests (at Rome usually associated with Mars), who performed ritual dances on certain occasions.
salsus, -a, -um, adj., *salted, witty, funny*
saltus, -ūs, m., *forest or mountain pasture, forest or mountain pass*
salvus, -a, -um, adj., *safe, alive, well*
sanguis, sanguinis, m., *blood*
sānus, -a, -um, adj., *healthy, sane*

sapienter, adv., *wisely*
sapiō, sapere, sapīvī, *have taste, be wise*
sapor, sapōris, m., *taste, flavor*
sarculum, -ī, n., *hoe*
satis, adv., *enough, sufficiently;* indecl. noun, *enough*
Satyrus, -ī, m., *satyr;* demi-god of wild places, especially forests, having the form of a man with some animal characteristics
saxum, -ī, n., *rock*
scandō, scandere, *climb, ascend, mount*
scelus, sceleris, n., *wrongdoing, crime, affliction*
scīlicet, adv., *evidently, of course, surely*
sciō, scīre, scīvī, scītum, *know*
scrībō, scrībere, scripsī, scriptum, *write*
sēcernō, sēcernere, sēcrēvī, sēcrētum, *separate, distinguish*
secō, secāre, secuī, sectum, *cut, divide, traverse*
sēcrētō, adv., *secretly*
sector, sectārī, sectātus sum, *pursue, chase*
secundus, -a, -um, adj., *following, second, favorable*
secus, adv., *otherwise, not so*
sed, conj., *but*
sedeō, sedēre, sēdī, sessum, *sit*
sēdēs, sēdis, f., *seat, site, home*
sēdulus, -a, -um, adj., *attentive, diligent*
semel, adv., *once, once and for all*
semper, adv., *always*
senecta, -ae, f., *old age*
sentiō, sentīre, sensī, sensum, *feel, sense, perceive, think, understand*
sequor, sequī, secūtus sum, *follow*
serēnus, -a, -um, adj., *calm*
seriēs, (-ēī), f., *series, sequence, succession*
sērius, adv., *later*
serpens, serpentis, m., f., *snake, serpent*
sērus, -a, -um, adj., *late, blossoming after the normal time*
servō, servāre, servāvī, servātum, *keep, protect, save*
servus, -ī, m., *slave*
seu, conj., *or if,* **seu . . . seu,** *whether . . . or*
sī, conj., *if*
sīc, adv., *so, thus, in this way*
Siculus, -a, -um, adj., *Sicilian*
sīcut, adv., *just as, as*

sīdus, sīderis, n., *star; sky* (pl.)

silva, -ae, f., *forest*

similis, -e, adj., *similar, like*

simplex, simplicis, adj., *simple, artless, plain*

simul, conj., *as soon as* (also with **atque**); adv., *at the same time, together*

sine, prep. with abl., *without*

Sīsyphus, -ī, m., *Sisyphus; son of Aeolus, committed various crimes and is punished in the underworld by forever having to roll a rock up a steep hill only to have it roll down again*

situs, -ūs, m., *site*

situs, -ūs, m., *deterioration, neglect*

sīve, conj., *or if,* **sīve . . . sīve,** *whether . . . or*

sōbrius, -a, -um, adj., *sober, moderate, sensible*

sodālis, sodālis, m., *companion*

sōl, sōlis, m., *sun, a day* (as determined by the rising of the sun)

soleō, solēre, solitus sum, *be accustomed*

solidus, -a, -um, adj., *solid, complete, entire*

sollicitō, sollicitāre, sollicitāvī, sollicitātum, *rouse, excite, shake up, disturb with repeated attacks*

solum, -ī, n., *ground, floor, land*

sōlus, -a, -um, adj., a*lone, lonely, deserted*

solvō, solvere, solvī, solūtum, *loosen, break up*

somnus, -ī, m., *sleep*

sonitus, -ūs, m., *sound*

sopor, sopōris, m., *sleep*

Sōracte, Sōractis, n., *Soracte, mountain in the south of Etruria*

sordēs, sordis, f., often used in pl., *dirt, squalor, baseness*

soror, sorōris, f., *sister*

sors, sortis, f., *lot, share*

sortior, sortīrī, sortītus sum, *cast lots over, choose*

sospes, sospitis, adj., *safe and sound, unhurt*

spatium, spatiī, n., *space, period of time*

spernō, spernere, sprēvī, sprētum, *remove, reject, scorn*

spērō, spērāre, spērāvī, spērātum, *hope, hope for, expect*

spēs, speī, f., *hope*

splendidus, -a, -um, adj., *bright, brilliant, glittering, illustrious*

sternō, sternere, strāvī, strātum, *stretch out, spread out, level, overthrow*

stō, stāre, stetī, statum, *stand*

suāviter, adv., *pleasantly, delightfully, nicely*

sub, prep. with acc. or abl., *under, below*

subeō, subīre, subiī, subitum, *go under, undergo*

sublīmis, -e, adj., *high, raised, elevated, sublime, lofty*

submoveō, submovēre, submōvī, submōtum, *move away, remove, ward off, banish*

subolēs, subolis, f., *offspring*

sūdor, sūdōris, m., *sweat*

sulcus, -ī, m., *a furrow, trench, track*

sum, esse, fuī, futūrus, *be*

summa, -ae, f., *sum, the whole*

summoveō = submoveō

summus, -a, -um, adj., *highest, topmost*

sūmō, sūmere, sumpsī, sumptum, *take, take on*

super, prep. with abl., *above*

superbia, -ae, f., *pride, arrogance*

superbus, -a, -um, adj., *proud, arrogant*

supercilium, superciliī, n., *eyebrow, nod*

superstes, superstitis, adj., *standing over, surviving*

superus, -a, -um, adj., *upper, higher*

suprēmus, -a, -um, adj., *last, final*

surgō, surgere, surrexī, surrectum, *get up, rise* (of heavenly bodies)

suscitō, suscitāre, suscitāvī, suscitātum, *rouse, awaken*

suspendō, suspendere, suspendī, suspensum, *hang up*

sustineō, sustinēre, sustinuī, sustentum, *hold up, support, withstand*

susurrus, -ī, m., *whispering*

suus, -a, -um, third person reflex. adj., *his, her, its, their* (own)

Syrius, -a, -um, adj., *Syrian*

Syrtis, Syrtis, f., *Syrtis* (especially pl.), name of two areas of sandy flats on the coast between Carthage and Cyrene; whole desert region next to this coast.

T

tabula, -ae, f., *board, plank, writing tablet,* (votive) *tablet*

taceō, tacēre, tacuī, tacitum, *be silent*

tacitus, -a, -um, adj., *silent*

tālus, -ī, m., *ankle bone, ankle, knuckle bone used in games*

tam, adv., *so*

tamen, adv., *nevertheless*

tandem, adv., *at last, finally*

tangō, tangere, tetigī, tactum, *touch*

tantum, adv., *so much, only*

tantummodo, adv., *only*

tardus, -a, -um, adj., *slow, late, moving slowly, dull*

taurus, -ī, m., *bull*

tectum, -ī, n., *roof, house*

tēcum = cum tē

Tēlephus, -ī, m., *Telephus,* man's name

tellūs, tellūris, f., *land, earth, country, ground*

Tempē, n. pl. *Tempe,* valley of the Peneus river between Ossa and Olympus in Thessaly, noted for its beauty; *any beautiful valley*

temperō, temperāre, temperāvī, temperātum, *moderate, hold back*

tempestīvus, -a, -um, adj., *timely, seasonable, ripe*

temptō, temptāre, temptāvī, temptātum, *try, attempt*

tempus, temporis, n., *time, occasion, proper time, an age or particular period in history, danger*

tendō, tendere, tetendī, tentum/tensum, *stretch out, extend, proceed, direct one's course*

tenebrae, -ārum, f. pl., *darkness*

teneō, tenēre, tenuī, tentum, *hold, persist*

tener, tenera, tenerum, adj., *tender, delicate, soft, young*

ter, adv., *three times*

teres, teretis, adj., *rounded, smooth, polished*

tergeminus, -a, -um, adj., *triple*

terminus, -ī, m., *boundary line, limit*

terra, -ae, f., *land, ground, country*

Thaliarchus, -ī, m., *Thaliarchus,* Greek man's name

Thēseus, Thēseī/Thēseos, m., *Theseus,* son of Aegeus or Poseidon; national hero of Athens

Thrācius, -a, -um, adj., *Thracian*

Thrēicius, -a, -um, adj., *Thracian*

Thressa, -ae, f., *a Thracian woman;* as fem. adj., *Thracian*

Thūrīnus, -a, -um, adj., *pertaining to the town of Thurii in southern Italy*

Tiberis, Tiberis, m., *the river Tiber*

tībia, -ae, f., *shin bone, tibia, pipe, flute*

tigris, tigris/tigridis, f., *tiger*

timeō, timēre, timuī, *fear, be afraid, be afraid of*

timor, timōris, m., *fear*

tinguō, tinguere, tinxī, tinctum, *wet, stain*

Tityos, -ī, m., *Tityus;* giant primarily known for attempting to rape Latona, mother of Apollo and Diana; punished in the underworld by being stretched over nine acres while two vultures or snakes ate his heart or liver

tollō, tollere, sustulī, sublātum, *lift, raise, extol, take away, destroy*

Torquātus, -ī, m., *Torquatus;* identity uncertain; a Torqutus, an orator, also appears as addressee of Horace *Epistle 1.5;* an orator; may be a son of Lucius Manlius Torquatus, consul in 65 BCE, the year in which Horace was born

torreō, torrēre, torruī, tostum, *burn, parch*

tōtus, -a, -um, adj., *the whole of, all*

trabs, trabis, f., *beam of wood, trunk of tree, ship*

tractō, tractāre, tractāvī, tractātum, *handle*

trādō, trādere, trādidī, trāditum, *hand over, deliver, introduce*

trans, prep. with acc., *across*

trecēnī, trecēnae, trecēna, pl. adj., *three hundred each, three hundred at a time*

tremō, tremere, tremuī, *tremble, quiver*

trepidō, trepidāre, trepidāvī, trepidātum, *be agitated, hurry*

trēs, tria, adj., *three*

tribuō, tribuere, tribuī, tribūtum, *allot, assign*

trīcēsimus, -a, -um, adj., *thirtieth*

trirēmis, trirēmis, f., *ship having three banks of oars; trireme*

tristis, -e, adj., *sad*

triumphus, -ī, m., *triumph, triumphal procession*

trivium, triviī, n., *meeting place of three roads, crossroads*

tū, tuī, tibi, tē, tē, pron., *you* (sing.)

tuba, -ae, f., *straight war trumpet*

Tullus, -ī, m., *Tullus Hostilius,* third king of Rome

tum, adv., *then*

tumeō, tumēre, tumuī, *swell*

tumultuōsus, -a, -um, adj., *full of commotion, turbulent*

tunc, adv., *then*

turba, -ae, f., *crowd*

turgidus, -a, -um, adj., *swollen, turgid*

turpis, -e, adj., *ugly, shameful, disgraceful*

turpō, turpāre, turpāvī, turpātum, *make ugly*

turris, -is, f., *tower*

tussis, tussis, f., *cough*

tūtus, -a, -um, adj., *safe, secure*

tuus, -a, -um, adj., *your* (sing.)

Tyrrhēnus, -a, -um, adj., *Tyrrhenian, Etruscan*

U

ubi, rel. adv., *where, when;* interr. adv., *where*

ūdus, -a, -um, adj., *wet, pliant*

ulcerōsus, -a, -um, adj., *full of ulcers or sores*

ullus, -a, -um, adj., *any*

ultimus, -a, -um, adj., *last, farthest, extreme*

ultrā, prep. with acc., *beyond*

umbra, -ae, f., *shade, shadow, ghost*

umbrōsus, -a, -um, adj., *shady*

umerus, -ī, m., *shoulder*

ūmor, ūmōris, m., *moisture, liquid*

unda, -ae, f., *wave, water*

unde, interr. and rel. adv., *from where, from whom, from which*

undique, adv., *on all sides, everywhere*

unguentum, -ī, n., *ointment, perfume*

ūnus, -a, -um, adj., *one, sole*

urbs, urbis, f., *city; the city of Rome*

urgeō, urgēre, ursī, *push, press upon*

urna, -ae, f., *urn*

ūrō, ūrere, ussī, ustum, *burn;* in pass., *be on fire*

usque, adv., *continuously, continually, all the way*

ūsus, -ūs, m., *use, enjoyment*

ut, conj. with indic., *as, like, when, considering how;* with subj., *so that, that, to;* interr. adv., *how*

ūtor, ūtī, ūsus sum (with abl.), *use, enjoy*

utrimque, adv., *on both sides*

ūvidus, -a, -um, adj., *wet*

uxor, uxōris, f., *wife*

V

vacuus, -a, -um, adj., *empty, free, available*

vador, vadārī, vadātus sum, (of a plaintiff) *accept a guarantee from the other party that the party will appear or reappear in court at an appointed date*

vae, interj., *alas, woe*

vagor, vagārī, vagātus sum, *wander*

vagus, -a, -um, adj., *roaming, wandering*

valeō, valēre, valuī, valitum, *be powerful, be strong enough to, be well*

vallēs, vallis, f., *valley*

vānus, -a, -um, adj., *empty, groundless, imaginary*

Varius, Variī, m., *L.Varius Rufus,* writer of epic and tragedy, important literary friend of Horace

vātēs, vātis, c., *prophet, singer, poet*

-ve, conj., *or*

vel, conj., *or*

vellō, vellere, vellī, vulsum, *pull, tug at*

vēlum, -ī, n., *sail*

velut, adv., *as, just as*

vēnātor, vēnātōris, m., *hunter*

venēnātus, -a, -um, adj., *poisonous*

venēnum, -ī, n., *poison, magical or medicinal potion*

veniō, venīre, vēnī, ventum, *come*

ventus, -ī, m., *wind*

venus, veneris, f., *Venus,* Roman goddess of love; *love, charm, sexual activity; best throw at dice*

vēr, vēris, n., *spring*

verberō, verberāre, verberāvī, verberātum, *beat, lash*

Vergilius, Vergiliī, m., *Publius Vergilius Maro* (70–19 BCE)

vēritās, vēritātis, f., *truth*

vērō, adv., *in fact, indeed, certainly, truly*

verrō, verrere, versum, *sweep together, collect*

versō, versāre, versāvī, versātum, *keep turning, stir*

versus, -ūs, m., *line of verse*

vertex, verticis, m., *head, summit*

vērus, -a, -um, adj., *true, real*

vescor, vescī, *enjoy, feed on, eat* (with abl.)

Vesta, -ae, f., *Vesta,* Roman goddess of the domestic hearth; *temple or shrine of Vesta*

vestīmentum, -ī, n., *clothes, garments*

vetus, veteris, adj., *old*

via, -ae, f., *road, street, way*

vicis (gen.), f., *turn, succession, alternation*

victima, -ae, f., *victim, sacrifice*

victor, victōris, m., *victor, winner, conqueror*

vīcus, -ī, m., *group of dwellings, village; block of houses, street, group of streets,* often forming a social or administrative unit (used of specific districts in Rome)

videō, vidēre, vīdī, vīsum, *see*

vigeō, vigēre, viguī, *flourish, thrive*

villa, -ae, f., *country-house, estate, farm*

vincō, vincere, vīcī, victum, *conquer, defeat*

vinculum, -ī, n., *chain, bond*

vīnea, -ae, f., *vineyard*

vīnum, -ī, n., *wine*

violens, violentis, adj., *violent, vehement*

vir, -ī, m., *man, husband*

vireō, virēre, viruī, *be green, youthful, fresh*

virga, -ae, f., *staff, wand*

virgō, virginis, f., *girl of marriageable age, young woman, virgin*

viridis, -e, adj., *green, fresh, young*

virtūs, virtūtis, f., *manhood, courage, valor, virtue*

Viscus, -ī, m., *Viscus;* there were two brothers with this name; both were literary figures and friends of Horace and Maecenas.

vīsō, vīsere, vīsī, *look at, go and see*

vīta, -ae, f., *life*

vītis, vītis, f., *vine*

vītō, vītāre, vītāvī, vītātum, *avoid, shun*

vitrum, -ī, n., *glass*

vīvō, vīvere, vixī, victum, *live*

vix, adv., *hardly, scarcely*

volens, volentis, adj., *willing*

volgus, -ī, n., *the common people, the general public, crowd*

volō, velle, voluī, *wish, want, be willing*

volō, volāre, volāvī, volātum, *fly, speed*

voltus, -ūs, m., *face, expression*

vōmer, vōmeris, m., *plowshare;* by metonymy, *the plow*

vōtīva, -a, -um, *votive, relating to a vow*

vox, vōcis, f., *voice*

Z

Zephyrus, -ī, m., *west wind, zephyr*

MORE ON HORACE

HORACE: Selected Odes and Satire 1.9, 2nd edition
Ronnie Ancona

Horace was a talented and innovative literary craftsman whose lyrics reveal an extraordinary facility and playfulness with the Latin language. Informed by the latest in Horatian scholarship, *Horace Selected Odes and Satire 1.9* presents twenty significant odes and one satire for advanced Latin students. The format includes line-by-line notes and vocabulary and a variety of enhancements, making it easily accessible to both teachers and students.

A separate Teacher's Guide includes enlarged version of the Latin text for reproduction, literal translations of the poems, discussion and sample test questions, and an annotated bibliography.

Student Text: xxxiv + 174 pp. (2005, second edition) 6" x 9" Paperback, ISBN 978-0-86516-608-0
Teacher's Guide: vi + 82 pp. (2005, second edition) 8 ½" x 11" Paperback, ISBN 978-0-86516-612-7

HORACE FULLY PARSED WORD BY WORD
Books I and II of Horace Odes
Grammatically Analyzed and Literally Translated
Introduction by Thomas J. Sienkewicz

This is the ideal reference for every teacher and independent scholar of Horace. The Latin text of Books I and II of Horace's *Odes* is included along with notes for each word. The notes give complete information: grammatical, syntactical, mythological, geographical, historical, and vocabulary. A literal translation of each ode is included at the back of the book.

vi + 282 pp. (2003 reprint of 1917 edition) 6" x 9" Paperback, ISBN 978-0-86516-552-6

WHY HORACE? A Collection of Interpretations
William S. Anderson

The lyrical voice of Horace is as fresh today as it was among his contemporaries. This collection of essays is an excellent resource for enriching the modern reader's experience with some of the finest poetry of literature's Golden Age. This edition includes:

- An introduction by William Anderson
- 21 essays by Horace scholars
- a select bibliography on Horace

xvi + 264 pp. (1999)
Paperback, ISBN 978-0-86516-417-8 • Hardbound, ISBN 978-0-86516-434-5

BOLCHAZY-CARDUCCI PUBLISHERS, INC.
WWW.BOLCHAZY.COM

Made in the USA
Lexington, KY
23 March 2016